PARTNER, Peter. Renaissance Rome, 1500–1559: a portrait of a society. California, 1977 (c1976). 241p ill bibl index 75-13154. 14.95 ISBN 0-520-03026-5

CHOICE   OCT. '77

History, Geography &

Travel

Europe

Partner, a scholar known for his work on papal administration in the 15th century, has advanced his attentions to the Rome of the High Renaissance. The only recent attempt in English to cover this complex and intriguing period in the long history of the city is Bonner Mitchell's short but lively and informative *Rome in the High Renaissance: the age of Leo X* (CHOICE, Feb. 1974). Partner's work is not only more detailed in respect to the traditional institutional, religious, and cultural themes normally associated with Renaissance Rome but adds interesting materials illuminating the social and economic basis. His contention is that the Renaissance papacy had greater strength and stability than might appear from its sometimes turbulent history. There are errors that might have been avoided by a specialist in the 16th century, and the book somehow fails to convey the excitement of the epoch—the heights of its aspirations or the depth of its despairs. Nonetheless, it will be useful to upper-division students in Renaissance history and art courses. Very brief bibliography, adequate index.

Renaissance

R·O·M·E

1500-1559

PETER PARTNER, Assistant Master of Winchester College, England, has written several books, including *The Lands of St. Peter. The Papal State in the Middle Ages and the Early Renaissance* (California, 1972). He has also worked as a journalist in the Middle East, Italy, and North Africa. In the fall of 1976 77 Dr. Partner was in residence at the Institute of Advanced Study, Princeton.

Renaissance

R·O·M·E

1500-1559

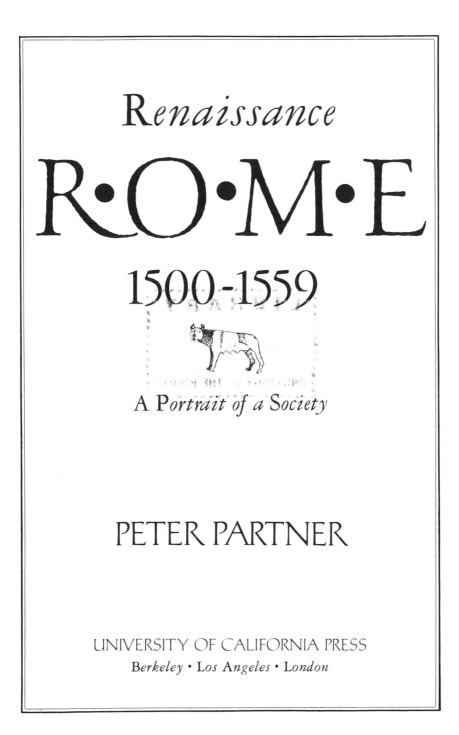

A Portrait of a Society

PETER PARTNER

UNIVERSITY OF CALIFORNIA PRESS
Berkeley • Los Angeles • London

UNIVERSITY OF CALIFORNIA PRESS
BERKELEY AND LOS ANGELES, CALIFORNIA

UNIVERSITY OF CALIFORNIA PRESS, LTD. LONDON, ENGLAND

COPYRIGHT © 1976 BY THE REGENTS OF THE UNIVERSITY OF CALIFORNIA

ISBN: 0-520-03026-5
LIBRARY OF CONGRESS CATALOG CARD NUMBER: 75-13154

DESIGNED BY KADI KARIST TINT
PRINTED IN THE UNITED STATES OF AMERICA

To Enzo Crea

Contents

Dates and Family Names of Renaissance Popes

POPE	DATES	FAMILY NAME
Nicholas V	1447–1455	Parentucelli
Calixtus III	1455–1458	Borgia
Pius II	1458–1464	Piccolomini
Paul II	1464–1471	Barbo
Sixtus IV	1471–1484	Riario
Innocent VIII	1484–1492	Cibo
Alexander VI	1492–1503	Borgia
Pius III	1503	Piccolomini
Julius II	1503–1513	Della Rovere
Leo X	1513–1521	Medici (Florence)
Adrian VI	1522–1523	Dedal
Clement VII	1523–1534	Medici (Florence)
Paul III	1534–1549	Farnese
Julius III	1550–1555	Del Monte
Marcellus II	1555	Cervini
Paul IV	1555–1559	Carafa
Pius IV	1559–1565	Medici (Milan)

Acknowledgements

I am grateful to Mark Stephenson, who helped me in the planning of this book, and to Gordon Pirie and Jo Bottkol, who pointed out to me some of the infelicities of the draft.

P.P.

Italy was once Lord of all the world, *Rome*, the Queen of Cities, vaunted herself of two myriads of inhabitants; now that all-commanding Country is possessed by petty Princes, *Rome*, a small Village in respect.

ROBERT BURTON,
THE ANATOMY OF MELANCHOLY

Thou stranger, which for *Rome* in *Rome* here seekest,
And nought of *Rome* in *Rome* perceiu'st at all,
These same olde walls, olde arches, which thou seest,
Olde palaces, is that which *Rome* men call.

Behold what wreake, what ruine, and what wast,
And how that she, which with her mightie powre
Tam'd all the world, hath tam'd herselfe at last,
The pray of time, which all things doth deuowre.

Rome now of *Rome* is th' only funerall,
And only *Rome* of *Rome* hath victorie;
Ne ought saue *Tyber* hastning to his fall
Remaines of all: O worlds inconstancie.

That which is firme doth flit and fall away,
And that is flitting, doth abide and stay.

SPENSER'S TRANSLATION FROM
JOACHIM DU BELLAY, *LES ANTIQUITEZ DE ROME*,
"NOUVEAU VENU QUI CHERCHES ROME EN ROME"

Renaissance
R·O·M·E
1500-1559

Introduction

THE RENAISSANCE
POPES
AND THEIR
SEE

I

In 1500 Rome was a city of towers. Towers surmounted the gates and scores of strongpoints along the twelve-mile circuit of walls; towers belonging to noble families were dotted all over the inhabited areas of the city; towers stood over most of the Tiber bridges; towers had been built onto many of the great ancient monuments which the Middle Ages had turned into fortresses. Alexander VI, the reigning pope in 1500, built towers when he re-fortified the Mausoleum of Hadrian, known as Castel Sant'Angelo, and he added another tower, known as the Borgia Tower, to the Vatican Palace. A great belltower of the Roman Commune dominated the Capitol or Campidoglio, just as the communal tower of the Palazzo della Signoria dominated the centre of Florence. The Roman Fora were overlooked by the thirteenth-century Torre delle Milizie. In addition, scores of belltowers of the Roman churches were there to convey messages of religion, of alarm, or of joy to the usually silent city. The belltower of S. Apollinare, part of the buildings of St Peter's, was the largest in Rome.

The fine streets and the orderly squares and public spaces which we associate with "old Rome" were almost entirely absent in 1500. The streets of the inhabited areas were so cramped, so deformed and interrupted by porticoes and outbuildings and spanning wooden bridges, that they were scarcely streets at all; it was more usual to name a *contrada* or district than a street. Very few churches or palaces existed in a form which we would today identify as "Renaissance". The Barbo palace at S. Marco was perhaps recognisable, as was the great Bramante palace of the Cancelleria, though it was still only half-built. St Peter's was a fourth-century basilica surrounded by medieval accretions; before it stood a vast atrium (the "paradise") in whose centre were a great decorative fountain and an antique bronze pinecone. Huge ancient monuments lay in profuse disorder all over Rome. Many ancient buildings could be seen which later vandalism destroyed, such as the Temple of Minerva in the Forum Transitorium or the Septizonium of Septimius Severus. Rome was pervaded by rusticity. Cows ruminated in the Forum; horses cropped the grass round the Columns of Trajan and Marcus Aurelius; sheep roamed over at least four of the Seven Hills. The Palatine Hill was covered by vineyards; the Circus Maximus was a market garden. For all its echoes of the Empire of the Caesars, for all the clerical pageantry of its priestly residents, Rome was only a large, medieval village, smelling of cows and hay.

The year 1500 was one of Jubilee in Rome. This custom meant the grant of special indulgences for pardon of the sins of pilgrims who came to Rome in that year. If fewer pilgrims came than had come in the last Jubilee years of 1450 and 1475, the reason was not the evil moral reputation of Pope Alexander VI, which was known to few ordinary Catholics, but the hazards experienced on the pilgrim roads due to the French wars in Italy. For most of the hundreds of thousands of pilgrims who still came to the Jubilee of 1500, Rome was not for the sightseeing of ancient monuments, nor did the pilgrims associate the Roman clergy with the dubious and worldly life led by Pope Alexander VI and his court. To them Rome meant the religious ceremonies of the Roman Church. The pilgrim followed the route which was prescribed by custom round the most ancient of the basilical churches. For the historical reason that the earliest Christian churches had tended to be in popular quarters on the periphery of ancient Rome, this route took the pilgrim far from the only intensively inhabited area of Renaissance Rome, which was between the Campidoglio and St Peter's. The pilgrim went to the ancient patriarchal church of St John Lateran, and on his knees climbed the holy stairway nearby; he visited the Church of S. Croce in Gerusalemme in the same area, and the churches of S. Lorenzo, S. Sebastiano and S. Paolo, all outside the walls of the city. All these ancient places were situated among vineyards or sheep pastures. The same was true of most of the ancient churches visited by the faithful in Lent for the ceremonies of the "stations", or of the routes of such great processions as that for St Mark's Day. When the pope himself went in procession from St Peter's to the mother church of St John Lateran, he rode for much of the way along a country lane.

In 1450 Rome had been even more bucolic than it was in 1500. The Jubilees which took place every twenty-five years encouraged the popes on each occasion to turn to the improvement of Rome as a city. In the mid-fifteenth century everything remained to be done. Rome was still a wilderness among crumbling ruins. One Spanish traveller remarked that outside the one or two small populated quarters Rome was so empty of people that "there are parts within the walls which look like thick woods, and wild beasts, hares, foxes, deer and even so it is said porcupines breed in the caves". Another, Alfonso de Palencia, making a comment which could still be made by Montaigne over a century later, said that only the tops of the ancient buildings protruded from the mountains of debris. It was a desolate city, whose inhabitants lived in what could only be termed huts, and who had nothing but contempt and mockery for their classical ancestors. They "neither knew nor cared about ancient Rome, and in modern Rome their interests were mainly in the wine shops".

Between the fall of the Western Empire and 1870 Rome was not a capital city in the modern sense of the phrase. Rome was the chief city of the papal state, but this was a minor matter. From the eighth century onwards all the other social and political functions of the city were submerged in the idea of Rome as the seat of the Roman bishop. The fortunes of Rome were the fortunes of the popes. Rome possessed its own civic consciousness, and, from the twelfth century onwards, its own civic government, but the economic and political power of the Roman people was puny compared with that of their bishops. The Romans found this out to their cost by the absence of the popes from Rome during the later Middle Ages.

Such absences had been quite frequent earlier in the Middle Ages, but from 1305 the popes accepted a displacement which lasted over seventy years. The alleged insecurity of the papal state was put forward, from 1305 onwards, as the excuse for the continuous absence of the popes from Rome, and for their location in Provence, in the city of Avignon. This long sojourn, known to some of its contemporary critics as the "Babylonian Captivity", was as much due to the Gallicizing of the clerks of the Roman court as to their fears of the perils of political life in Italy. After 1376 the popes attempted to return to Rome, only to expose themselves to a debilitating period of schism (1378–1417) during which two and eventually three clerks claimed the papal title at the same time. Not until three years after the Great Schism had been ended by the Council of Constance did Pope Martin V (1417–1431) return to Rome in 1420 to re-establish a line of truly "Roman" bishops, and to inaugurate a tradition of definite papal residence in Rome, under which the pope absented himself from the city (apart from summer residence in the nearby hills) only in the most exceptional circumstances.

During the Avignonese Papacy and the Great Schism, Rome had experienced decay, neglect and depopulation. The churches, even the greatest of them, had fallen into disrepair and ruin: the city had suffered from the absence of pilgrims and of the rich clerks of the Roman court, and from deprivation of the gold and silver with which Catholic Europe was wont to subsidise the papal institutions. After the Great Schism popes and people re-learned the lesson of Christian Rome. Continuous papal residence was absolutely necessary to the economic and social wellbeing of the city. Almost from the beginning the Roman bishops had subsidised the Roman people. Urban policy and urban development had existed only when the pope paid for them. The lesson was thoroughly learned: the only fifteenth-century pope to absent himself from Rome for a long period was Eugenius IV (1431–1447), who was driven away by the wars of the Italian mercenary generals. After his return to Rome in 1441, the only long absence of a pope from Rome, until Pius VII was abducted to France by Napoleon in 1809, was that of Clement VII, after the Sack of Rome in 1527.

II

The Italian cities enjoyed a noble tradition of urban planning and development, which went back to the great flowering of the Italian communes of the Middle Ages, and which continued strongly into the Renaissance and early modern period. In that tradition Rome and its bishops participated. Papal rule in Rome became more and more in tune with the general condition of Italian society and government, as they drifted from the constitutional oligarchy of the Middle Ages towards the princely autocracy of the Renaissance. The strong, conservative, ideologically coherent regime of the Roman popes was in many ways very suitable for the application of the Renaissance principles of town planning and development. But successful urban development needs not only strong and able government, but a vigorous society and a plentiful supply of capital. It may well be asked how, at a time of apparent weakness in which the Roman papacy confronted the new forces of the Renaissance and Reformation, at the moment, in fact, of their supreme trial and of the split of Catholic Christendom into two opposed blocks during the Reformation crisis, the Roman bishops were able to re-plan and reorganise their environment on a grand scale. It is an aim of this book to attempt an answer to that question.

The pace of Roman urban growth during the Renaissance was slow. Arguably a reasonable date for the end of "Renaissance Rome" is 1559, the year of the death of Pope Paul IV and of the conclusion of the Treaty of Cateau-Cambrésis, three years before the third session of the Council of Trent. By 1559 only the preliminaries had been completed for that great triumph of urban planning which we call "Counter-Reformation Rome". Nonetheless, these preliminaries were stylistically formative and administratively essential. Counter-Reformation and Baroque Rome grew from Renaissance Rome like a tree from a sapling. Yet Renaissance Rome was disorderly, unlucky, indeterminate, ruled by men who were not quite sure how to deal with their political and ideological situation, and who were at times overwhelmed by events they could neither understand nor control. The Renaissance popes who ruled for any length of time were almost all of them men of rather inferior moral stature; the only one with inflexible moral views, Pope Paul IV (1555–1559), was a self-deluding old bigot whose reign was a disaster for the court and a misery for the people. All the Renaissance popes but two were Italians, at a time when the Italian peninsula was first bloodily fought over by French and Spanish power, and then steadily absorbed by tyrannical and unscrupulous means into the orbit of the Hapsburg Empire. It is hard to believe that such popes, at such a time, could have re-founded one of the great urban centres of western Europe.

Part of the explanation for the success of Renaissance Rome lies simply in the trend of the times. Throughout sixteenth-century Europe, money and population flowed into the towns as they had not done since the first great urban boom of the thirteenth century. There is no single explanation for this phenomenon, which was subject to great regional variation and was far from universal in late Renaissance Italy. But in the case of Rome the answer is partly to be found in the resilient nature of the Roman papacy itself. It is easy to over-estimate the failure of the Renaissance papacy by over-estimating the success of the medieval papacy. Culturally and socially the medieval papacy was a staggering achievement; it was the domination of most of a continent by a small, privileged clerical class, and the imposition of cultural norms on the most disparate ethnic groups. But so far as governments were concerned, papal power was influence and persuasion rather than command. Typically, the popes influenced governments by the despatch of experienced clerical diplomatists and arbitrators, of whom Shakespeare's Cardinal Pandulph in *King John* is the English literary prototype. Even at the peak of papal power, papal "universal" policies often failed, in the sense that popes failed to exercise direct control over policies of lay rulers which were harmful to Church interests or incompatible with Church law. Viewed in this way, the failure of the popes in the later medieval and Renaissance periods was a failure as old as the papacy itself, and the resilience of the popes in face of the Reformation's threat is more easily understood. The failure to control the development of the Protestant schisms of the sixteenth century was a grave defeat for the popes, but their predecessors had experienced similar defeats and survived. At no point in the Renaissance or Reformation periods did the confidence of the popes waver that they were the guardians of apostolic tradition and the instruments of divinely wielded authority.

INTRODUCTION

Inevitably one tends to read back the failure of the popes of the Reformation period into the papal history of the fifteenth century. There is no doubt of the basic weaknesses of the papacy as an institution, nor that those weaknesses made themselves felt in the later Middle Ages. But the great faults of the late medieval popes were of lack of imagination and insight, rather than of neglect of their duties in the sense in which they understood them. When the popes of the century that preceded the Reformation are considered in the terms in which they saw themselves and their situation, rather than in the terms suggested by the great shipwreck of the Church in the sixteenth century, the picture that emerges is far from the conventional one of self-indulgent Italian lordlings. What mattered above all to the papacy was its own legal status. The fifteenth-century popes had defeated the attack on their legal authority made by the clerks of the Councils of Constance (1414–1418), Siena (1423) and Basle (1431–1437). It is possible to see the ecumenical achievements of Pope Eugenius IV's Council of Ferrara-Florence (1437–1439) and the understanding which Eugenius reached with the Greek Church as more important than the trifling administrative adjustments which the conciliars put forward as a plan of Church reform. When further efforts were made later in the fifteenth century to revive the conciliar movement against the popes, they failed. Judged by the aims they set themselves, the fifteenth-century popes were not unsuccessful.

To create or to take over control of popular religious movements, as the popes had done with the mendicant friars in the early thirteenth century, was no longer within the powers of the papacy. Sixtus IV (1471–1484) passed laws which strengthened the position of the now elderly mendicant orders against the bishops, and a certain amount was done to accede to the requests made for the reform of some orders of clerks regular and of some sections of the older religious orders. But though the popes were still able to support and control some of the reforming friars such as Bernardino of Siena or John of Capistrano, even such a relatively conservative reformer as the Florentine friar Savonarola was unable to come to terms with Alexander VI, and ended on the stake. The conservative and repressive attitude of the Holy See to popular religious movements in which it saw doctrinal danger was no development of the very end of the Middle Ages. From the late thirteenth century onwards the attitude of the Church to deviationist reform movements, such as the heresy of the "Fraticelli" among the Franciscans, had been similarly repressive. The *devotio moderna*, the pietist movement which was widespread among clerks regular and educated layfolk at the end of the Middle Ages, was tolerated by the popes without ever being vigorously taken up and encouraged by them. The lukewarmness of the Church to the *devotio moderna* can be seen in its hesitant attitude to the piety of Erasmus, who was the greatest product of the *devotio moderna*.

The fifteenth-century popes had three main aims: the defeat of attempts to subordinate their authority to that of Church Councils, the repression of heresy, in particular of the Hussite heresy in Bohemia, and the assertion of their temporal authority in central Italy so as to ensure their political and financial independence. In all these policies they enjoyed a moderate degree of success. The third aim, the reconstruction of the papal state, was the more important to the popes because of the drying up of many of the traditional sources of papal income. There was nothing new in the idea of asserting papal temporal power, which had been one of the main elements in papal policy since the eighth century. It is a mistake to suppose that Renaissance popes were "Italian princes" in a way that thirteenth-century popes were not. But the negativity of papal policy in other fields, and its failure in one or two other matters like that of the Crusade, threw the function of the popes as Italian political leaders into greater prominence. Sixtus IV's apparently aggressive aims for the papal state, his vigorous prosecution of the wars of Tuscany and Ferrara, his favouring his nephews with papal lands and offices, all drew a great deal of attention. Contemporaries could not have known that Sixtus IV, this supposedly warlike pope of the late fifteenth century, spent a far smaller proportion of his income on warfare than Pope John XXII had been spending in the early fourteenth century.

Sixtus IV erred as a churchman in devoting huge sums of Church money to his family, just as Martin V had done earlier in that century, and as most of Sixtus's successors were to do for three-quarters of a century after him. But his nepotism or "carnality" were naturally in his own eyes a subordinate factor, and were thought to contribute to certain ends of papal policy, not to conflict with them. Only in the case of one Renaissance pope, Alexander VI, can it be convincingly argued that nepotism led rather than followed other papal policies.

But the whole social relationship of a noble family to the Church benefices which it controlled implied nepotism, both in the Middle Ages and in the Renaissance. To "build Zion on the blood relationships of one's kindred"* was an idea which went deeply into the medieval church, and it is a mistake to suppose that Renaissance popes were especially wicked, or different from their medieval predecessors, in practising it. The only difference in the Renaissance period was that the crumbling away of some of the "universal" fabric of the papacy left the local foundations on which it had always rested more blatantly exposed to view.

The pontificate of Alexander VI (1492–1503) marks a watershed in the Renaissance papacy, though perhaps not for the reasons that are commonly supposed. The place of Alexander VI in papal history is not determined by his flaunting his own children in the Vatican and glutting them with the lands and money of the Church, nor by his open and shameless simony. Both these things were practised by Renaissance popes after him, and notably, as to the first, by his protégé Alessandro Farnese (Paul III, 1534–1549). What above all marked the pontificate of Alexander VI was the French invasion of Italy of 1494, and the conversion of Italy to a cockpit for the squabbles of the great powers. The re-appearance of foreign power in Italy on a massive scale was utilised by Alexander and his son Cesare Borgia for the same purpose that Frankish power had been harnessed by the popes in the eighth century and that French power had been used by the popes after 1266: for the recuperation of papal temporal claims in the papal state. More than any other state in the Italian peninsula, the papal state was in a good position to harness foreign invading forces for local purposes. These forces also provided an umbrella which usually protected the pope if his political calculations went wrong, though startling leaks were to develop in this protection during the early sixteenth century. But the success of Cesare Borgia in subduing the papal state between 1500 and 1503 was due not only to the much-lauded *virtù* or personal capacity of that remarkable individual, but to French power.

---

*See Micah 3:10. The meaning of the Vulgate phrase "in sanguinibus" ("You who build Zion with blood, Jerusalem with crime") was twisted by some medieval commentators to mean "You who build Zion with the help of your blood-relations", thus distorting the true sense of the phrase.

The pontificate of Sixtus IV's nephew, Julius II (1503–1513), was remarkable first for the energetic prosecution of papal claims in the papal state, which were carried so far as almost to amount to a re-foundation of that venerable institution, and secondly for the successful resistance of the papacy to one of the most dangerous manifestations of traditional anti-papalism, the Gallican Council of Pisa-Milan (1511–1513). The position of Julius was rendered doubly hazardous by the intervention of Spain as well as of France in Italy; the situation was now set up which was to endure until the Peace of Cateau-Cambrésis in 1559, that of competing French and Spanish arms and claims in Italy. Julius II's idea of papal leadership of an Italian coalition which would "free Italy from the barbarians" and expel the ultramontane* invaders from Italy was a dangerous political illusion which flickered before the minds of many of the Renaissance popes. Julius II's moment of maximum peril came after the French victory at the Battle of Ravenna in 1512, which appeared to presage his unseating from the papacy by the French army and the French conciliarists. But fortunately for Julius the French army was too exhausted, after the death of Gaston de Foix and its enormous losses in the battle, to march on Rome. Three weeks after the Battle of Ravenna Julius opened his own Lateran Council in Rome, which was intended to meet the challenge of the French-inspired Council of Pisa and to show the willingness of the Roman See to sponsor the reform of the Church.

The wider policies of the Renaissance popes were not without significance for Rome. The recovery and re-organisation of the papal state had the greatest importance for papal finances. It was on papal-state taxation that the whole apparatus of papal finance and credit was, in the course of the sixteenth century, to be pinned. Julius II's firm imposition of his temporal authority was felt by the Roman barons, whose feudal power had to be broken if Rome was to emerge as an orderly and well-governed unit. The baronial family of Colonna inspired a revolt of noble Roman families in 1511, whose suppression by Julius II meant also the extinction of the last flicker of Roman civic independence.

*I use the word in the sense of peoples living north of the Alps, and so "ultramontane" to Italians. The word was, of course, used quite differently by clerical circles of the nineteenth and early twentieth century.

III

The relation of the papacy to the new humanist learning of the Renaissance period was central to the papal mission. The hegemony of the Roman Church in Europe was essentially that of a cultural elite. It was dependent on literary communication and on the effective transmission of ideas as well as on the preservation of popular religious and cultural patterns. Overlaid though it was by all sorts of accretions, late-antique Latin culture was still in a sense *the* culture of the Roman Church. The revival of late-antique culture was bound to affect the transmission of the message of the church. In the papal court the secretaries were using the humanist literary idiom in some papal letters almost as soon as such an idiom can be said to have existed. From the beginning the papal court was one of the great centres of humanist learning. Even in fourteenth-century Avignon the role of the papal court had not been negligible for the great humanist poet Petrarch. When Pope John XXIII moved from Bologna to Constance in 1414 to preside at the Council that was to deprive him of the papacy, he was accompanied by the best humanists and men of letters of his time. It was inevitable, given the clerical control of medieval education and culture, the financial and cultural resources of the papal court, and the professional needs of the papal bureaux, that humanists should find patronage and employment in Rome.

The popes were the patrons and employers of humanists from the moment that such a term can be used, and for centuries they remained so. When the young John Milton visited Rome in 1638 he came as a humanist to one of the great European centres of humanism, which had never ceased to be so from the beginnings of the "revival of letters". There was never a time in the sixteenth century when the continued saturation of the papal court by humanist culture was for a moment in doubt. Objections to the "pagan" tendencies of humanists were made by some theologians, but the popes themselves were troubled about the matter only at the time of the supposed conspiracy of the Roman Academy under Paul II (1468). The real cause of this conspiracy seems to have been the pope's attempt to reduce the number of venal offices in the curia; and accusations of "paganism" were made against the conspirators only in the usual way that heresy charges followed accusations of rebellion against the Church. The

Church seldom treated the question of "pagan" tendencies in classical scholars as more than a minor one, and it was arguably right in doing so. For the papal government the powers of literary expression released by the revival of classical learning were in the first place something to be harnessed to traditional political ends. The advent of humanist culture in the late fourteenth century coincided almost exactly with the advent of a new papal secretariat. Such pioneer humanists as Poggio Bracciolini (1380–1459) made careers in the papal curia. By the mid-fifteenth century the papal secretariat had begun to take the shape it had in the later Renaissance period; by this time there were already a script and a diplomatic form in use in the papal offices which were proper to the humanist correspondence of the secretaries.

Posterity, because of an almost invincible prejudice which attaches "humanism" to that which is "modern", and by consequence "anti-medieval", has until recently found it difficult to accept the idea of a papal court permeated by humanists. Aeneas Sylvius Piccolomini, who was one of the most distinguished humanists employed in the papal court in the mid-fifteenth century, became pope under the title of Pius II (1458–1464). He has often been called in modern times "the humanist pope", though Pope Marcellus II, who was pope for a short time in 1555 in the middle of the period of the Council of Trent, was just as much a "humanist pope" as Pius, in the sense that he also was preoccupied with accurate classical scholarship. But Pius II and Marcellus II were both also men of business, as were most of the humanists in papal employment in the fifteenth and sixteenth centuries. Pius II was not *the* humanist pope, but the first humanist to become pope. The idea that there is some sort of paradox in the very notion of a humanist pope is mistaken.

Humanism was not an ideological programme but a body of literary knowledge and linguistic skills based on the "revival of good letters", which was a revival of late-antique philology and grammar. This is how the word "humanist" was understood by contemporaries, and if scholars would agree to accept the word in this sense rather than in the sense in which it was used in the nineteenth century we might be spared a good deal of useless argument. That humanism had profound social and even political consequences for the life of the Italian courts is not to be doubted. But the idea that as a movement it was in some direct way inimical to the Church, or to the conservative social order in general, is one that has been put forward for a century and more without any substantial proof being offered. The nineteenth-century historian Jacob Burckhardt, in his classic work *The Civilisation of the Renaissance in Italy*, noted as a "curious fact" that some men of the new culture were "men of the strictest piety, or even ascetics". If he had meditated more deeply on the meaning of the careers of such great religious humanists as Ambrogio Traversari (1386–1439), the General of the Camaldolese Order, perhaps he would not have gone on to describe humanism in unqualified terms as "pagan", and thus helped to precipitate a century of infertile debate about the possible existence of something called "Christian humanism" which ought to be opposed to "pagan humanism".

From Petrarch onwards the climate in which many humanists lived was markedly religious. Crude and destructive anti-clericalism was exhibited only by a few, philosophical scepticism by hardly any. Words like "unbelief" or "paganism" can be applied only to a tiny minority of writers and thinkers educated in the new humanist culture. Some humanists of the early fifteenth century like Lorenzo Valla showed tendencies which would later have been described as "evangelical", and would a century later have brought their owners at least to the fringes of Protestantism. But a far more common tendency was the religious Platonism which was so widespread in the circles of Tuscan humanism in the later fifteenth century. When expressed in certain strong forms this religious Platonism weakened belief in conservative Catholic theology. It also led to the study of early Greek fathers whose influence had been dormant in the Church for centuries. The revival of the study of Origen at the turn of the fifteenth century was an example. On the other hand, Platonism had for centuries played a part in the philosophy of medieval Catholicism, and the Platonism of the humanists was by no means bound to lead to religious revolution. The elaborate religious symbolism which was so dear to Renaissance Platonists, and which plays such a tremendous part in Renaissance art, was only a sequel to the equally elaborate religious symbolism of earlier generations. For a short time at the beginning of the sixteenth century there were theologians in the papal court who pursued, as the art historian Edgar Wind has written, "a bold and erudite, poetically learned theology, which drew from some of the Greek and Latin fathers the authority to revive apocryphal traditions". Such men drew up the imaginative and recondite programmes which lie behind the Sistine ceiling of Michelangelo. Such men also looked forward, under Julius II and Leo X (1513–1521), to the "fulfilment of all things" (*plenitudo temporum*). Giles of Viterbo, who was a learned and clever man (if also something of a pompous windbag), wrote that the splendour of the Roman See under Julius II had reached a point comparable to the state of Israel under Solomon: from this point it could only decline. Giles reflected an uncertainty common among men of his time, who were unsure whether the "fulfilment of all things" would come in some splendid triumph of religion, or whether in some apocalyptic judgement like that preached by Savonarola.

From the pontificate of Pope Nicholas V onwards (1447–1455), the popes began to show themselves once more sensitive, as the Avignonese popes had been, to the prestige which art and architecture could confer on them. In the deathbed speech attributed to Nicholas V, the pope who had organised the great Jubilee of 1450, the power of buildings to speak to the illiterate was argued:

> Only the learned who have studied the origin and development of the authority of the Roman Church can really understand its greatness. Thus, to create solid and stable convictions in the minds of the uncultured masses, there must be something which appeals to the eye; a popular faith, sustained only on doctrines, will never be anything but feeble and vacillating. But if the authority of the Holy See were visibly displayed in majestic buildings, imperishable memorials and witnesses seemingly planted by the hand of God himself, belief would grow and strengthen from one generation to another, and all the world would accept and revere it. Noble edifices combining taste and beauty with imposing proportions would immensely conduce to the exaltation of the chair of St Peter.

There is nothing specifically humanist in this judgement, which is only a rhetorical statement of the practice of the Church during the whole of the Middle Ages. But "taste and beauty" imply an artistic canon accepted by the educated. The architectural advisor of Nicholas V was Leon Battista Alberti, the most original theorist of art and architecture of his generation. It was probably to Alberti that Nicholas

V owed the idea, which he never lived to execute, of demolishing and rebuilding the great church of St Peter. Given the position which the papacy occupied in the world of Italian humanist culture, it was inevitable that when it turned to great projects of building and decoration, they would be executed according to the canons of humanist taste. On the other hand, though the taste which inspired these works was that of the educated, the public which they sought to impress was illiterate. The opinions attributed to Nicholas V contemplated people like the pilgrims who in 1450 were sleeping in the porticoes of the Roman churches and in the vineyards within the walls of the city.

Pope Sixtus IV (1471–1484) spoke in 1474 of the depopulation of the city of Rome, though we do not know with what earlier period he was comparing it. The long pontificate of Sixtus was in many ways a decisive one for the future of Rome as a city. The Roman population had for centuries been penned into a narrow corner of the city between the Campidoglio and the Tiber, with little contact with either of the two inhabited areas on the other side of the river, the Leonine Borgo and Trastevere, which in turn had no road connecting one with the other. The bridge at Castel Sant'Angelo (Ponte Elio) connected with one of the two main arteries of the city, the Via Papale which ran to the Campidoglio. The other main artery, the Via Lata, followed the course of the upper part of the present Via del Corso. The bridges connecting the Tiber island with the two banks were remote from the main centres of habitation. By the construction of a new bridge (Ponte Sisto), Sixtus gave a new axis leading from the Trastevere side of the river to the ancient centre of the city (Via dei Pettinari). He also encouraged the development of the quarter of "Ponte" which became the heart of Renaissance Rome. But probably the most important local measure of Sixtus was that which concerned the law governing the descent of real property. By protecting the legal position of the heirs of clerks who bought or built houses in Rome with money derived from Church benefices, Sixtus gave a powerful incentive to the rich curial clerks to invest their money in urban development. Until this time such investments had been liable to government confiscation after the death of the clerk concerned; the security which Sixtus supplied gave an immense impulse to building.

The second major urban change of the fifteenth century came only right at its end, when Alexander VI (1492–1503) took up the work

(17)

begun by Sixtus IV in the rationalisation of the huddled buildings on the Vatican side of the river which comprised the Leonine Borgo, and started (again in view of the concourse of pilgrims for the Jubilee) the clearance of the "Via Alessandrina" which cut from the river to St Peter's and the Vatican Palace. By the standards of the time the Via Alessandrina was a fine street, superior to the earlier parallel cutting made by Sixtus (the then Via Sistina)—superior also, if the comparison is possible, to the vandalistic activities of Mussolini and Pius XI in 1937 which were responsible for the Via della Conciliazione.

The replacement of ramshackle houses and old-fashioned fortresses in Rome was a long process which cannot be attributed merely to Sixtus IV. The Barbo cardinals (one of whom became pope as Paul II) began the construction of Palazzo Venezia in the middle of the fifteenth century; of the same date or earlier was the palace of Cardinal Guillaume d'Estouteville near S. Agostino which the Florentine Giovanni Rucellai in 1450 said was "walled in the modern manner". The style of these palaces was not yet that of the Tuscan architects. But though they were invisible to outsiders like the Spaniard Alfonso de Palencia, there were educated Romans who saw themselves as inheritors of a classical tradition. In 1468 under Paul II the Roman Lorenzo de' Manili built a house near the Portico of Octavia with an inscription so "classical" in style and lettering as to be a manifesto: *Urbe Roma in pristinam formam renascente* ("[Built] at the time when Rome was being reborn in its former shape . . .") it begins, reflecting the aggressive classicism of the Roman Academy of the time.

The requirements of rich cardinals whose style of life was spacious and magnificent were, however, more important than the ideas of theoretical Romanizers. Each pontificate, after the mid-century, gave favoured clerical courtiers the means to buy and build. In 1461 Cardinal Francesco Todeschini-Piccolomini bought and rebuilt a palace on the site now occupied by the church of S. Andrea della Valle, which was to be judged "as suitable to a cardinal's dignity as to the frugal way of life of a priest".

Not all Renaissance cardinals, particularly those who were blood relations of the popes, managed to maintain this difficult balance. The family of Sixtus IV, whether clerical or lay, was hardly more remarkable for moderation than the family of Alexander VI (1492–1503). Sixtus's nephew, Cardinal Raffaele Riario, built an immense palace at his church of San Lorenzo in Damaso, which, like the Palazzo Venezia of the Barbo cardinals at San Marco in Rome, actually absorbed the cardinal's titular church in the main building. The Palazzo della Cancelleria, so known from Raffaele's post as Apostolic Vice-Chancellor, was not begun until five years after the death of Pope Sixtus IV in 1484, and was not completed until 1511. This huge but elegant building was the most imposing of all the early Renaissance palaces in Rome outside the Vatican. The Lombard-trained architect Bramante, who was to be so important to Roman Cinquecento architecture, was called in to advise on the construction only at a late stage, and the identity of the architects responsible for the rather monotonous façade remains unknown. The scale and style of the Cancelleria announced, though they did not dictate, the new architectural idioms of the Roman sixteenth century.

Although the cardinals and their great palaces were important in the development of Rome as a city, they were always subordinate to the papal office itself. In Rome the papal policies were explained to the world not only through Church ceremonies but by art, architecture and urban policy. One of Sixtus IV's main political aims was the vindication of the papal supreme power against the renewal of the "conciliar" challenge by Andrew Zamometič and attacks on papal power in Germany by Gregory of Heimburg. Sixtus's success is proclaimed in the frescoes of the newly built Sistine Chapel in the Vatican Palace. One of these, by Botticelli, depicts the punishment of Korah and his sons for rebellion and heresy taking place in front of the Arch of the Emperor Constantine, the protector of the Church. Another of Sixtus's aims was inspired by his concern for the mendicant orders, and his desire to reconcile their "observant" and "conventual" wings. In Rome a result of this was Sixtus's enthusiastic patronage of the Augustinian observants, and his conversion of their church of S. Maria del Popolo from an eremite centre remote from the turmoil of the city into a rich and fashionable church rebuilt in the modern style, the centre of a new movement of urban development. Sixtus's concern for the Roman pilgrimage led him completely to rebuild the great pilgrim hostel of Santo Spirito, and to decorate it with splendid paintings which again celebrated his policies. But the explicitly propagandist iconography is not to be set apart from the works of urban development and improvement whose object was eventually the same. In restoring the aqueducts for the Roman water supply, by improving the Roman port, by re-fortifying the city and its outer defences, Sixtus was pursuing the same general policy of proclaiming papal power and glory as was reflected in his propagandist use of the arts. In a semi-literate culture these public works had a function infinitely more important than in the modern period when governments have other ways of impressing their power on the governed. It was also important that, although the adoption of Tuscan architectural usages had not even begun in Rome at this time, the whole Sixtine programme tended to be conceived in the framework of humanist language. In Melozzo da Forlí's painting which celebrated the opening of the Vatican Library under Sixtus, the humanist prefect of the Library, Platina, is shown together with his epigram which celebrates not the services of Sixtus to humanist culture but his urbanist programme in Rome.

Pope Innocent VIII (1484–1492), who followed Sixtus, was relatively unimportant in the history of Rome. Alexander VI was considerably more active as a builder and patron, and his clearing of the Via Alessandrina marked a further step forward in the rationalising of the Roman street pattern. But the planning, the style, and, if the word can be used, the temperament of Renaissance Rome owe most to Sixtus IV's nephew, Giuliano della Rovere, who was pope from 1503 until 1513 as Julius II. "Excluded from heaven", as Erasmus satirically suggested, Julius may have been. But as a builder, an administrator, a propagandist, he possessed a power and dynamism which placed his personal stamp on Rome and its social and urban organisation. No pope until Sixtus V (1585–1590) did more to shape early modern Rome. The robust energy of Julius II was more fitted to effect social and political aims than to act according to the precept of his court preacher Giles of Viterbo, at the opening of the Lateran Council, that "men must be transformed by religion, not religion transformed by men". But if Julius was only a rather ordinary Renaissance bishop, he was an extraordinary man. At a moment when every other Italian power was being engulfed or threatened by foreign conquest, Julius prosecuted a temporal policy which gave the ancient and rickety papal state new life and energy. When the French government conjured the venerable bogey of an anti-papal Church Council out of its long sleep, and set up against Julius the "Gallican" Council of Pisa, Julius replied with a policy so energetic as rapidly to make the Pisan fathers into figures of scorn. Though in the long run its achievements were disappointing, the Fifth Lateran Council summoned by Julius in 1512 was in appearance at least the imposing achievement of a Christendom brought together under Julius in the unity of the faith and in fear of the Turkish danger.

Julius II had the confidence and courage to proceed with the greatest Roman architectural work of the sixteenth century, which his uncle and his two other predecessors had suspended, the demolition of the ancient basilica of Constantine, and the construction of a new church of St Peter. Typically enough, the reason which impelled Julius to go ahead with the new St Peter's seems to have been the need for a definite home for his own tomb. But the great work he put in hand was to engage the hardly interrupted attention of his successors for over a century, and to require the expense of over a million and a half gold ducats.* Within a few years of Julius's death the methods

*The popes issued both gold and silver coins. From the late fifteenth century until 1530 the main gold coinage of the papal mint was the ducat known as the "gold ducat of the Chamber" (so called from the Apostolic Chamber, which was the principal financial bureau of the papacy). These ducats were approximately the same in value as the older gold money known as the "gold florin of the Chamber" which continued to be used as a money of account. In 1530 the papal mint issued a new gold coin, the *scudo* (properly the *scudo d'oro in oro*). The *scudo* was of slightly less value, though not substantially less, than the earlier papal ducat. The main thing for the modern reader to remember is that the *scudo*, ducat and florin were all roughly of the same value.

It is of interest to the modern reader to try to obtain a ratio between the papal ducat and the Tudor pound sterling. The relationship between the two currencies was indirect, since the papal ducat was a gold coin of issue, whereas the sixteenth-century pound sterling was a money of account representing a nominal unit of fine silver. If we bear these qualifications in mind, we can say that a Tudor pound sterling was the rough equivalent of three papal ducats.

Trying to obtain equivalents to archaic currencies in units of modern money is a notoriously frustrating business which will not be attempted here. The sort of annual money income on which a modest parson or schoolmaster might have expected to live in the early sixteenth century was, perhaps, twenty-five to thirty ducats. All these calculations, however, are very rough-and-ready. Some of the difficulties which confront modern historians in dealing with sixteenth-century references to sums of money are concisely explained in a note by the greatest historian of this period, F. Braudel, in *The Mediterranean and the Mediterranean World in the Age of Philip II* (1972), I, p. 420.

used to raise money for the rebuilding were to be the immediate cause of one of the most severe setbacks the Roman Church had known since the days of paganism. But he would be a bold man who claimed, even today, that the new St Peter's has yet finished its part in the propagation of the Roman faith.

Julius's most important enterprise in the city of Rome was the construction of the Via Giulia, a fine new street running from Sixtus IV's bridge to the Florentine church of S. Giovanni on the next bend of the river. This street gave shape and dignity to a new quarter of curialists and bankers. As originally planned there would have been in the middle of the present street a great "Julian Palace" in which all the courts of the Roman Curia would have been centralised; in front of this building there would have been a wide square. Only some of the foundations of the "Julian Palace" survive, but the Via Giulia remains the most noble of the existing streets of Renaissance Rome.

The artists and architects employed by Julius gave a new imprint to Rome. They were by no means all Tuscans, but essentially the nature of this cultural regime was that of Tuscan humanism. The architect Bramante, who was entrusted with the first designs of the new St Peter's, was the key man for the change of style. Until Bramante, Rome had participated in the revival of the classical style in architecture largely through a rough-and-ready approximation to the idioms of classical architecture which could be seen in the Roman ruins. The materials at hand, particularly the travertine blocks, were not well adapted for the smooth-surfaced facades typical of the Tuscan classicizing architects. Bramante brought at last to the Roman court the theoretical architecture of Renaissance humanism: his *tempietto* at S. Pietro in Montorio announced this change on a small scale, as the designs for St Peter's announced it on a scale for giants. At the same time he began the Belvedere in the Vatican—part-garden, part-villa, part-theatre, part-fortress—which added to the ostentation and convenience of the papal court on an equally immense scale. It needed another megalomaniac pope, Sixtus V, to close the Belvedere half-way down its immense length and to deny to succeeding generations the sight of the grandeur of Julius II's original concept.

In decorating the rooms of the Vatican Palace with paintings by Tuscan-influenced artists, Julius was less of an innovator; the walls of his uncle's Sistine Chapel were already splendid with the paintings of Botticelli, Ghirlandaio and Rosselli. And indeed the great painter called to Rome by Julius was not Tuscan but from the Appenine part of the papal state, as Pintoricchio, who had done so much in Rome and in the Vatican Palace, had been. But if Raffaello Sanzio of Urbino (Raphael) was no Florentine, his artistic formation was partly Tuscan, and Tuscan above all was his capacity to represent the iconography of classical humanism in a new pictorial balance. There begins to emerge in the early sixteenth century a sort of synthetic tradition in the visual arts in the peninsula. Rome was, because of the changed political conditions of the peninsula since the French and Spanish invasions at the end of the fifteenth century, the most suitable home for this tradition. It was fitting that Raphael and Michelangelo should be called to Rome by Julius, and that they should lead the way in giving Rome a central place in the arts in Italy which it had never enjoyed before. Julius called on Raphael to design, in the state rooms of the Vatican Palace, a series of frescoes which celebrate that fusion of humanist learning with traditional theology and papalist doctrine which Julius considered to be the cultural achievement of his own court. He called on Michelangelo to make him a tomb which he hoped would immortalise the heroic manner with which he had tried to exercise his office. Julius employed in Rome not only Bramante but the other Tuscan architects who were to work on the formative stages of his gigantic project of a new St Peter's: Sangallo the Younger, Peruzzi and Michelangelo. The Roman Church under Julius stood on the edge of catastrophe. But no one could accuse him of leading it in a near-sighted or pusillanimous way; "failure of nerve" is not an accusation that can be flung at him.

Chapter One

ROME
AND PAPAL
POLICY,
1513-1559

I

The social, the economic, the cultural destinies of Rome were all bound up with the fortunes of the papacy. The position of the popes was much weakened by the outbreak of the German Schism at the end of the second decade of the sixteenth century, which by the end of the fourth decade had turned into the Protestant Reformation. The gravity of the Lutheran crisis was not much mistaken by the popes. Leo X (1513–1521) made serious errors at the outset of the Lutheran quarrel, but his successors had no illusions about it. The notorious indecision of Leo's relative, the second Medici pope, Clement VII (1523–1534), was partly due to his consciousness of the critical nature of the issues. And the long delay of the popes in convening an effective reforming council was partly due to their fears that such a council would be used as a weapon against them by schismatics and other political enemies.

While the spiritual authority of the popes in Christendom was gravely affected, their political position in Italy became in some ways more important than in the past. The French invasion of Italy in 1494 began the long agony of the Italian states, both the city-states and the feudal kingdom of Naples. By the opening of the second decade of the sixteenth century the role of the Italian powers had been transformed.

Milan, Florence and the Neapolitan kingdom had become the instruments of the European policies of the great powers. Venice, which had for a time seemed to stand out alone, was after the catastrophe of the Battle of Agnadello (1509) reduced to a spectator's role. The papacy, though materially weak (for the reconquest of the papal state was of little account in the politics of the peninsula), alone among Italian governments retained a dignity and pre-eminence which could secure a place in the councils of the great powers of Europe. Great Italians, such as Machiavelli and Guicciardini, deplored the temporal influence which the spiritual power gave to the church, but both were realists in their own manner, and Machiavelli dedicated *The Prince* to Leo X's nephew, while Guicciardini spent most of his political life in papal service. Rome became the lung, even if a diseased one, through which Italy breathed. Genovese bankers, Lombard industrialists and Neapolitan nobles retained a social role, but only in the context of foreign power. Only in Rome could Italian intellectuals and politicians influence European politics on the grand scale as the agents of a government which was normally ruled by an Italian. When the papal historiographer Paolo Giovio in 1552 contemplated the unpleasant fate which seemed to face the papacy, he remarked that the "miserable Roman Court" was nevertheless the "sustainer of so many excellent talents". Its collapse would be "an insult to poor Italy, which still preserved the honour due to the ancient Empire by means of the spiritual obedience due to the papacy, an obedience bringing with it prosperity and temporal prestige".

The historic connection between the city of Florence and the papacy stretched far back into the period of the Italian communes, to the Guelph-Ghibelline conflicts of the thirteenth century. The intertwining of Tuscan banks with papal financial power was accomplished during the Angevin wars in Italy after 1266. The papal-Tuscan relationship underwent every kind of vicissitude in the late medieval and early modern period, but it never ceased to be important. Its manifestations were more than financial: Tuscan men of letters and administrators held important posts in the papal government throughout the Renaissance period.

The Renaissance popes never gave Tuscan banking or Tuscan culture a monopoly, even after the election of the first Medici pope in 1513. Leo X's court was as remarkable for the number of Germans it contained as for the number of Tuscans. The Genovese and German bankers retained a substantial role in the finances of the Medici popes: Agostino Chigi, the greatest banker at Leo X's court, was a Sienese and not a Florentine, even if he was a Tuscan. The election of Leo X was in most ways a confirmation of the general political and cultural direction of the papal court, not a variation. Practically all the important bureaucrats under Leo X, including Cardinals Armellini and Pucci, the two directors of financial policy, were already holding important curial office when Leo was elected.

The leadership of the Church exercised by Renaissance popes is usually pushed into obscure corners of the books written about them. Leo X was above all the continuator of the work done by Julius II in the Fifth Lateran Council, which was continued and concluded by Leo. The failure of this council to conceive or execute the great Church reforms necessary need not be wondered at. Hardly any churchman in 1512–1517 had a real conception of the complete rebuilding of the structure of the Church which reform entailed. Before proper reform could be planned, let alone put into practice, men had not only to realise the threat of extinction which the Church faced, but to re-think the basic ideas behind it. Such a task was the work of decades. Leo X asked for reform as he understood it. That he failed, for example, to ask for the ending of clerical pluralism is regrettable, but it must be remembered that seven years after the end of the Council of Trent the income of the cardinals from benefices was over a million scudi.

The fact remains that the election of a pope of the former Florentine ruling dynasty in 1513 gave a new stamp to the whole nature of papal policies and to the nature also of Roman curialist society. Papal policy was geared for twenty years (with the exception of the brief pontificate of Adrian VI from 1521 to 1523) to the needs of the Tuscan dynasty. Leo X's election led almost immediately to the overthrow of the Soderini regime in Florence and the reversal of the revolution which had exiled his dynasty from that city in 1494. It meant the needless squandering of papal troops and money on the Urbino war of 1517, whose only aim was to place Leo's nephew in possession of a duchy peacefully possessed by Francesco Maria della Rovere. This war cost Florence and the papacy three-quarters of a million ducats, though it was less financially and politically ruinous than the war to reduce the Florentine republic of 1527, waged in 1529–1530 by Leo's relative Clement VII. The Siege of Florence came at a terrible time for the papacy, just ruined by the Sack of Rome which had also been the stimulus to the anti-Medici revolution in Florence. But in spite of the general clerical crisis—for this was also the decisive period of the Lutheran and English schisms—sums of perhaps as much as a million gold florins, or two-thirds of the whole cost of rebuilding St Peter's, were expended by Clement on the siege of his native city. The pope devoted most of his attention to this military operation for two important years.

But if Medici interests deflected papal policy from time to time, the great catastrophe of sixteenth-century Rome owed little or nothing to their influence. The battle of Pavia in 1525 and the capture of Francis I of France by the Emperor Charles V upset the balance of power in Italy on which all the minor Italian powers, the papacy included, depended for their effective independence. After Pavia the margins within which the sixteenth-century popes had so far operated were so curtailed as to disappear altogether. Spanish power in Italy was now overwhelming. The only two remaining Italian governments which could pretend to a vestige of independence were Venice and the papacy, but unless they mobilised such military force as they still possessed to challenge the victorious imperial army, they were bound to accept indefinite servitude. This was the argument of some of the best minds in Italy, including the Florentine politician in papal service, Francesco Guicciardini, and the papal datary Gian Matteo Giberti, who was distinguished as much by his intelligence as by his moral probity. The great mental powers of Machiavelli approved the same policy.

The policy of resistance to Charles V in Italy hinged on a single practical factor, which seemed to offer great opportunities but was eventually to bring the policy and its authors down in ruin. This was the disorganisation and penury of the imperial armies in Italy, which seemed to be, and to some extent was, a weakness which could be exploited by a Venetian-papal alliance. But it could be exploited only by a united and powerful leadership. The hard facts were that Clement VII was just as penurious as the emperor, and that far from displaying grim determination, he showed only the same hot-and-cold hesitancy which had distinguished his whole pontificate up to that point. "A sheep instead of a shepherd" Aretino called him. It was useless for the anti-French faction in the papal curia to try to whip Clement into a determination which would harden into the ferocious aggressiveness of a Julius II. Guicciardini and Giberti had mistaken—as they often sadly regretted—their man: Clement VII was no leader for a great alliance to expel the German barbarians from Italy. Machiavelli's fierce injunction to "extirpate these wild beasts [of imperialists] who have only the faces and voices of men" was in effect accepted by Guicciardini and Giberti, but the attempt to return to the violence of Julius II's days was too much for a Medici pope to stomach. The Treaty of Cognac signed between Clement VII, Venice and the Sforza Duke of Milan on 22 May 1526 was directed against the emperor, but Clement never executed the treaty with the vigour needed to give it effect.

The pope's military weakness was exposed in the later summer of 1526 by one of the oldest phenomena of Roman medieval history, the revolt of the Roman baronial families. The imperial ambassador encouraged the Colonna to revolt, just as French agents had fomented the fatal revolt of Sciarra Colonna against Pope Boniface VIII in 1305. Though not quite as immediately disastrous as the outrage of Anagni against Boniface some two centuries earlier, the results of the Colonna revolt were humiliating for the pope. On 20 September the Colonna levies broke into Rome and looted the Vatican palace. Though they withdrew in a couple of days, they broke Clement's feeble nerve; he shortly afterwards concluded a truce with the imperialist forces in Italy. The sequel was a series of truces, often broken on either side. But the pope failed to realise that truces signed with imperialist forces in the south of Italy were of absolutely no avail to protect him from the undisciplined and unpaid hordes of imperialist troops in north Italy. When the northern imperialist army under the Duke of Bourbon started to march south early in 1527 there was nothing to defend the papal state but a few scraps of paper signed by dishonest mercenaries. Clement VII's blindness and pusillanimity prevented him from seeing a danger like that run by the popes from the murderous mercenary companies who terrorised Italy in the fourteenth century.

Bourbon entered the papal state early in March 1527. Attempts by the pope and the imperial viceroy of Naples to deflect his march on Rome were entirely fruitless. The only armed forces available to the pope were some hastily levied mercenaries under a second-rank commander, Renzo da Ceri. Giovanni de' Medici, the able leader of the "black bands", had died of wounds in the preceding year. Though the pope at the twenty-fourth hour renewed his alliance with Venice, the army of the League under the Duke of Urbino was still in Tuscany. No one resisted Bourbon in the Appenine passes; on 5 May his army was outside Rome, and on 6 May he launched an assault. Though he fell in the first stage of the operation, his starving and desperate army pressed on, took the Leonine Borgo and poured over the bridges, which the defenders had neglected to cut, into the city.

The Sack of Rome was only one of the catastrophes which afflicted Italy in the nasty third decade of the sixteenth century. Milan had already by 1527 been reduced to a miserable condition by plague and war; Naples was little better off; Florence suffered horribly in the siege of 1529–1530. But sixteenth-century men saw the justice of God executed in the spoiling of the city of the Vicar of Christ by the half-Lutheran imperial soldiery. Churchmen and bankers were tortured and ransomed, churches and monasteries were looted, women were raped and murdered—though this was no novelty in the Italy of those years. Nor was there anything new in the plight of the Romans who, even when they managed to fly from the city "like rats coming out of their holes", were hunted like wild beasts by the peasants of the Roman Campagna as they tried to get through the passes of the surrounding hills. Rome was sacked twice, first by the imperialist army and then by the savages levied in the Campagna by the Orsini Abbot of Farfa. The terror and disorder in Rome lasted over a year; plague and famine seized the city, and in the winter of 1527–1528 doors, windows and woodwork in the city, even to many of the roofbeams, had been burned, every piece of ironwork torn out even to the nails. But these again were the commonplace misfortunes of war. The victims were cardinals and nobles in chains at one end of the social scale; at the other were the wretched Jewish rabbis who had "no shirts on their backs, no bread, no wood in the house". The squalor was indescribable. "The rich shops of the merchants are turned into stables; the most splendid palaces are stripped bare; many houses are burnt to the ground; in others the doors and windows are broken and carried away; the streets are changed into dunghills. The stench of dead bodies is terrible; men and beasts have a common grave, and in the churches I have seen corpses that dogs have gnawed." But the lesson for Europe lay not in the squalor of war, which most people knew all too well, but in "the justice of God, who forgets not, even if his coming tarries. In Rome all sins are committed openly: sodomy, simony, idolatry, hypocrisy, fraud. Well may we believe that what has come to pass has not been by chance but by the judgement of God." This was the commonplace judgement of the century. It was expressed by the libertine satirist, Pietro Aretino, and by Clement VII himself. It was endorsed by the austere Cardinal Giles of Viterbo, who, using the language of the twelfth-century mystic Joachim of Flora, saw Charles V as the "new Cyrus" whose mission was to execute divine judgement through his armies.

The primary meaning of the Sack of Rome was thus that of God's judgement on his unworthy ministers. This is the language of religious symbolism and not of politics. From a narrowly political point of view, the Sack proved only what had been shown to be true many times before: that there were limits to the extent to which the Holy See could obstruct the policies of a great power which possessed preponderant military force in Italy. Rome had, after all, been sacked by the Normans in 1084 at a time when the Gregorian Reform was about to triumph in the Church. Rome only narrowly escaped a new sack, again at the hands of Spanish troops, thirty years after 1527, when the pope was not the worldly Clement VII but the fanatically religious Paul IV. In 1527 a political and military event took on a dimension above all religious and moral. Anticipation of an apocalyptic end to all things was widespread in the early sixteenth century, and not only among religious enthusiasts and extremists. The power of the pope as Christ's vicar was attacked among Christians as it never had been before: hundreds of thousands of believers had seen him named and depicted as the Anti-Christ; one wonders, too, what the effect of the news of the Sack of Rome would have had on those who had seen the engraving of the papal monster, the pope-ass, standing in front of Castel Sant'Angelo, which had been issued by Luther and Melanchthon four years earlier. In that castle Pope Clement lay, in May 1527, with the demoralised remnants of his government, the helpless victim of an anarchic army.

The papal datary Giberti had a year before the Sack anticipated the judgement of history, remarking that if his policies failed then it would be held in the history books that in Pope Clement's time the Holy See was ruined and that all Italy went amiss. He added the optimistic rider that historians would take into consideration that Clement had acted in the interests of justice to save Italy from slavery and tyranny, and had acted also with prudence, in that the princes, and especially the king of England, had encouraged him to do so. Historians have not, on the whole, treated Giberti's policies as kindly as he would have liked. But they have on the whole agreed with him about the implications of his failure. The Sack of Rome had a religious meaning for Catholicism but it also had a political meaning for Italy.

The Sack of Rome had consequences which were not only political and religious but cultural as well. Fifteen months after the Sack, the great scholar Erasmus wrote from Basle to the humanist churchman Sadoleto to console him on the plunder of his Roman library. For Erasmus the disaster of the Sack was one which affected "all nations", since Rome was not only "the fortress of the Christian religion and the kindly mother of literary talent, but the most tranquil home of the Muses, and indeed the common mother of all peoples". Twelve years before the Sack, Erasmus had expressed his nostalgia for the Rome he had visited in 1509, for its freedom, its libraries, for the conversation of the learned which was to be found there. Now he viewed with horror the brutal destruction of much of that which humanist churchmen all over Europe had held dear.

Erasmus's phrase "the common mother of all peoples" was an adaptation of an already common saying; Romans themselves, when talking about the cosmopolitan nature of their population, referred to the city as "the common domicile of the world". When Erasmus called the Sack a disaster for learning and the arts, he expressed a horror felt by all but the most passionately anti-papal of humanists. The effect of the Sack was to disperse a whole generation of artists and scholars, and to break up the learned circles, equivalent of the later salons, which had congregated in the villas and gardens of such churchman patrons as Angelo Colocci or the Luxemburger John Goritz. After a few years the learned returned to Rome, and the villas were rebuilt and re-furbished with ancient statues and works of art; one of the most elegant, Villa Lante on the Janiculum, which was built by Giulio Romano for the papal datary Baldassare Turini, still exists, as do the frescoes which were painted for it before the Sack. But at the time the scholars felt the Sack as a devastating blow. Giovanni Pierio Valeriano wrote a treatise on their misfortunes, and wrote another to justify the wearing of beards by priests, many of whom had sworn like Clement VII to wear them in token of mourning for the events of 1527. The barbarian devastation of that year marks a gap in the economic and cultural life of Rome no less than in its demographic development.

In the history of art and architecture the Sack of Rome is important not as a catastrophe but as the motive for a dispersion which propagated in Italy the "Roman" style of the community of artists and architects which had grown up there in the past decade. Polidoro da Caravaggio, the decorator of the façades of the Roman palaces, left Rome for ever; Giovan Battista Rosso and the architect Baldassare Peruzzi were tortured before they escaped; Giulio Romano and Jacopo Sansovino, also propagators of the Mannerist style, took their talents to other princely courts. Viewed in this light, the Sack can be judged to have been as much a cultural bonus for Italy as a cultural disaster for Rome.

II

There seems, then, to be no good reason for making a clean break in the social history of sixteenth-century Rome on account of the Sack of 1527. That it created a gap can hardly be denied. For eight or nine years building almost stopped; house prices fell; the great boom of the earlier Medici period was at an end. To the evils of the Sack and the plague were added those of the great Tiber flood of 1530 and the famine of 1532. The income of the pope and his court declined because of the general religious crisis; the gross income of Clement VII in 1525 may have been double the income drawn by his successor Paul III early in his pontificate. Aretino cynically suggested that though the *monsignori* in Rome tried to starve their servants after the Sack on the pretence of poverty they were in reality richer than ever, but this is overdrawn. Camilla Gonzaga described Rome as "still beautiful, in spite of the Sack" in 1533. Construction of the fine

Palazzo Massimo alle Colonne had begun by 1532, and one of the Gaddi palaces was rebuilt almost as soon as the Sack was over; the beautiful Cesi chapel in S. Maria della Pace was executed by Sangallo in 1530. By the time of his death in 1536 the architect Baldassare Peruzzi had not only built Palazzo Massimo, but had reconstructed the Savelli palace above the Theatre of Marcellus, and had been engaged by the pope with Antonio da Sangallo the Younger to re-commence the great works at St Peter's.

Alessandro Farnese, (Pope Paul III, 1534–1549) was the first mem-ber of the great Roman families to become pope since Martin V of the Colonna family in the preceding century (1417–1431), and was directly in the tradition of the great Roman magnate popes of the Middle Ages. Like them, he "carnally" indulged his relatives with the monies and privileges of the church, making the shifty Pier Luigi Farnese Duke of Parma and Piacenza, giving his grandchildren fifty or a hundred ducats at a time from the papal privy purse to gamble at the Roman Carnival. From minor barons of the Papal Patrimony and the Neapolitan kingdom, whose main boast was to have led a few hundred troops under the papal banner, the Farnese became one of the great families of sixteenth-century Europe, the close relatives of kings and emperors. The pope employed Antonio da Sangallo and Michelangelo to make the palace he had already been constructing for himself as a cardinal near Campo dei Fiori into the most splendid in Rome. His grandsons, Cardinals Alessandro and Ranuccio Farnese, built at the family seat at Caprarola the finest of the palace-villas of the Roman Campagna. In the Palazzo Farnese and the Palazzo della Cancelleria in Rome, and in the state rooms at Caprarola, great artists painted scenes which announced with vulgar ostentation the triumph of the Farnese family. Perhaps the pope whom Paul III most resem-bled was the thirteenth-century Orsini, Pope Nicholas III, whose great castle of Soriano stood only a few miles from Caprarola.

Paul III was born in 1468, and belonged to the generation which produced almost all the later Renaissance popes. He was by seven years the senior of Leo X, and by ten years the senior of his predeces-sor Clement VII. If we except Adrian VI (b. 1459), who belonged to an earlier generation, and Marcellus II, who reigned for only a few weeks, all the popes to reign from 1513 to 1559 were born between 1468 and 1487. Paul IV, the "Counter-Reformation" Pope (1555–

1559), was only a year the junior of Leo X and two years the senior of Clement VII. That all these popes were adult by the early years of Pope Julius II helped to make the social history of Rome in this period more homogeneous.

Paul III's main aims at his accession were the pacification of Europe, the assembly of a General Council to reform the Church, and a war against the Turks. As a Roman, as the former protégé of Alexander VI, and as the former pupil of Paolo Cortese, who had formed the ideal picture of the humanist Italian cardinal, Paul was entirely convinced of the superiority of Roman culture and civic life. He was the practical exponent of the dignified, polished way of life of the Roman court in which his whole career had been spent. Paul III's reconstruction of the Roman Campidoglio, executed in part by Michelangelo, was inspired by the idea of the grandeur of Rome and the Roman people, and the universal nature of Roman rule. That Paul subjected the Roman civic government to stern papal despotism did not affect this attribution of leadership to Roman ideas. The culture of Paul III's court was directly continuous with that of his Medici predecessors, and, beyond them, with that of Julius II and the patron of the Farnese, Alexander VI, whose anniversary Paul III meticulously celebrated in his chapel.

The first assertion of Roman recovery under Paul III was made at the time of the visit of the Emperor Charles V to Rome at Easter 1536. Although, as Aretino ironically observed, when Charles V inspected the ruins of Rome he saw not only the ancient ruins but the new ones his own troops had made nine years earlier, and although the Romans trembled when they saw among his troops some of the hated faces of their tormentors of the days of the Sack, the imperial visit was still an occasion for grave and solemn pomp. The wretched Romans were taxed by the pope to finance a big programme of road clearance in the Forum; scores if not hundreds of houses were demolished so that the imperial procession could ride from the Colosseum and along the Via Triumphalis. The Campidoglio was still a heap of ruined buildings, and instead of pausing there the emperor rode down the Via Papale to the Vatican. The antiquities were pointed out to him by Latino Giovenale Manetti and the other papal humanists; the man who had destroyed the city was received as an honoured guest. But the splendour of the temporary triumphal arches erected by Antonio da Sangallo and others in the square of S. Marco, at the entrance to the Borgo and elsewhere, proclaimed, with the rest of the pompous apparatus, that Rome was no longer convalescent after the sickness of the Sack, but was once more free and splendid. The reception of the emperor was, naturally, a reflection of the independence which Paul III claimed as between Francis I of France and Charles V. The emperor's speech before the papal Consistory attacked this independence, and called on the pope to choose between himself and France, but in vain.

To re-assert prestige costs money. So did such great works as the building of the Farnese palace and the resumption of work on St Peter's. Nor was the calling of an ecumenical council something that could be done without expense. The Turkish danger was in the 1530s a real threat to security in central Italy, and not a mere occasion to assert the principle of Christian communal interest. Since Paul III's initial income was so modest, he had to borrow to meet all these calls on his revenues. To secure these loans he multiplied and pledged the venal offices; in the middle decade of his pontificate he borrowed the equivalent of two years' ordinary papal income in this way. Another year's income was borrowed by floating new stock in the papal *Monte della Fede*, a system which is explained in Chapter II. To finance these loans, and to push papal income back towards and then above its level before the Sack, Paul III turned to the expedient on which all later papal finance was to be based, the taxation of the subjects of the papal state. This policy met with resistance, and to implement it he had to fight the so-called salt-war with the Perugians and with the baronial family of Colonna in 1540–1541. But the eventual result was the imposition of a huge annual tax, the so-called Triennial Subsidy, which having first been imposed for a three-year period in 1543 was renewed by Paul III and by all subsequent popes of the period, so that it became the basic papal tax. By these means the income at the pope's disposal at the beginning of Paul's pontificate in 1534 was almost trebled by 1551, two years after Paul's death. As in so many other matters, Paul III laid down the main lines of the policies to be followed by successive popes for the rest of the century.

Once the prejudice of the nineteenth century against Mannerist art is discarded, there is little reason for thinking the pontificate of Paul III culturally inferior to that of the Medici popes, nor for considering the Rome of his day a sort of pale Indian summer after the splendours of the "High" Renaissance. Paul's own works in the Palazzo Farnese, on the Campidoglio, and in the adjoining papal villa, in the fortification of the Leonine City, in St Peter's, were costly constructions executed by master architects. The gardens of the Belvedere in the Vatican palace were given fine walks and enriched by the statues excavated from the Baths of Caracalla. But Rome was adorned by many other builders than Paul. Palaces were built on a scale that far more than sufficed to replace those destroyed in the Sack: the two Mattei palaces, the elegant Sangallo palaces in Via Giulia, Palazzo Ricci, many others in the regions frequented by bankers and merchants. Churches were built: the important church of Santo Spirito in Sassia and confraternity churches such as those of San Giovanni Decollato and the Oratory of the Gonfalone. Distinguished painters were employed to decorate these constructions, among whom were Francesco Salviati, Jacopino del Conte and Taddeo Zuccaro. And over all Rome brooded the spirit of Michelangelo, who had made the whole city into a workshop to contain the architectural meditations of a noble and wise old man. This Rome was not a city run by a frivolous old clerk from the court of Alexander Borgia who had outlived his own period; it was a city controlled by a deeply civilised and intelligent man, which reflected the highest aspirations of the culture of his time.

III

It has been claimed that as early as the time of Pope Paul III the papacy gained in moral and political authority from the general collapse and uncertainty about religious and ethical norms which the Reformation brought with it. It is true, perhaps, that the Catholic generation which was first confronted by the unethical politics which can be loosely called "Machiavellianism" tended to turn to the principles of Ignatius Loyola, and that behind St Ignatius stood Pope Paul III, who gave legal status to the Society of Jesus. But other judges have seen Paul III as a man who can only with reservations be viewed as the first pope of the Catholic Reformation. If Paul stood firmly for the calling of a Catholic Reform Council, it was largely because he was clever enough to see that in the eyes of European public opinion the Roman Church could not morally survive without it. When Paul III saw that Catholic reform was right and expedient, he was only making a judgement which had already been made, under different political circumstances, and without acting upon it, by his mentor Pope Alexander VI.

In Paul III's time all Europe lay under the shadow of Hapsburg power. The figure of Charles V has been rather idealised by some twentieth-century biographers. It ought to be emphasised that, if he is a patron saint of European unity, he is a very brutal one. Hapsburg authority was imposed by military force, by arbitrary criminal justice, and by religious persecution. The Sack of Rome was only one example of the exercise of Hapsburg terror in Italy. Lombardy and Naples experienced the same terror repeatedly; in Tuscany Cosimo de' Medici was hardly more than its agent; in the mid-century Siena was ground cruelly into the dust for daring to re-assert the ancient communal liberties of the free Italian city-states. It is not surprising that the predominant emotion of the popes about Charles V was fear, sometimes even physical fear. Not only was Paul III frightened of Charles, but Pope Julius III (1550–1555) had been as Cardinal del Monte one of the ill-treated cardinal-hostages handed over to the imperialists in 1527 when Clement VII was besieged in Castel Sant'Angelo; the German soldiers had hung up Cardinal del Monte by his hair. Charles V was not above threatening to repeat the Sack of Rome, a menace he several times made to papal ambassadors, if only in grim jest.

The Reform Council was first summoned to Mantua in 1537, and first met in Trent in 1542. Its tortuous history reflects a political situation in which, far from being united in their determination to defend and reform the faith, the papacy and the Hapsburg Empire pursued divergent and often hostile courses. If Paul III's attitude to Charles V was characterized by fear, that of Charles V towards Paul was dictated by hate. In spite of the marriage of convenience which Charles V enforced on his bastard daughter Margaret with the depraved grandson of Paul III, Ottavio Farnese, the emperor regarded the Farnese family with a sentiment much stronger than dislike. Charles V never willingly accepted the neutrality of the papal court in the great quarrel between the houses of Hapsburg and Valois, and he became increasingly impatient of the papacy's attempt to act in its traditional role of mediator between Christian rulers. Charles saw himself as the only great princely champion of the Catholic faith, and viewed Francis I and Henry II, allies of the infidel Turk and the German Protestants, as unworthy and unchristian princes. Even so, he treated his Valois opponents with a chivalrous respect which he denied to the popes.

Charles's bitterness towards the popes was first given full vent in the speech he made before the papal Consistory in Rome in 1536. Subsequently, from the negotiations at Nice in 1538 to those at Brussels in 1553–1554, Charles V gave only a grudging and often hostile reception to the many clerical diplomats in papal service who tried to mediate between Hapsburg and Valois. In the complex diplomacy of the war years, and in the equally complex diplomacy of the Council, papal aims and positions changed many times. They came nearest to those of the emperor while he was preparing for the war against the German Protestants in 1546, but even after the papal-imperial alliance of June of that year, at the high tide of their diplomatic amity, pope and emperor continued to treat one another with distrust. Paul III's immoderate ambitions for his own family, which he hoped to satisfy by bending imperial power in Italy to his own ends, did not help matters. His attempts to secure Milan for the unprepossessing Ottavio Farnese got nowhere. His creating Pierluigi Farnese papal Duke of Parma and Piacenza, cities to which the emperor also claimed title, created a groundswell of imperial resentment.

"Summit meetings" between pope and emperor were not lacking. The most impressive, after the imperial coronation of Charles V in Bologna by Pope Clement VII in 1530, was the great state visit of the emperor to Rome in 1536. On this occasion, as in 1530, the whole apparatus of Renaissance pomp and splendour was deployed in "triumphs". The triple meeting of Paul III, Charles V and Francis I at Nice in 1538 was on a less grand scale, largely because the participants were housed on board ship in galleys. The meetings at Nice were in any case rendered slightly farcical by the refusal of Francis I to meet Charles V face to face. But Nice was perhaps more productive of diplomatic results than Rome, since it led to the conclusion of the Franco-imperial truce. There were further papal-imperial meetings, of an entirely business-like nature, at Lucca in 1541 and at Busseto, near Parma, in 1543. At the last encounter the proposal for a Farnese candidature for the Duchy of Milan was discussed and left undecided, but in effect rejected. The most important decision taken at Busseto was that to suspend the Council then sitting at Trent. Taken all in all, Paul III's returns from his personal meetings with the emperor were small.

In both the papal and the imperial bureaux there were long traditions of mutual hostility. The "Erasmian" humanist tradition of moralistic scepticism in the imperial household was in the 1540s beginning to turn into a new tradition of *raison d'état*, equally critical of the popes. In 1543, when Paul III was trying to persuade Charles V to grant Milan to his grandson Ottavio Farnese, Diego Mendoza wrote a violent memorandum against the pope, asking the emperor, who had worked more evil against him than Paul III, and advising him to proceed in Milan on the principle that "might is right". On the papal side the medieval tradition of "Guelph" hostility to imperial policy in Italy still endured. A year after Mendoza wrote his memorial, in the papal court Claudio Tolomei composed a "Discourse on whether the pope should declare himself for the imperialists or for the French", in which he strongly recommended the latter course. Tolomei indicted the anti-papal policies of Charles V, which he represented as the logical continuation of the policies of earlier emperors who had also desired the ruin of the Church. Tolomei incited Paul III to take vengeance on Charles V for the Sack of Rome. Paul III was far too cautious to act on such advice, but clearly in 1544 the Sack was not forgotten.

For Rome the most important thing about a Catholic Reform Council was that it could not take place there; the main city of Christendom was excluded from being the seat of its reformation. While Luther's demand for a "free Council on German soil" was never conceded, European and especially imperial opinion was unwilling to accept some new version of the Lateran Council of Julius II and Leo X. If the Council of Reform was also going to be the Council of Union, to bring back the Protestants into the church, then it had to sit in a German-speaking town. For these and other reasons neither the original summoning of the Council to Mantua in 1537 nor the transfer from Trent to the papal city of Bologna in 1547 was accepted by the imperialists. The idea of Roman Councils, which in medieval

Christianity went back to the Roman Lenten Synods held by Gregory VII in the eleventh century, seemed to be dead.

IV

In the 1550s these same questions of the Council and of imperial policy in Italy presented themselves to the popes with increasing urgency. Cardinal del Monte, who had succeeded Paul III as Julius III in 1550, was not a man of heroic stature; he was described by one of the imperial envoys as "a rabbit". Julius III was widely said to want a quiet and agreeable life as pope. He did not add to his reputation by his making a corrupt little fifteen year old retainer, who had kept his pet monkey, into a cardinal of the Roman Church. Julius III also has been claimed as a pope of the Catholic Reformation, but the reservations to be applied to his case are surely as great as those to be applied to Paul III.

The Franco-imperial conflict created serious political and security problems in Rome itself. Most cardinals were pensioners either of the French or of the imperialists, and the two hostile factions among the cardinals, with their dependent prelates and diplomats, and the similarly opposed factions of the Roman aristocracy, were like two rival headquarters set up in Rome. Great diplomatic functions, such as the celebration of the birth of a son to the king of France, were often made into political demonstrations by one Roman party against the other. One of the arts of papal government was to pick a way among the hostilities of the Francophile and imperial factions in the Roman Court; the contemporary historian Paolo Giovio gives especial praise to Pope Paul III for his skill in this difficult field of papal policy. Julius III, who like his predecessor Paul had the justified reputation of being more or less pro-French in his general opinions, was no less skilful than Paul in dissembling his real views. The support given by Henry II of France to the rebellion of Ottavio Farnese against the Holy See made Julius, in any case, less benevolently inclined towards France than he had been as a cardinal. Like Paul, Julius saw the absolute necessity of bringing the Council to a successful conclusion, and the major achievement of Julius's pontificate was the re-opening of the Council at Trent in 1551.

The two main political trends under Julius outside the Council were the breakdown of papal attempts to mediate between Valois and Hapsburg, and the collapse of the Italian policies of the Renaissance popes. Charles V was determined in his last years not to suffer any more the kind of mediation which he attributed to Paul III, and which he described as "like the trick employed by cloak sneak-thieves in Spain, where one man steals your cloak, and two others come and assault you, 'to make peace between you', when the first man has already taken your cloak". Charles made clear in this image an intention, which he put into effect, not to trust or to follow the advice of papal mediators in their attempts to end the Hapsburg-Valois war.

But the most important change for Rome in the 1550s was the end of anything resembling "Italian liberty" in the face of imperial power, and the end of a truly independent papal state. From 1552 the rebellion of Siena against the empire, its acceptance of a French garrison and the attempt to put the city under papal protection marked the last episode in the long series of attempts by the papacy, which went back to the policies of Julius II at the beginning of the century, to assert Italian autonomy against ultramontane intervention. Julius III aimed at a neutral status for central Italy which would protect the papal state from the constant threat of military encirclement by imperial troops from Tuscany in the north and Naples in the south. Failing this, he was willing to connive at the imperial reduction of Siena. The march of the imperial troops from Naples through the papal state in the early spring of 1553, passing near Rome on the Via Casilina, was an evil omen for the future. But Julius did not act willingly; he saw himself as the "slave bound hand and foot" of the ultramontane "tyrants". His attempts to guarantee Sienese neutrality by means of a papal protectorate were fruitless. The imperial masters did not give up their subjects so easily. At the same time Rome and the Romans lived in constant fear of imperial aggression.

V

Julius III died in 1555 without solving any of his political problems. His immediate successor, Marcellus II, reigned for only three weeks.

On 23 May 1555 Gian Pietro Carafa was elected pope at the age of seventy-nine years, the last pope of the generation which began with Leo X in 1513, and so the last pope to have been adult in the court of Alexander VI. Paul IV was the zealot who had been waiting in the wings of the papal court for his moment for over half a century. A member of the Oratory of Divine Love from its foundation and the head of the Theatine Order, he considered his own orthodoxy unimpeachable and his judgement of the orthodoxy of others infallible—so much so that he had intrigued against the election of the imperialist Cardinal Pole to the papacy on the grounds that Pole was a heretic. A great deal has been made of Carafa's passionate southern blood, but his mother's family had been tyrants of Aquila, which is only just over the border from the papal state; the Carafa of Madaloni were a family of Neapolitan courtiers stemming from the region of Benevento. Perhaps the key to his temperament may be found in the ferocious independence of the mountaineer.

Politically, Paul IV was the last of the Renaissance popes in that he was the last pope to make the freedom of Italy from ultramontane interference into the cornerstone of his policy. He was not merely Francophile and Germanophobe but passionately Italian. Early in the pontificate he protested to the Venetian ambassador that once ultramontane people had only been employed in Italy as cooks, bakers and grooms (referring to the main traditional employments of Germans in Rome and the papal court), but that now they ruled Italy, to the ruin and shame of the Italians. The emperor was a heretic, a tyrant, a schismatic, who regarded Rome and all Italy as his own property. Like his predecessors, Paul IV looked back and referred constantly to the Sack of Rome, but this time inspired not by fear but by hatred of imperial power. Early in his pontificate he signed the offensive alliance with France before which his predecessors had all recoiled. Little wonder that when St Ignatius Loyola learned of Carafa's election he felt in his horror that all the bones in his body had been wrung.

The armistice of Vaucelles, concluded between France and the Hapsburgs in February 1556, showed clearly to the world how irrelevant papal policy had become to the great powers that dominated Europe. The Council of Trent had been suspended. The Franco-imperial truce which papal mediators had for years sought to sponsor was concluded, not merely without the help of papal mediation but at a time when the pope wanted war with the Hapsburgs. The pontificate of the zealous Paul IV was not a time of the triumphant assertion of Catholic principle, but one of bitterness and humiliation for the pope and for the city he ruled. The policies of the pope were in themselves mistaken, but their application was made even more disastrous in practice by the corruption of the pope's nephew Carlo Carafa, who had been made from a soldier into a cardinal by a procedure hardly more defensible than that which had made a boy monkey-keeper into a cardinal under Julius III, and with results far more serious for the welfare of Rome and the Holy See.

The war with the Spanish regime in Naples which broke out in the early autumn of 1556 was just the disaster for Rome and the papal state which might have been anticipated. The poet Joachim du Bellay, who was in Rome at this time in the suite of Cardinal du Bellay, described the city as dark and gloomy, full of the sound of drums and the clash of arms. The Duke of Alba occupied Ostia and the south of the papal state immediately. There was a short respite as a result of renewed French military intervention, but in the summer of 1557 all resistance to Spanish military power in the papal state collapsed. At the end of August Alba brought his army almost to the walls of Rome, and probably only refrained from storming and sacking the city out of fear of the unfavourable consequences for Spain in European public opinion. Paul IV's attempt to play the part of the warlike Julius II was over.

Paul IV passed most of his pontificate in a state of delusion about political realities. Rather cruelly, fate permitted him to discover, in the New Year of 1559, the extent of the moral corruption of the Carafa nephews who had for four years been all-powerful in secular policy. The disgrace of the papal nephews in January 1559 was not the end of papal nepotism, but it was the end of papal nepotism in its Renaissance form. Paul IV died on 18 August 1559. On 3 April 1559 the signature of the Treaty of Cateau-Cambrésis had finally transformed the political world into which Gian Pietro Carafa had come as a young clerk in the 1490s. French power was finally excluded from southern and central Italy. The time of Italian liberty was over; Rome, like the rest of Italy, was entirely dependent on Spanish power. The role of the papacy in European politics was not over, but it was entering yet another phase of its long history.

VI

The pontificate of the Carafa pope was one of the lowest points of sixteenth-century Roman history. The Spanish war alone was a major disaster, since it meant two years in which Rome was practically cut off from its hinterland, found it difficult to import foodstuffs, could not receive pilgrims or tourists, and had to pay huge emergency taxes for purposes of defence. Natural disasters were added to these man-made ones. In September 1557 Rome experienced the worst Tiber flood since that of 1530. Mills and bridges were destroyed, and most of the reserves of food which had been built up against a siege were spoiled. Prices of staples were already very high in Rome, but the flood losses sent them to famine levels. Paul IV never took much in-terest in the fate of the poor, whose conditions of life his policies made intolerable. His government in 1555 tried to expel all able-bodied tramps and beggars, and when famine hit the city three years later the agricultural workers from the countryside were also expelled, even though many of them must have been refugees from areas devastated by the war.

The pontificate of Paul IV was in some respects a reign of terror. The powers and instructions given to the Roman Inquisition by Paul, and the secret and arbitrary procedure of the tribunal, meant that widespread accusation, imprisonment and torture of innocent persons were practised in a way never before customary in Rome. The in-structions to the Inquisition to pursue sodomy and simony as well as heresy meant that there were relatively few persons in the Roman court free from suspicion. Absolutely, the number of persons judged and sentenced by the Inquisition may not have been large, but its operation cannot be called other than despotic and terrorising. The persecution of the Jews was equally harsh and frightening. Fierce restrictions of a social and an economic kind were placed on the whole Jewish community, including the confiscation of their real property and the physical confinement of the Roman Jews in a new "ghetto".

Most of Paul IV's measures had depressing social and economic effects. This was also true of the new issue of the Index of Prohibited Books, which was drawn up in such a way and on such a scale as to make the printing press practically superfluous. Perhaps the most sadly significant of all the intellectual prohibitions was that against all the works of Erasmus. When his works were prohibited in Rome, the Renaissance might be said to have come to an end.

Paul IV's place in the history of Rome is thus almost entirely negative. The Roman people showed their opinion of him immediately after his death by tearing his statue down from the Campidoglio and knocking it to pieces, by destroying the Palace of the Inquisition, and by defacing the Carafa arms all over Rome. The pasquinades uttered against him and his family are more ferocious and obscene than any others in a fierce and obscene tradition. Yet it is doubtful whether his pontificate was more than an unfortunate parenthesis in the history of sixteenth-century Rome, and a far less drastic parenthesis than the Sack of 1527. If Paul marked a serious recession in Roman urban order and prosperity, his predecessor Julius III had not. Under Julius the building and planning which had begun under Paul III had continued. Not only had new palaces and streets developed, but the new concept of the "suburban villa" had begun for the first time to assume an important place in the lives of the greatest figures of the Roman court. The pope himself led the way, emulating Leo X's Villa Madama by his construction outside the walls of Rome of his great "Villa di papa Giulio". At the same time Cardinal Ippolito d'Este was beginning at Tivoli one of the finest of all Renaissance villas in the Roman area.

Paul IV's pontificate was the watershed. Two years after his death the development of Rome under Pope Pius IV was described with enthusiasm: "The city is unfolding itself in its fullest beauty. The pope promised at the beginning of his reign to protect religion, peace and justice, and to provide for the material needs of his capital, and he has kept his word. Rome has a superabundance of grain, wine and other necessaries, and the feeling of general contentment is universal".* The development of sixteenth-century Rome was tied to high ideals and great matters. But the price of a loaf of bread and a flask of wine was never unimportant to those who lived there.

*Quoted by L. von Pastor, *History of the Popes*, xv (English trans. 1928), p. 130.

Chapter Two

THE ECONOMIC BASIS OF ROMAN LIFE

I

Rome was far from the greatest even of the Italian cities of the early sixteenth century. Naples was far more populous; Florence and Venice had more developed and decorous traditions of urbanism and civic life. Rome was a mere reflection of the power and the ostentatious courtly life of its bishop. Like the other notable Italian cities, it was the capital of an Italian state; it owed this position not to the diligent and warlike qualities of its citizens but to the ancient political guile of the Roman clergy. Rome neither produced nor manufactured goods of primary importance. Its textile industry was negligible beside the great centres of north and central Italy. In so far as it profited from the agriculture of the surrounding Roman Campagna, it participated in a rural life which was at this time entering a long period of decline. Rome contained none of those streets of industrious artisans, of saddlers and cordwainers and ironworkers, which marked the urban plans of Paris or London or Cordova, or of Aleppo and Damascus and Fez in the Muslim world. The typical Roman industries were luxury and service industries: jewellers, silversmiths, painters, me-

dallionists; bankers and innkeepers; masons, architects, land speculators. The hub of Roman life was the Roman court, a great service
industry dedicated to the administration of the clergy of Catholic
Europe. Round this primary activity revolved all the rest. Roman life
was the life of the court in a way typical of no other city of the time,
save perhaps of Madrid in the later part of the sixteenth century. The
French poet Joachim du Bellay wrote that Roman life consisted of
courtiers and bankers, and that what mattered in Rome was to know
how to borrow money, and how to baffle or deceive other courtiers
with an enigmatic "messer si", "messer non".

The origins of Rome's place in Christendom are to be found in the
traditions of the early Middle Ages. The Roman bishop was the
guardian of the pilgrimage to the tombs and holy places of the martyrs, the custodian of the deposit of faith, the primate of the Latin
bishops. On this basis had arisen the great structure of medieval
papalism, and the legal and administrative machinery which papalism
brought into existence. The practical consequence of papalism was a
network of courts and offices, small by twentieth-century standards,
but complex, numerous and costly by those of the sixteenth. The centre of the web was the great papal "family" of seven hundred or so
persons in the Vatican Palace, though other offices such as the
Chancery and the Penitentiary were outside the Vatican, and the
papal bureaux as a whole cannot have employed less than a thousand
persons.

But though the papal bureaux were the heart of the Roman clerical
establishment, they were far from all of it. Twenty-five or thirty resident cardinals, with an average "family" of a hundred and fifty persons for each cardinal, and an agreed minimum income requirement
of 6,000 ducats annually, were a part of the historic Roman Church.
So were the titular churches of the cardinals, the great Roman basilicas including St Peter and St John Lateran, the monasteries and
nunneries, the hundred and thirty parish churches, upwards of two
hundred other churches. So were the hospitals and asylums, whose
history went back collectively, though not individually, to the Roman
Church of the late Empire. The number of secular priests and religious of both sexes in Rome in 1609 was over 6,000 out of a total
population of 100,000; at the beginning of the sixteenth century,

(48)

when the population was half that of a century later, the total is unlikely to have been less than 3,000.

Banking dominated the economic side of Roman lay life. Some bankers occupied posts such as that of "depositary" to the Apostolic Chamber, the main financial agency of the papacy, or one of its branches. But the main concern of the bankers was the transmission of money to Rome, and especially the settlement of the papal taxation on benefices. The systems of "annates" and of papal "provisions" to benefices throughout Europe were intricately tied up with the bankers, who were often given custody of the papal bulls of appointment or of the consistorial notes (cedulae) of appointment to a benefice until the money due to the papacy had been settled. By this means the Apostolic Chamber collected dues from places as far afield as Scotland and Poland. The banker dealt with the clerk who was obtaining the benefice or with his proctor in Rome, with the Apostolic Chamber and the Chamber of the College of Cardinals, and in the case of "consistorial" benefices with the cardinal who proposed the appointment in consistory.

The raising of long- and short-term credit by the papal government was almost entirely the concern of the banks. Bankers "farmed" most of the more important papal revenues—the alum mines, the customs of Rome, the salt monopoly. They advanced large sums to the popes on the security of the "assignment" of the spiritual revenues. They made loans of a more old-fashioned kind on the security of papal jewels and treasures. They kept their fingers firmly in the profitable pie offered by the sale of papal offices, in which they facilitated individual or corporate investment. They floated the later papal loans or monti on behalf of the popes. They also offered important services to the cardinals and to the papal courtiers and diplomats in general, in fact to everyone frequenting the Roman court, including the European governments and their representatives. Little wonder that bankers settled in Rome from all the important banking centres of Italy—especially from Florence, Genoa and Siena—and from the German firm of Fugger. There were also families of Roman bankers, some of ancient lineage. There were lesser fry such as the twenty or thirty Jewish banking firms, and the smaller Christian moneychangers known as "bancherotti". There was, finally, the activity of the

(49)

Roman papal mint, which was normally managed by a banker. The "holy martyrs Rossus and Albinus", the red gold and the white silver, were still two of the main patron saints of Rome.

As financial operators the bankers were by no means alone. Beyond the monies which came to the pope and the main papal officials in their directly official capacities, lay an enormous and practically undefinable field of financial practice carried out by members of the papal court, especially in so far as they were clerks who owned church benefices in other parts of Italy or elsewhere in Europe. Clerical pluralism and clerical absenteeism were an integral part of papal government; papal control of the benefices of Catholic Europe, and papal collection of information about what happened to these benefices, turned the papal court into an immense market for church offices. The system of allowing favoured clerks to hold numbers of abbeys in commendam, and to administer numbers of bishoprics and draw their revenues, led to huge accumulations of clerical income in the hands of a few prelates. Cardinal Willem van Enckenvoirt (1464–1534), the datary of Pope Adrian VI, controlled at least twenty-six bishoprics, without taking count of abbeys or of minor benefices. The value of the revenues thus acquired was vast, and the freedom to dispose of them surprising. Van Enckenvoirt had papal permission to dispose by will of income from his benefices up to a total of 25,000 ducats annually. Cardinal Alfonso Carafa (1540–1565), the young nephew of Paul IV, was after the disgrace of the Carafa in 1560 allowed to put his benefices up to auction so that he could pay the required fine of 60,000 scudi. Cardinal Ippolito d'Este was attacked by Alfonso's uncle, Paul IV, as a man who had bills of exchange in his pocket to the value of one or two hundred thousand scudi, and who could grant benefices worth from 50,000 to 60,000 scudi annually. When Giulio de' Medici was elected pope as Clement VII in 1523 he distributed his benefices among the cardinals on his accession; they represented an annual nominal value of 60,000 ducats (though his real income was only a third of this sum). The young Cardinal Carlo Borromeo, destined but not yet qualified for sainthood, had an annual income of 50,000 gold scudi.

The number of higher clergy who enjoyed these really monstrous accumulations of income was small, smaller perhaps than even the total number of cardinals. But practically every member of the papal bureaucracy of any influence or importance enjoyed some kind of accumulated clerical patronage, and the total of the monies controlled by the clerical bureaucracy must be reckoned as having exceeded, perhaps even doubled, the monies directly controlled by the papal central government.

It will be clear that the Holy See and its satellite organisations could not exist without good communications. The pluralists in the Roman court laboured only by putting pen to paper. They could collect the fruits of their pluralism only by ceaseless correspondence with the rest of Italy and the rest of Europe. Everything in Rome was turned to the outside. Papal diplomacy was complex, expensive, and equally dependent on good communications. There was no system of permanent papal ambassadors, but the papal *nunzio*, who might be either a clerk or a layman, was beginning to be a semi-permanent feature in the courts of France, Germany and Spain. Over thirty papal *nunzi* were despatched to the French court between 1525 and 1534. The cost of these missions was not negligible; the popes budgeted to spend between 16,000 to 20,000 scudi a year for this purpose. The papal legate was a more traditional and more dignified envoy, whose despatch was even more expensive. The Apostolic Chamber, the main financial agency, sent its own agents abroad as "Apostolic Collectors": the last of these to visit England, under Henry VII, was Pietro Griffi. All these papal agents were continuous sources of information for the papal court, and so the essential cogs of papal central administration. Every time a major benefice was vacated in France or Spain, couriers sped down the roads to Rome to inform the papal court whether its rights were involved.

In essence communications were unchanged from earlier centuries, but this does not mean that they were poor; within the technical possibilities of the times, Roman communications were good. The establishment of a regular postal service by the papal master of the posts dates from the second half of the sixteenth century. But the office itself dates to the first part of the century, and the maintenance of a relay system of post horses along the main lines of communication was already one of his main duties. Gerardo Mattia di San Cassiano, the papal postmaster, was powerful enough to be a formidable enemy of St Ignatius Loyola, who had placed his mistress in a hostel. The kings of France and Spain both kept "masters of the posts" in Rome, with large staffs, and Rome became eventually the centre of the whole Hapsburg postal service. The Roman banks maintained their own courier service, which was usually at the service of the pope; the Florentine banks ran a particularly important service between Rome, Florence and Lyons, and the Genovese banks had a parallel service. By the ordinary services Rome was a week from Milan and Genoa, four or five days from Venice, three or four from Bologna, Florence or Naples. Paris was a distance of three weeks, Brussels the same, London almost four weeks, Madrid a month, Vienna a fortnight. Special messengers could at considerable expense cover distances in a far shorter time.

Rome was a great mart for the exchange of political information. As a diplomatic centre it was as important as Paris, or as Madrid by the mid-century. The advent of standing embassies during the later fifteenth century, and the development of a legal and social status for the standing ambassador which brought him from being a barely tolerated spy to being a specially accredited permanent negotiator, gave Rome great advantages. The sixteenth-century popes appreciated the importance of diplomatic representation at Rome. Paul III was praised for having admitted Roman nobles to some ceremonies at his coronation to which Clement VII had admitted "only the ambassadors". Rome was the natural diplomatic forum for Catholic powers, not only for matters concerning religion (and what important political issues did not involve religion in the sixteenth century?) but for the affairs of Italy, and for matters involving the Ottomans and the eastern Mediterranean. All the Italian powers, not only the important ones such as Milan and Venice, but minor ones such as Siena and Mantua, kept ambassadors or agents in Rome. Only the Florentines seemed to find that their relations with the Holy See were already too close for an embassy to be necessary, though they prized the concession of a consulate to look after the interests of their nationals in Rome. Imperial diplomatic rights in Rome dated back to the early Middle Ages. France spent large sums on her Roman embassies. Portugal maintained an embassy which gave the name of Portugal to a triumphal arch spanning the Corso, though at the time of the Sack the Portuguese embassy was located in the Theatre of Marcellus. The most notable power to fail to maintain some form of semi-permanent diplomatic representation in Rome was England, which, with perhaps momentous consequences for English relations with Rome, stuck to the old-fashioned method of pensioning a curial cardinal or a Roman notable to look after its interests.

The ambassador was by profession a lavish spender. His household was unlikely to number less than seventy or eighty persons, unless he was merely an observer for an Italian city. The state entries and exits of ambassadors to and from Rome were opportunities to display the wealth of host and guest; an ambassador of importance would on such occasions be escorted by gaudily caparisoned processions of cardinals and Roman nobles. The receptions an ambassador gave, the banquets to which all the major clergy and gentry must be asked, were marked by ostentation and magnificence. The birth of a son to Henry II and Catherine de' Medici in 1549 was the occasion for an entertainment by the French ambassador which included a bullfight and a mock siege of a wooden castle specially erected in the Piazza dei Santi Apostoli. The protests made by Cardinal Gian Pietro Carafa (the future Paul IV) against such an exhibition taking place in Lent did not prevent it.

Conspicuous hospitality of this kind marked the power and prestige of the host government, and might also be an occasion for the display of the political support which it could command among the Roman nobility. The Renaissance feast, with its attendant theatrical entertainments, dances, music-making, was the occasion for the expenditure of large sums of money. The scenography for the "intermezzo", or entertainment given between the scenes of a play, could be an elaborate stage set for which artists of great talent were employed. For the banquets, immense quantities of gold and silver plate were used. The honesty of the guests was by no means above suspicion, and Agostino Chigi's famous device of having the plate flung into the Tiber (where it was caught in nets) may well have been a means of protecting it from his guests. The whole process of diplomacy brought money to the Roman economy. When the young Charles de Guise, newly designated as a cardinal, came to Rome to receive the red hat in 1547, he brought with him eighty followers, and 30,000 écus for "honourable expenses".

Ambassadors were pompous and extravagant, but Rome could live without them. She could not live without the pilgrimage; the *romapeti* or *romei* were the visible sign that Rome was what it claimed to be.

Without them the great churches were meaningless shells. The pilgrimage reached its seasonal height in Holy Week of any year. Every twenty-five years, the indulgences associated with the Roman Jubilees which had been instituted by Pope Boniface VIII in 1300 brought far greater crowds. The total numbers of pilgrims cannot be known more than very approximately, but it seems that in a year in which the pilgrim influx was unaffected by war or plague, the grain consumed in Rome was reckoned to exceed by a half the amount which would have been consumed by the stable population of the city. If the latter is reckoned at fifty or sixty thousand, and if allowance is made for the short stay in Rome of the average pilgrim, it is hard to place the annual influx at fewer than 100,000 pilgrims. No doubt the humble pilgrim who could not afford to stay in an inn, but slept on a straw palliasse which he bought in the precincts of St Peter's and took to a dossing house, made only a tiny contribution to the Roman economy; if he was housed without charge in a pilgrim hostel it would have been even less. But the economic benefits of the pilgrimage were still vital to Roman life. Upwards of 120 inns properly so called existed in the 1520s, and the total number of establishments offering accommodation of one sort or another was probably as high as 500; in a Jubilee year it could rise as high as 1,000 and still not satisfy the demand. But in a civilisation whose culture was largely oral, the pilgrim had a function beyond the economic one; he took back with him the image of Rome, devotion to Roman saints, reverence for the Roman bishop. These were more important than the religious trinkets sold him by the paternoster vendors.

The Lutherans denounced pilgrimages and indulgences as frauds. The outbreak of Lutheranism coincided with a period of instability in the Roman area: the plague of 1522, renewed plague epidemics and the Colonna rebellion of 1525, the operation of French and imperialist armies in the Campagna, the disastrous Sack of Rome of 1527 and its sequel combined to make the third decade of the sixteenth century a terrible one for the peaceful traveller. In northern Italy the miserable conditions of the Milanese Duchy in the mid-twenties made the northern pilgrim roads equally unpleasant. Small wonder that the Jubilee of 1525 was a failure. Yet even if the first part of the sixteenth century saw a decline of the Roman pilgrimage, the building of hostels and the provision of other facilities for the pilgrim went on.

Important for the future was the foundation by S. Filippo Neri of the Trinità dei Pellegrini in 1549. The Jubilee of 1550 was a modest affair for the same reasons as that of 1525; only by 1575 had the peace of Italy, the progress of Catholic reform and the rebuilding of Rome combined to bring the Roman pilgrimage back into favour with the masses of Catholic Europe. There is, however, no reason to believe that the stream of pilgrims in Rome ever came near to drying up, save in the exceptional conditions of 1527–1530.

If there was a certain thinning out of early sixteenth-century pilgrims, there was also an influx into Rome of a new kind of visitor, the educated or semi-educated tourist. The gradual adoption by the European governing classes of humanist educational programmes meant a new attitude to the antiquities of Rome. Baldassare Castiglione was the author of the *Cortegiano*, the *Courtier*, a book which influenced social and educational attitudes as much as any other published during the sixteenth century. He was also the Mantuan agent at Rome, a papal courtier and *nunzio*, and the author with the painter Raphael of a pamphlet on the antiquities of Rome and the relation of the modern artist to antique models, which influenced aesthetic theory almost as much as his own book influenced social behaviour. Earlier in the century the Roman clerk Paolo Cortese in his book on the cardinalate had laid down an equally humanist programme for the governing ranks of the clergy. To see the remains of ancient Rome, and to acquire Roman "antiquities" for his own use, were gradually becoming normal desires of an educated man of means. It is true that the popularisation of this trend did not begin until the mid-century. For the first half of the sixteenth century the printers were still bringing out only new versions of the medieval *Marvels of the City of Rome* for the popular market; antiquarian accounts of Roman antiquities existed, but they were written in Latin. Only in 1556 did Lucio Mauro's *Le antichità della città di Roma* begin the stream of guide-books written in the vulgar tongues.

It is too early, in the sixteenth century, to make a sharp distinction between the pilgrim and the cultured gentleman, the forerunner of the itinerant gentry who made the Grand Tour in the eighteenth century. There was, however, even in the early sixteenth century, a sort of superficial "cultural" tourism which was noticed by Aretino. One of his prostitutes uses her arts on foreigners who "came to spend only

eight or ten days in Rome", and who when they had seen the antiquities or the "old stuff" *(le anticaglie)* wanted to see the bits of skirt
or the "new stuff" *(le modernaglie, cioè le signore).* Berni in his bur-
lesque verse told folk not to bother to go on pilgrimage to Rome any
more, either with the idea of climbing the Holy Stairs on their knees
or to look at triumphal arches, the Colosseum, Roman bridges and
aqueducts and so on. Whether they went to Rome out of piety or out
of a desire to look at antiquities, they would still do better to come to
his tavern in Florence. *(Se vanno là per fede, o per disio / Di cose vec-
chie.)* The reference to popular rather than learned tourism is as clear
as in Aretino. These anonymous tourists were more important for the
Roman economy than the distinguished learned men who came to
Rome and left their mark in the written records.

II

Rome was an appendage of the Roman court, and the finances of
Rome were in the last analysis the papal finances. These monies were
linked to the universal powers claimed by the popes, as Luther noticed
when the Dominican Tetzel preached an indulgence for the rebuilding of the church of St Peter. Luther was not interested in accounts,
and he would have treated an analysis of the papal budget with the
same contempt that he treated Tetzel. But for Roman society the real
sources of papal income, as opposed to the folk-myth sources, were
not a matter of indifference. If Protestant propaganda about papal
blood-sucking had been right, the inhabitants of Rome and the papal
state could have rejoiced. The realities gave them considerably less
cause for celebration.

The income drawn by forty-one cardinals from benefices at the
beginning of the sixteenth century amounted to 350,000 gold ducats
annually, or at least as much as the gross papal income of the same
period. The revenues of seventy cardinals from benefices in 1571
amounted to the huge sum of a million gold scudi, or half as much
again as the total papal income of the time. If we consider that besides
the cardinals there were usually thirty or forty curial bishops, and as
many prelates again, who, while neither cardinals nor bishops, were

enjoying the incomes of major benefices, the total monies coming into the Roman court from benefices can hardly have been, in the period of the Council of Trent, less than double the whole of the income which came to the papal government proper. This is a not untypical illustration, for the sixteenth century, of the superior wealth and power of oligarchies as contrasted with governments. It was also one of the main proved grievances of critics of the papal system.

The monies received by curial officials as fees from the users of the Roman court were small when compared with the incomes of benefice-holders. Curial officials' fees are thought to have been in the region of 150,000 gold cameral ducats in 1520–1521, and substantially less, about 130,000 gold scudi, in 1561. The real value of the fees was lower than this, as the estimates of their value were made in gold, but they were actually collected in silver, and often in coinages foreign to Rome and of an inferior quality. The value of silver in terms of gold declined, moreover, throughout the sixteenth century. Though the fees were fiercely resented by those who paid them, their total value amounted only to a tenth or less of the total monies coming into the papal court from all sources.

The finances of the papal government were to some extent fixed by tradition and custom, but in the end they were controlled by the pope's own personal policy. The areas in which the pope's decisions were especially important were the control of government borrowing (which included the sale of offices), the facility with which the papal court granted "graces" or dispensations, and the willingness of the pope to create new cardinals and so to cause the "vacation" of many of the offices and benefices which the new cardinals had held before their promotion. A city full of bankers and office-holders was very sensitive to financial policy. The bankers and men of money were naturally happiest with a policy of heavy government spending. When Pope Adrian VI (1522–1523) adopted a policy of retrenchment and economy after the end of the spendthrift pontificate of Leo X, the Dutch pope was abused by every section of Roman society. Many of the Tuscan bankers and some of Leo X's curial officials left Rome; the great artistic and building enterprises of Leo were put aside, and the artists followed the bankers out of Rome. German financial management took over the papal court. Adrian's biggest offence was his desire to restrict public credit and to stop the runaway indebtedness of

the previous pontificate. Adrian had little success in restricting transactions in the venal offices, though the mere knowledge that he had
consulted Cardinal Campeggio about the possibility of suppressing
them led to disquiet and discontent. Adrian was a blight for the Roman builders; his severity in sequestrating the houses of courtiers
who died in Rome was complained of because "no one wants to build
any more". This reversal of Sixtus IV's decision to let curial clerks
bequeath real property in Rome to their heirs menaced the whole legal
basis on which Roman urban development rested. It is not surprising
that after Adrian's death a paper was attached to the papal doctor's
door which hailed him as the saviour of his country.

Like most sixteenth-century rulers, the pope drew his revenue from
sources which were basically those approved by ancient custom, but
which had been in recent times modified by the cautious exercise of
arbitrary power. Like other rulers, the pope was busy building a ramshackle structure of improvised public credit, whose main materials
were the sale of government offices. And like the rest, the pope from
the mid-century onwards had to deal with a decline in the value of
silver in relation to gold, and a rise in the prices of many goods.

It was usual to distinguish between the revenues which the pope
drew from his "spiritual" and his "temporal" power, though the distinction could be misleading. Many of the ancient "spiritual" revenues were obsolete and could no longer be collected. The demise of
"Peter's Pence" from England was a small loss, but the inability of the
popes to raise tenths, or assessed income taxes on clerical revenues,
from the clergy anywhere save in Italy and Spain (and even there only
with the permission of the lay governments) was a great one. These
"tenths" were requested only for "crusade" purposes, but the crusade
in the sense of the war against the Turks was a real and permanent
charge on the papal budget.

In the early modern period the revenues of the spiritual power were
principally from "annates" and "common services". Both were assessed value taxes on benefices which were bestowed through papal
action; the most important were those conferred through the process
of the papal consistory. "Common services" were shared between
pope and cardinals equally, and the cardinals had their own collegiate
financial office to deal with these revenues—which, for any individual
cardinal, were very modest in amount. The annates were in real terms

a declining revenue, because the assessments either remained constant at those reached in the fifteenth century, or were reduced. They resembled in this the "tenths and fifteenths" collected from the counties by the English parliaments of the same period. The annates were still large enough to be reckoned as substantial in papal sixteenth-century budgets; by the seventeenth century they had declined to insignificance.

Another substantial "spiritual" revenue was that from "compositions". These were essentially an expedient resorted to by fifteenth-century popes when other sources of income were drying up. When a "grace" was conceded to a supplicant by the papal court, he might have to make a "composition" with the papal officers about the amount due to be paid for it; the amount of this composition was determined by the official known as the datary, who by the early sixteenth century was one of the main officials of the papal court and also of the papal household. The competence of the datary was extremely wide, and extended to other papal departments such as that of the Penitentiary. The papal budget of 1525 remarked that the revenues from compositions amounted to more or less "according to the exigencies of the moment"; if the pope cared to "open his fist" (*alarghare la mano*), he could concede dispensations more liberally and so enlarge the compositions revenue. The whole practice represented a decline from the high standards of legality and good accounting which had been set by the medieval popes, especially since the compositions were from a legal point of view so arbitrary.

From the early fifteenth century onwards the monies from compositions had tended to be handled by the pope's personal household financial officers (the "Secret Treasury") and to be at the pope's personal disposal. By the time of Pope Paul II the outgoings of the monies handled by the datary were almost identical with those of the private household accounts. These were not the household accounts in the sense of the expenses of the Apostolic Palace; the papal wine and meat bills were settled in other ways. But the Secret Treasury represented the pope's personal spending money—"il vivere delli pontefici" as Pope Paul IV described it. The datary was the pope's poor box, and between 15 and 20 per cent of its monies went for alms for the poor. But far larger sums from datary funds were spent on the needs and pleasures of the pope's own relations. It was from this source that

Paul III found 600 scudi for his grandson Ottaviano Farnese to spend in the Roman Carnival of 1540.

Though the income from compositions was not enormous (it came to 64,500 scudi annually averaged for the period 1534–1565), it was important because it was ready money of a kind never assigned either to office-holders, bankers, or to shareholders in the papal debt. Nor was it used to finance papal building projects. There were periods when the compositions represented between half and a third of the entire disposable balance of the papal income. It was therefore extremely hard for successive popes to give way to the criticisms made by theologians of the principle involved in charging money for papal "graces"; whether the money was simoniacally acquired or not, the popes could not do without it. So although reform of the compositions was asked for by the Reform Commission of 1536–1537 and subsequently, no radical changes were made. In the seventeenth century the compositions income increased, though changes in monetary values may have been responsible for this.

The datary also managed the sale of offices, which was the main method of raising long-term credit for the papal government in the first half of the sixteenth century. The sale of office in a bishop's court may seem shocking by the standards of modern administrative practice, but it was not indisputably so in the sixteenth century, when most lay governments raised money in this way. Only one or two papal offices, such as that of Papal Chamberlain, were not venal in the Renaissance period, and all were venal by the end of the sixteenth century. The system followed was to sell the office as something amounting to a life annuity, the emoluments of the office providing the annuity payment. The office might be re-sold after it had been "vacated", on the payment of a forfeit percentage charge to the papal government. The purchase of offices might with papal permission be financed by companies (societates officiorum) on behalf of individuals.

From the last two decades of the fifteenth century popes set up new "colleges" of sinecure offices, whose titularies had either merely honorific duties or none. Such new offices might in appearance be part of the curial bureaucracy, such as the 101 sollicitatores (banteringly known as "Janissaries") first established by Sixtus IV (1471–1484), or have a half-curial, half-honorific nature such as the sixty chamberlains (*cubicularii*), or be frankly snobbish in intention such as the college of 400 "knights of St Peter" set up by Leo X in 1520. The last category allowed such humble persons as the painter Baccio Bandinelli, who had been lampooned for his creation as a knight by the Emperor Charles V, to become a knight papal as well as imperial. But whether the offices were honorific or not, assignments of papal revenue had to be made to make them into reasonable investments for the purchaser. Some colleges of "officials" such as the shareholders in the Roman port taxes (*portionarii Ripae*) seem to have been specifically directed at the small investor, as not more than two shares could be held, and the office could not be sold. From an early stage property in the venal offices was spread over a wide social range: the papal gendarmerie, the body of *servientes armorum*, was staffed largely by barbers, smiths, bakers and other artisans. Women were able to purchase a few offices.

The great leap forward in the expansion of the venal offices was made by Pope Leo X. At the end of the pontificate of Julius II (1503–1513) the number of venal offices was under a thousand. By the end of Leo's pontificate in 1521 they had been more than doubled in number; the number of venal offices now amounted to three times the number of people actually resident in the papal court. The invested capital in the offices in 1521 represented 2,500,000 gold ducats in round figures, and the rent due to the officers came to 300,000 ducats annually. This rent was raised partly through assignments made on the revenues of the papal state (110,000 ducats), partly from the papal share of the annates and common services (40,000 ducats) and partly from the fees paid by the users of the Roman court to the officers concerned (roughly 150,000 ducats). A third of the papal income was thus devoted to payment of rents to office-holders. The fees paid by users of the Roman court to officials had doubled by 1521 since the beginning of the century, a fact which did not go unnoticed.

One social consequence of the sale of offices may easily be imagined; the office-holders did not feel under a strong obligation to work! Even in the offices like those of secretary or abbreviator of apostolic letters where the task clearly had to be carried out, leave of absence was often given to execute other duties. The purchase of several curial offices by the same person was frequent, although attempts were made to restrict the practice; and pluralism cut down even further the work done by officials. The wonder is not that the system worked badly, but that it worked at all. That the pope was able to attract to his service men not fanatically religious and of the greatest talents, that they were in spite of this cumbrous system willing to devote their lives to his administration, and to riding the muddy and uncomfortable roads of Europe as his emissaries, shows that Rome still had power over men and exercised fascination upon them. Self-interest was not, of course, absent; the plums of the Roman court were still worth eating. A system which made self-indulgent men like Paolo Giovio or Giovanni della Casa into bishops of the church was not one which turned the greedy away.

Many sixteenth-century popes added to the burden of papal debt assumed through the venal offices. Clement VII adopted the new expedient of borrowing on the *monti*, which is discussed below, but Paul III instituted four new colleges of "knights", which were added to by Pius IV (1559–1565). Quite clearly, the papal ideas of the time of the Council of Trent were in no way opposed to venal offices. By 1564 the total capital invested in the offices had risen to 3,300,000 gold scudi, and the rents due to the investors to 342,000 scudi annually, representing a return on invested capital of 10.7 per cent, and absorbing about 30 per cent of papal revenue for repayments. The practice reached its peak during the sixteenth century under Sixtus V (1585–1590), who not only instituted a new college but confirmed and strengthened the rule that promotion to a new ecclesiastical dignity entailed the loss of all the offices a person held. By this means he was enabled to promote ecclesiastics into bankruptcy.

Except at moments when whole new colleges of offices were floated, the revenue from the sale of offices was uncertain, since it depended on the casual factors of the deaths and promotions of office-holders. Vasari in his *Lives of the Painters* reproaches the painter Francesco Salviati with having made a bad investment in buying offices, since he did not live to enjoy them and his heirs got nothing. Leo X took very large sums from new offices: 400,000 ducats from the "Knights of St Peter" alone. Under Clement VII the revenues from the sale of offices were lower after the Sack of Rome, perhaps 50,000 ducats annually; under Paul III they were about 77,000 scudi; and under Paul IV again about 50,000. The average for the whole period

1535–1565 was 78,300 scudi, about 10–15 per cent of total papal revenues.

The total of the annual payments due to the office-holders was practically double the average annual amount which could be considered as borrowed from them. Such a situation was only acceptable because the rate of interest paid by the popes on loans secured in other ways was often in the region of 18 per cent. The popes also used the offices themselves as pledges to their bankers, so that the system lent itself to a double series of loans. About a third of the office-holders rendered services to the popes for which a salary was appropriate, so a part of the payments made to them should in modern terms be counted as wages rather than as interest repayment. But this kind of reasoning is misplaced for the sixteenth century, which made no social distinction between active employments and sinecures. All governments of the period borrowed from their servants, many of them by means of the sale of offices. The papal government was no exception.

The sale of offices still did not provide enough income for papal needs. In 1526 Clement VII had recourse to a system of borrowing which was new for the popes, but very old for the Italian cities: the system of state loans known as *monti*. The *Monte della Fede* floated by Clement had an initial capital of 200,000 gold ducats split into 2,000 shares or *luoghi di monti* of a hundred ducats each. The loan bore 10 per cent annual interest, and was secured on the revenues of the customs dues of Rome. Paul III doubled the capital of the *monte* and reduced the rate of interest to $7\frac{1}{2}$ per cent. Some *monti* holdings were extinguished by the death or ecclesiastical promotion of the holder, but most were held in full property and were subject to transmission to heirs by will.

From 1550 onwards the system of *monti* became as important as the venal offices to papal finance. Julius III (1550–1555) launched a whole series of loans of this kind, and by 1564 the popes had borrowed in this way something like 1,500,000 silver scudi, and 400,000 scudi in gold. The pioneer researches of Delumeau* led him to con-

---

*Vie économique et sociale de Rome dans la seconde moitié du XVI siècle (Paris, 1957–1959).

clude that between 1526 and 1605 the papal government borrowed 10,750,000 silver scudi and substantially over 1,500,000 scudi in gold. These huge sums made Rome into one of the most important money markets in sixteenth-century Europe. Though the market was only fully developed at the end of the century, the Genovese and Tuscan bankers and the German firm of Fugger were fully entrenched in Rome at its beginning. The Fugger and the Genovese connected the financial world of the papal court with that of the Hapsburg Empire.

Few sixteenth-century states were able to raise loans without earmarking specific government income to cover the interest payments. The papal government made specific assignments of this kind to cover both the payment of salaries of the venal offices and the interest due on the government loans or *monti*. The nature of these assignments reveals the basis of the whole papal financial system of the sixteenth and seventeenth centuries. The assignments were made only to a negligible extent on the "spiritual" revenues which came from Europe in general. One "college" of officials only, the "annatisti" whose payments were secured to the extent of about 40,000 ducats annually on the first fruits or annates, depended on assignments of the "spiritual" revenues. But most of the colleges were paid from papal-state revenues which had been specially marked for the purpose. In 1520 rather more than half the interest on the venal offices was payable from papal-state sources; in later periods the proportion was even higher. The interest due on the papal *monti* was to an even greater extent secured on the revenues of the papal state. The first *monte* of 1526 was secured on the customs dues of the city of Rome, and this arrangement merely pointed the way to later ones. The *monti* of the early 1550s were secured on the same source of revenue, and those of the second half of the same decade, floated by Pius IV, were secured on other taxes in the papal state, or on the revenues of the papal alum mines. The borrowing of the second half of the century was entirely secured on papal-state revenues, and the burden of taxation on the population of the papal state rose in proportion. Rome, it is true, drew great economic benefits from the papacy, but the papal state as a whole was not strong enough to bear the economic burden which the high destiny of the papacy thrust on it.

III

One part of the papal state was too closely linked with the Roman economy to be left out of a discussion of the foundations of Roman economic life. The Campagna Romana, the countryside surrounding the city, was largely owned and exploited by landowners who lived in or had houses in the city, as was true for any Italian city of the period. The extent of the Roman District was legally defined by the list of the smaller communes who paid their salt tax through the Roman communal authorities. The effective economic control of Roman magnates, bankers and "barons" who more or less took an active part in Roman court and political life extended further even than the Roman "District". The Farnese family, for example, under Paul III carried out some of their most intense building and political activity in the Duchy of Castro, in the extreme north of the papal state. The papal government for some administrative purposes treated the agricultural area of the Campagna Romana as that within fifty leagues of the city. It is probably best to treat the whole area of the coastal provinces of the papal state between the northern border of Castro and the southern border of Terracina as being in one sense or another part of the agricultural domain of Rome.

Most of the richer classes of Rome were landowners in the Roman Campagna in one way or another. The clergy themselves, in so far as they were attached to or profited by the great spiritual corporations of the city, owned enormous tracts of land in the Campagna. The great churches, not excluding St Peter's itself, the monasteries, greater hospitals, titular churches of cardinals, were all proprietors of estates, some of them of enormous antiquity and huge extent. Much church property had been secularised at Rome in the later Middle Ages, as it had been elsewhere, but the amount remaining under clerical control was vast, even though the process of secularisation was far from finished.

The "Roman barons" were the feudal class of the Roman area, or more exactly the feudal class of the papal provinces of the Patrimony of St Peter in Tuscany, of Campagna and the Maritime Province, of Sabina or part of it, and of the immediate Roman area. The part played by this class in Roman political life had always fluctuated; in spite of the imposing Roman palaces of such families as the Caetani,

Colonna, Orsini or Savelli in the sixteenth century, the period was one in which their urban political influence was in eclipse. But as long as such great lords had houses or palaces in Rome, and formed part of the papal court and of the papal political system, their wide lands could be said to form part of the Roman economy.

The urban aristocracy, much of which would not a century earlier have called itself noble, was a landowning class more than a merchant class, though the great banking families must be excepted. But the bankers were also landowners, even the non-Roman bankers. Agostino Chigi, the Sienese banker, was said to have owned 300 horses, 300 cattle and 12,000 sheep on his estates north of Rome. The great estate of Longhezza in the Tivoli area, formerly church property, went to the Medici family under Leo X and to another family of Florentine bankers, the Strozzi, under Clement VII: it remained with the Strozzi until the nineteenth century. The Roman family of Massimi were landowners as well as bankers; so were the Altoviti and the Mattei. Such families bought estates in the Campagna with the profits of their financial operations in Rome. Other more conservative Roman families might perhaps be considered more landowners than anything else, and some of the great sprawling "palaces" in Rome of such families as the Altieri, Iacobacci or (on a more modest scale) the Boccapaduli, with their conglomerations of stables, barns and labourers' quarters, were as much great farmhouses as "palaces". Great flocks of sheep would be brought down from the hills in October to winter not only near but within the walls of Rome; the shepherds of the highland area of Norcia who cared for them are recorded in the Roman census. At a lower level there was an important class of landowners, stockbreeders and grain merchants who would at a slightly later phase of Roman urban history be known as "mercanti di Campagna". The guild of stockbreeders, or *bovattieri*, united great magnates with such small men. There was also a substantial agriculture, especially wine-growing, practised within the walls of Rome itself.

The most important benefit of the agriculture of the Roman Campagna was that in the first half of the sixteenth century under normal political and agrarian conditions Rome was fully supplied with grain from its own countryside. The rest of the papal state was a net exporter of grain, and not only the March of Ancona on the other side of the Appenines, but even areas relatively close to Rome such as Chiusi, the granary of Perugia, did not normally supply Rome. The high costs of road or even river transport made it more economical to import from Sicily to Rome than from the papal March of Ancona. The northern part of the Patrimony of St Peter in Tuscany, the grain-growing areas round Castro and Tuscania, would normally reckon to export a part of their crop through the ports of Corneto (Tarquinia) and Civitavecchia. The cereals of the papal state, especially the wheat, were not of top quality, and much of the crop was in oats, barley and spelt. But except under circumstances like those of the Sack of 1527 or of the floods of 1530 or the famine of 1538–1539, Rome would not expect to import cereals on a large scale, beyond those supplied by its own hinterland.

Stockbreeding and sheepfarming were as important as cereals in the agriculture of the Roman area. The rough pasture and *macchia* which formed a large part of the Campagna, and which were un-forgettably described in the hunting handbook of Boccamazza, the papal huntsman of Leo X, lent themselves to the raising of horses and cattle which pastured wild. Other large areas were given over to transhumance sheepfarming, the beasts pasturing in the high Appenine in the summer, and being driven down in huge herds to pasture in the coastal lowlands such as the areas around Corneto (Tarquinia) in the autumn.

Like other contemporary governments, the papal government was concerned about the depopulation and the decline in cereal produc-tion which it feared would follow the turnover from arable cultivation to pasture; like the English Tudors it feared that sheep would eat men. There was legislation under Julius II, Clement VII and Paul III to en-courage the agricultural tenants of the Roman Campagna to put a third of their holdings under the plough, whether the landlord agreed or not. Under certain circumstances peasants could occupy a holding without the owner's consent, provided they cultivated it, and paid him a proportion varying from a fifth to a tenth of the produce. Not unnaturally the landlords resisted this law; their arguments were not received by the papal government, but their practical power over their tenants was so great that it may be doubted whether the law was very effective. The profits to be made from cereal growing were con-siderable, but the poor standards of soil cultivation probably cut them heavily, and it was suspected by contemporaries that landlords re-stricted the arable land in order to keep up grain prices. However, the cattle and sheep raising which enriched the *mercanti di campagna* brought economic benefits to Rome, even if it failed to soothe the fears of the papal government about possibilities of famine.

Whatever form of cultivation was used, the product was taxed by the government if it entered the market. Movement of grain in bulk needed government permission, and was subject to tax (the *tratta*); some concession was made to small cultivators by charging them a lower rate when grain prices were low. Movement of beasts from one pasture to another was taxed (the *fida*), and when the sheep came down from the hills they had to be pastured in lands authorised by the tax authorities, for which a further tax was due (the *dogana dei pascoli*). All these were standard forms of taxation employed by many Italian governments, though those used by the Neapolitan regime to tax transhumance sheepfarming were most similar to papal methods.

Rome consumed enormous quantities of wine, and apart from the inns there were several hundred wineshops. Much of this wine, both the luxury and even the less costly kinds, was imported. The wine dealers with warehouses at the port of Rome (the *Ripa Grande*) were important enough to have their own guild. But very large quantities of cheap Roman wine came from the Roman Campagna, where both to the south and the north of Rome wine-growing had been practised on a large scale from ancient times. The handling of wine in bulk in Rome was carried out by a guild of specially accredited *sensali*. The government taxed all wine moved into the city, and from the proceeds the Roman University was financed.

Without the agriculture of the Campagna, Roman life would swift-ly have broken down, as indeed it did break down during the two years following the Sack of 1527. Not only grain and wine, but enor-mous quantities of meat and olive oil were supplied by the Cam-pagna. Less obvious to a modern observer than these were the huge quantities of firewood consumed by a sixteenth-century city. Delu-meau has estimated the annual consumption of firewood in Rome towards the end of the century at something like a million cubic metres. Vast quantities of wood, most of it of a much higher quality, were consumed by the Roman building industry. Anyone looking up at the enormous timbered ceilings of the sixteenth century in some

Roman churches—in Santa Maria Maggiore, notably, which was timbered and gilded by Alexander VI—may well be reduced to awe both by the bulk of the wood employed and by the immense length of the beams. Whole forests were felled to provide wood for the great Renaissance churches and palaces, from the slopes of the Monti Lepini in the south to the great alpine woods of the area called Massa Trabaria in the north of the papal state. It is not surprising that one of the first papal prohibitions against the felling of woods in the papal state is dated 1518. The Campagna also supplied Rome with minerals; iron was mined in the southern part, and the papal alum mines at Tolfa north of Rome were the most important in Europe. Alum mines were far more important, however, for their direct contribution to the papal budget, than for any importance they may have had for the small Roman textile industry.

The relation between the Italian cities of the early modern period and the countrysides surrounding them was a most complex and delicately organised social phenomenon. An older generation of historians, influenced directly or indirectly by the sharp agrarian conflicts of late nineteenth-century Italy, saw the cities as exploiting their surrounding country districts with simple brutality. That such exploitation had existed at Rome, and continued to exist in the sixteenth century, can hardly be denied; its symbolic manifestation was the salt-tax payable to Rome, and the obligation of villages and towns in the Roman District to supply men and materials for the games held in the annual Roman Carnival. On the other hand, that so many Romans were themselves landowners and stockbreeders in the Campagna meant that agricultural interests were not invariably subordinated to urban ones. The papal government's sporadic attempts at drainage and improvement schemes in the Pontine marshes were not very significant; its legislation on behalf of small cultivators was more important. There was also, by the mid-century, a new tendency for great clerks and nobles to move into the countryside and to build themselves great villas, parks and pleasaunces. These operations brought the countryside both economic benefit and loss. The sixteenth-century villa in the Campagna was not necessarily a centre for estate management as it usually was in Tuscany; the villas at Frascati were expensive playgrounds which can have brought little benefit to the peasantry of the area. But the great Farnese building programmes on their estates at Castro, Capodimonte and Caprarola brought prosperity and employment to some.

But the real scourge of the papal state was the severe and inequitable taxation, which gathered force from the second decade of the sixteenth century onwards, and from the middle years of Pope Paul III became acute. Taxes on consumption were typical of early modern Europe, but the Roman taxes, from the time of the oppressive *stadera* or general consumption tax which Cardinal Armellini imposed under Leo X, were especially severe. When to the many indirect taxes Pope Paul III added the direct "Triennial Subsidy", he set up the machine which his successors used to finance an indefinitely increasing burden of debt. One cannot really separate cities from countryside in assessing the results of this fiscal policy, which was against the interests of both.

IV

Money supply and prices were important for the agricultural sector of the Roman economy, but even more so for the curial sector. As the most important European financial centre of the late Middle Ages, the Roman court had maintained a good and abundant supply of gold and silver money. The Roman Mint *(Zecca)* was one of the vital centres of curial activity. The Mint was reconstructed by Bramante for Julius II in the middle of the financial and trading region of Ponte, next to Bramante's church of S. Celso; it was then again remodelled by Antonio da Sangallo the Younger. Sangallo's façade remains on this building, which is now occupied by the Banco di Santo Spirito. The Mint was farmed by the Apostolic Chamber to bankers, sometimes to individuals, but on some occasions in the Medicean period to the Florentine community in Rome. The technical ability of the artists and artisans of the Mint was of the highest order, and they produced not only a very beautiful coinage, but medals and medallions which can be described as great works of art.

From the early Middle Ages the papal court had been able to lay hands on an adequate supply of gold. The offerings of the faithful in St Peter's and the Roman churches were mostly in silver, but offerings of princes tended to be in gold. From the time of the development of the financial system for the conferment and taxing of benefices, payment was due to the Apostolic Chamber in its own gold coinage, which has been thought by some modern historians to have assured to the Roman court a supply of gold quite out of proportion to its true European economic importance. Contemporaries put the matter more bluntly by asserting that Roman priests were bleeding their countries white.

The papal treasury and the Roman churches tended to accumulate masses of precious objects, reliquaries, monstrances, jewels and so on. Fewer of the most precious gold objects were preserved than might be supposed. The vicissitudes of the Great Schism (1378–1417) had disposed of most of the accumulated treasures of the medieval popes. The sparse finances of fifteenth-century popes meant that many remaining treasures were pledged or melted down. When the sepulchre of a noble lady of Imperial Rome was uncovered under Innocent VIII, the pope hastened to have the gold brocade of her robes melted down in the papal mint. But on the other hand the popes were from the time of Paul II (1464–1471) onwards collectors of antique objects, jewels, cameos and coins, and in spite of sales and losses these tastes added to the value of the contents of papal palaces. The Medici popes were indefatigable and extravagant collectors, though their family tastes were for ancient gems and cameos rather than for bullion.

The direct financial role of papal treasure was not very important. Papal tiaras, jewels and gold objects were pledged in moments of emergency: at the financially troubled end of Leo X's pontificate, a loan of 10,000 ducats was obtained in this way, but the sum was negligible compared with papal debts. The almost complete loss of papal treasures in the Sack of Rome in 1527 seems to have had no direct effect on papal finance; in fact in the period after 1530 Clement VII was spending very large sums with Benvenuto Cellini and other jewellers to replace some of the lost objects. Paul III seems to have relied to some extent on silver gilt to make what modern Italians call a *bella figura*; his accounts very often mention silver objects sent to be gilt.

The most important papal need was for a plentiful issue of good money. The two main influences on this were the state of German and American silver production, and the flow of coin into Rome and into the papal offices. In the first half of the century there were two revaluations of papal coinage, the first to the profit of the papacy and the second not. In 1504 Julius II dealt with the problem of payments to the papal court made in depreciated or mixed silver money by replacing the small silver coins known as *carlini*, whose nominal value was 10:1 ducat but whose real value was 13½:1, by a new issue which came to be known as *giulii*, based on the ratio 10:1 gold ducat of 24-carat gold weighing 3.386 gr. The immediate result of this new issue was to improve papal income for all dues payable in silver in the proportion 10:13½.

The issue of the *scudo d'oro in oro* in 1530, which was of 22 carats and weighed 3.094 gr., is to be explained not by the Sack of Rome but by papal imitation of Spanish and French currencies. The small silver money issued by the papal mint, the *baiocco*, was, however, fairly seriously debased in this period. The silver giulio was also valued in 1532 at a rather lower ratio to gold than in 1504 (3.338 gr. of fine silver instead of 3.634 gr.). From 1538–1542 there was something of a financial crisis in Rome, which is perhaps to be attributed to the first overspill of American silver on the European money markets. The nominal ratio of gold to silver had been about 1:10.76. From 1538 silver fell mildly in terms of gold. The fall was attributed by contemporaries to poor and mixed silver money, and Paul III tried to stop it by reissuing the giulio with the higher silver content of 3.634 gr. But efforts to stabilise the gold-silver ratio at the old rate failed, and the gold scudo was in the end revalued at 11 giulii of 3.338 gr. of fine silver, instead of the former rate of 10 giulii. This ratio obtained until there was a further slide in value of silver in terms of gold in the 1560s.

The idea of a devaluation in the proportion of 10.76:11.0 scarcely makes a twentieth-century heart beat faster, even if it troubled creditor-debtor relations in Rome from 1538–1542. The money market in Rome seems to have been extremely stable in the first half of the century: it was only in the last three decades of the sixteenth century that price rises, bank failures, and the indebtedness of the state and of the great families made the money market a more dangerous, if still profitable, occupation.

It is hard to talk about *the* price rise in the first half of the sixteenth century in Rome. The prices of many commodities remained stable. On the other hand, some staples such as wheat, wine and oil suffered from such a succession of poor years in the period 1528–1560 as to push up the average price of these products to a level far above that of the first quarter of the century, though still below that of the last quarter. The most severe period of the price rise at the end of the century saw prices for some staples five times their level at its beginning. But the thirties, forties and fifties were still a period of dearth. The price of wheat considered normal in 1524 was 18 giulii for one *rubbio*. A rubbio was the average annual individual grain consumption per "mouth"; it amounted to roughly 200 kgs. or 2.30 hectolitres. From 1528 onwards the price of grain frequently reached 52 giulii for a rubbio or more. The years 1528–1533, 1538–1539, 1545, 1550 and 1556–1558 were all periods of severe dearth, and the last of these periods, that of Spanish aggression in the papal state, was as disastrous as any.

This steep rise in the prices of basic foods was clearly unfavourable to the lower classes in Rome. Their conditions deteriorated in the 1540s and 1550s, and the problem of Roman beggars became much worse. The need for more effective charitable action was clear in those years to great apostles of social charity like St Ignatius Loyola and S. Filippo Neri. The combination of high prices of basic foods with severe indirect taxation was no formula for a just society. Nor did things improve under the Counter-Reformation popes. In the last part of the century the vertiginous rise of prices, the decline of cereal cultivation in the Campagna, and the rise of urban population combined to produce a situation far more unfavourable to the Roman poor. A not dissimilar situation obtained in Naples, where the revolt of 1585 owed something to the misery of the people in the same conditions of price rise and high taxation. To the intolerant, harshly policed, overcrowded society of Sixtus V's Rome, with its feverish building boom and its decayed agriculture, looking back to the easy-going and cheap life under the Medici popes must have been like looking back from early Victorian England to the England of George III.

Chapter Three

THE
ROMAN
PEOPLE

I

"Only a minority of the Roman people are Romans." The Roman
Capitoline official, Marcello Alberini, the diarist of the Sack of Rome,
supplies with this remark the key to the understanding of Roman
society. Sixteenth-century Rome was a city of immigrants, which in
turn lived off a floating population of pilgrims and tourists. Of
roughly 3,600 Christian heads of households in the Roman census of
1526–1527 whose place of origin is known, only 747 (23.8 per cent)
originated in Rome or in the papal provinces lying to the north and
south of the city.* Of the remainder, 57.6 per cent came from other
parts of Italy (including Sicily, Corsica and Sardinia), and 18.6 per
cent originated outside Italy. The information is far from complete, as
only in 40.6 per cent of Roman Christian households in the census is
the place of origin of the householder indicated or easily ascertainable.
But it seems reasonable to treat this 40.6 per cent as a random sample,
and reasonable also to assume their households to have been predominantly Roman. If we do so then we may assume that not more

---

*The Roman "census" of 1526–27 was published by Gnoli in *Archivio della
Società Romana di Storia Patria*, XVII (1894). There is also an important section on
Roman population in K.J. Beloch, *Bevölkerungsgeschichte Italiens* (Berlin, Leipzig,
1939), II. I have found it necessary to make a new analysis of the document published by Gnoli, and I intend to publish the detailed results in due course.

than a quarter of the population resident in Rome in 1526–1527 had been born either in Rome or the Roman Campagna.

The causes of some of the waves of immigration into Renaissance Rome are known. The pontificates of the Aragonese popes Calixtus III (1455–1458) and Alexander VI (1492–1503), and the contiguity of the Aragonese Kingdom of Naples, led to the Spanish colony in Rome being the most important linguistic element among the non-Italians. The largest occupational groups were Spanish officials in the Roman court and Spanish prostitutes, and the two groups do not appear to have kept strictly apart. Spanish cardinals had plays performed in Castilian before their guests, amongst whom, in the first decade of the century at least, courtesans were to be found. The novelist and playwright Bartolomé de Torres Naharro set several of his works in Rome, and one of the best-known Spanish plays of the century, *La Lozana Andalusa*, is an account written by a Spanish clerk of the life of a Spanish prostitute in Rome.

French immigrants in Rome were numerous in the papal court, and among innkeepers, musicians and notaries. French cardinals in Rome brought French households. The illegitimate children of Cardinal d'Estouteville (who died in 1483) settled in Rome to become an accepted family of Roman notables. But the cynicism and disgust which Roman life inspired in the poet Joachim du Bellay in the mid-sixteenth century show that it did not charm every Frenchman. Corsicans had been present in Rome since the early Middle Ages; in the Renaissance period they controlled the Roman port, and also had an unenviable reputation for banditry and unmanageable violence. Another of the ancient colonies, that of the English whose original burgh near St Peter's dated to the eighth century, had by the sixteenth century dwindled away to nothing. Numbers of English wool merchants were to be found in Rome in the late fourteenth century, and English proctors worked in the Roman court in the fifteenth, but neither group is to be found in Renaissance Rome. In spite of the brief greatness of the English Cardinal Bainbridge under Julius II, there seems not to have been a single Englishman at the court of Clement VII, and apart from the few priests of the English College only one Englishman and one English woman are recorded in the Roman census of 1526–1527. Germans, on the other hand, were numerous and powerful in Rome. In the fifteenth century, curialists such as Sanders von Northeim and the papal master of ceremonies Burckhardt were typical. They built substantial houses, and helped to endow the German national hospice of S. Maria dell'Anima. German bankers, above all the Fuggers, were important; German cardinals such as Matthias Schinner were rich if not numerous. German innkeepers, cooks and bakers were very frequent.

It would be wrong to call the Jewish community in Rome immigrant, since its origins there were more ancient than those of the Christians. But Jewish immigration into Rome in the Renaissance period was so heavy that in 1524 Pope Clement VII was appealed to by Roman Jews to settle the quarrels between "Italian" Jews and "ultramontane" newcomers. The 1,738 Jewish mouths recorded in the 1526–1527 Roman census represent about 3.1 per cent of the total population. The immigrant Jews had come, usually after persecution or expulsion, from places all over the western Mediterranean—from Sicily, Naples, Provence, Aragon, Castile, Portugal, and even from Muslim Tunis. Some of these immigrant families, such as the Lattes of Montpellier, were rich and powerful; others were poor artisans. Jewish occupations in Rome included those of the bankers, the doctors and musicians of the papal court, tailors, clothiers, old clothes and junk merchants, and furniture dealers. There were learned but far from opulent rabbis.

Catholic Albanians and Slavs from the eastern Adriatic had formed part of Roman population from the time of the Turkish conquest of the late fourteenth century, and had continued to arrive during the wars of Skanderbeg in the fifteenth. There was a quarter in Campo Marzio containing the "Slav" hostel of S. Girolamo degli Schiavoni, and there were a few merchants from the Adriatic port of Ragusa, which traded with the papal state and also relied to some extent on papal diplomatic support.

Of the peninsular Italian population in Rome the north Italian element was much the largest, and was equal in size to that of the indigenous Romans. This can be set down, as can so many factors in Roman growth, to the misfortunes of Italy. The wars and plagues of the second and third decades of the sixteenth century drove out from Piedmont and Lombardy thousands of skilled and semi-skilled workers who could get a living in Rome. The most important industry to occupy them was the construction and decoration of buildings. Lombard "masons", a term which includes artisans, architects and some painters such as Polidoro da Caravaggio, were numerous in Rome from Sixtus IV's time onwards. They came both to get business and to learn it. The Ferrarese painter Benvenuto Tisi (called Garofalo) was bitterly disappointed when the Duke of Ferrara stopped him from returning to Rome to resume his pupillage under Raphael. Artists found in Medicean Rome a society which would accept almost anyone with talent; the Lombard painter Sodoma (Giovanni Antonio Bazzi), who painted the wonderfully sensual "Alexander and Roxana" for Agostino Chigi in the Villa Farnesina, could glory in his homosexual nickname in papal Rome as he could not in puritan Florence.

An area in the Campo Marzio region was thickly settled by Lombard artisans from the town of Caravaggio, the home not only of the painter Polidoro but of the architect Francesco del Pozzo. Other popular Lombard trades were those of currier and tanner, of baker, butcher, wine-seller, smith, textile-worker, potter, armourer. Lombard workers came seasonally to harvest the Roman vineyards and work on the Roman building sites. Most Lombards in Rome were artisans or labourers; few were to be found in the well-to-do quarters.

Most Genovese in Rome were also humble folk; predominantly they were sailors in the Roman port. But the rich Genovese bankers of the Ponte quarter gave their nation an importance beyond their numbers; the Ligurian popes, Sixtus IV and Julius II, had not ruled in vain. Neapolitans were few in Rome earlier in the century, probably because of tensions between the papal state and the Spanish-controlled kingdom of Naples. In any case Naples was three or four times as populous as Rome, and could absorb immigrants more easily. There was some Neapolitan immigration at mid-century under the southerner Paul IV.

Immigration from other parts of the papal state into Rome was modest and seasonal. Immigrants from Viterbo were not unwelcome; they were on the whole substantial people concerned with trade between this rich little town and Rome. The mountaineers of Amatrice and Norcia stayed in Rome in the winter when they brought their sheep down from the hills; so did the shepherds from Aquila in the Neapolitan kingdom. The shepherd with his bagpipes was one of the typical figures of the Epiphany season in Rome from the Middle Ages until the late nineteenth century. But the government did not favour this kind of peasant immigration, which filled the city with smelly and dirty livestock, and tended to accentuate just those rustic elements in Roman life which papal policy was trying to reduce. During the famine of 1558, the agricultural workers from Norcia and the Ciociaria (the hills south of Rome) were given twenty-four hours to leave the city. But even if they annoyed the government occasionally, the mountaineers were few. The mass arrival of immigrants from other parts of the papal state, notably from Bologna and the March of Ancona, did not take place until the great spurt of Roman population in the 1570s and 1580s.

The Tuscans were, under the second Medici pope, Clement VII, at the height of their wealth and power in Rome. At that time they numbered about 12.5 per cent of the Christian population, roughly half the number of indigenous "Romans". Their roots went deep into Roman society; Tuscans such as the curialist families of Cortesi and Mattei, or the banking family of Altoviti, had entered the city in the fifteenth century. Wealth, taste and power, not labour or craftsmanship, were the essence of the Tuscan position in Rome. The two Medici pontificates saw the establishment not only of a tremendously powerful group of Florentine families in Rome, but also of great Sienese bankers like the Sauli and Chigi. The historic origins of the Sienese position in Rome were linked with the Sienese popes Pius II and Pius III, but the advantages thus gained were not lost. The Tuscan bankers, of whom there were twenty or thirty major firms, had almost a stranglehold on Roman city life and on papal finance. They were not merely bankers in the modern sense but "merchants"; they dealt in luxury textiles, held the monopoly concession of the papal alum mines at Tolfa, acted for the pope and the civic authorities in provisioning Rome with grain, acted singly or in concert to handle the papal mint (the *Zecca*).

The less rich Tuscans plied occupations which on the whole fitted in with those of the great. Tuscans were jewellers, sculptors, painters, dealers in *objets d'art*, booksellers. The patronage of rich Tuscans helped them, as Benvenuto Cellini was helped by the patronage of the Gaddi family. The Tuscans were not spread thickly in the artisan quarters of Arenula (Regola) and Parione, as the Lombards were; the Tuscan areas were the rich regions of Ponte, the centre of financial and trading life, and Borgo, next to the papal palace.

The two great catastrophes—the Sack of Rome in 1527 and the Siege of Florence in 1529–1530—dealt a great blow to Tuscan power in Rome; in fact it might be argued that what was ended by the Sack was not Renaissance Rome but Tuscan Rome. But Tuscan wealth and power were too firmly entrenched to be destroyed. Tuscans continued to control the papal court until Pope Clement VII died in 1534. Even after his death the Tuscan families with one foot in banking and another in papal administration, like the Gaddi or Strozzi, remained powerful. One of the most striking examples of the Tuscan official in the papal court was the conservative Apostolic Penitentiary, Cardinal Lorenzo Pucci, the bane of Catholic reformers of the 1530s. Able Tuscan curialists like Monsignor Giovanni della Casa, and the papal treasurer, the future Cardinal Giovanni Ricci, made their way under Paul III and reached the height of their power in mid-century. But Paul III's pontificate nevertheless marked the waning of Tuscan predominance in the curia. Paul was from the Roman Campagna, and his immediate entourage, the papal "family", ceased to be Tuscan. Tuscan influence remained, but Tuscan rule was ended, and Tuscan numbers in Rome dropped, though perhaps only proportionately as all Roman population dropped after the Sack. Tuscan institutions in Rome survived. The Florentine consulate granted by Leo X, which possessed extra-territorial powers, was an envied special privilege. Florentine guilds and churches in Rome were established and honoured. In the 1530s the paintings of Francesco Salviati in the Florentine guild church of San Giovanni Decollato trumpeted the new style of Roman Mannerism. Until mid-century Michelangelo was engaged in planning and re-planning the Florentine church of San Giovanni, adjoining the consulate, which was the centre of a whole complex of Florentine business and charitable enterprises.

II

The populations of Renaissance cities were subject to disasters whose violence is now hard to appreciate. The most obviously terrifying was plague. The medical definition of what was termed "plague" in the sixteenth century is not easy, but bubonic plague, typhus, dysentery and malaria all had their part to play. Scholars do not yet agree about the nature and the degree of the damage inflicted by pestilence on Renaissance towns. But in a city like Rome in which only a quarter of the population had put down substantial roots, the displacement effected by plague could have been just as important as losses directly due to sickness. We know that many painters, architects and men of letters left Rome because of the plague of 1523, and that by no means all of them had returned by 1527.

Famine was also a potent control on Renaissance populations. Usually cities of the importance of Rome were able to defend themselves against it by means of stockpiling and state purchase. Perhaps only once in the sixteenth century did Rome experience true famine, in the dreadful period of 1527–1529 in which the normal organisation of city life broke down at a time when the countryside which usually supplied it was also paralysed by disorder and dearth. But viewed as catastrophes for the lower classes, the dearth periods of 1538–1539 and 1558–1559 both ran the Sack close.

Another regular menace to Roman life was the Tiber in flood. There was no embankment of the river by way of flood control. In a few hours whole quarters could be flooded to a depth of three or four metres, filled with stinking mud, and exposed to the danger of typhoid and other infections. Rome, as a popular poem of 1527 put it, became a marsh. Such a flood occurred approximately once in every decade. Even if the direct loss of human life was not always great, the economic disasters of a flood could be colossal, especially for the poor living in one-storey tenements in the quarters of Arenula (whose very name means "silt") or Campo Marzio. Benvenuto Cellini's shop partially escaped the 1530 flood because it backed onto Monte Giordano, but he cautiously took his stock of jewelery to the slope of the Quirinal ("Monte Cavallo").

War was a control on Renaissance populations which cannot be ignored. War had distressed the Roman area even in the years preceding the Sack of 1527. From the time of the operations of the duke of Albany in the Roman Campagna in 1525 to that of the revolt of the Colonna against papal government in 1526 there was no security in the Roman area, and in 1526 there was fighting inside as well as outside the city. Already by the time of the Roman census of 1526–1527 the most important Roman barons had withdrawn their households to their fortresses in the Campagna, and their great palaces in Rome were either empty or let to foreigners. A similar situation of disorder and fear obtained in 1557, when French troops were trying to garrison Rome, and the whole Roman Campagna was being attacked and plundered by the troops of the Duke of Alba.

When we consider these natural and man-made disasters, the lustre of the pontificate of Pope Leo X becomes understandable not only as the triumph of civilisation and art, but as a period of peace and of fortunate exemption from the scourges of nature. Julius II had done much for Rome, but he stood for policies of war and aggression, and in 1511 he had experienced a rebellion of the Roman nobles not unlike that against Clement VII in 1526. Leo X's only war, that against Urbino, was waged far from Rome in the Appenine passes. He spent and borrowed recklessly and taxed ruthlessly, but the Romans saw something for their money. And Leo also managed to bribe or intimidate the Roman nobles into keeping quiet.

The total population of Rome in the census of 1526–1527 is given as in the region of 54,000 "mouths", a figure which excludes unweaned babies, and in the case of the very large households was obtained only approximately and in round figures. The "corrected" figure of 53,897 is therefore still only an approximation. A decade earlier the curialist historian Paolo Giovio had estimated the Roman population at 85,000. This figure has been treated with scepticism by historians, though it deserves more respect than they have given it, especially as Giovio would have had access to census figures. Giovio's population estimate for 1530 is usually accepted, and it is strange that his estimate for the earlier period is so often rejected. We possess only fragments of a census taken in 1517, and it is unlikely that the population under Leo X will ever be correctly known. But it is far from impossible that the natural and political misfortunes of Clement VII's reign had drastically reduced Roman population, perhaps even by as much as a third, before the Sack of Rome took place.

The estimated figures for the Roman population after the Sack are very modest. The great flood of 1530 and the disastrous harvests of 1533 and 1538–1539 impeded Roman recovery. In 1530 the Roman population was perhaps 32,000, in 1545 45,000, and even in 1560 not much over 50,000. Not until 1580 did population reach the level of 80,000, which it may well have already touched under Leo X, and not until 1600 did it top the 100,000 mark, which brought it to the population level of contemporary London. The pattern of Roman Renaissance population seems thus to have been largely a political one. The last period of Clement VII's pontificate, from 1527 to 1534, was a period of political humiliation and distress which is reflected in the reduction of population to hardly more than a third of the probable numbers under Leo X. Under Paul III, in spite of the recovery of papal prestige and policy, and in spite of rising papal income, recovery of population was only modest. During the 1550s, which are sometimes reckoned as a period of Catholic Reformation and recovery, the poor political and military conditions in the Roman area still kept the population down. Only with the Peace of Cateau-Cambrésis in 1559 were political conditions established in Italy which enabled the popes to launch new policies of urban development in Rome, and which promoted population growth up to and beyond the level reached in the second decade of the century.

The mean size of a household in Rome in 1526–1527 was high for the period—5.77. If, however, we take out the households of the pope, the cardinals, and twenty-one other households numbering fifty or more, we get the much lower mean figure of 5.15. It is noticeable, however, that "Roman" households in the narrower sense, that is households whose head is known to have originated in Rome or the Roman Campagna, were much larger than others. Even if households numbering fifty or more are excluded from the sum, the mean size of the "Roman" household in this narrow sense was 7.34.

Habitation in Rome was concentrated overwhelmingly in the regions between the Campidoglio and the Tiber (Campo Marzio, Ponte, Parione, Arenula). These four of the thirteen regions contained 49.4 per cent of the total population. The region of Monti, on the other hand, while it comprised nearly a quarter of the total area of Rome, contained only 5.1 per cent of its population. Not until Sixtus V (1585–1590) was a big effort made to build up and populate the region of Monti. The two most densely inhabited regions were Ponte, which contained 7,626 "mouths", and Parione which counted 6,336. If a ratio is obtained between population and surface area, Ponte was the most densely populated, and Parione in second place.

The social classes were not strictly segregated in Renaissance Rome. Some areas of the city were predominantly artisan, especially the regions of Arenula (Regola) and Sant'Angelo. These regions included the Jewish quarters and were also the home of many of the more humble prostitutes. Parione, Ponte and Borgo tended to contain the more solid tradespeople. Campo Marzio was inhabited by more modest folk, though there were one or two great palaces like Palazzo Cardelli. In general the classes were mixed throughout Rome. Cardinals and nobles would let out rooms on the ground floor of their palaces to traders and prostitutes, or lease wooden stalls in the squares surrounding their palaces to small dealers. The greatest households were like small villages, sheltering scores or even hundreds of humble servants who would live far from the great state rooms. When the great French classical historian Jerome Carcopino went to the École Française in Palazzo Farnese at the end of the last century, the domestics of the palace's Bourbon owners still kept flocks of chickens on the attic terraces. Such rustic little colonies in the attics are likely to have been common in sixteenth-century Rome.

III

From the point of view of the papal government, the problem of population was basically one of food supply, or even more narrowly of grain supply. It was with these requirements in mind that the government caused censuses to be made; what interested them was the number of mouths capable of eating bread. The grain in question was wheat; barley, maize and spelt were mixed in with the bread eaten in country districts, but in cities even the poor wanted wheaten bread. A clerk of the Apostolic Chamber acted as "President of the Annona" or head of the corn supply office, and another papal agency subjected all movements of grain to government permit and made them subject to tax (the *tratta del grano*, controlled by the *dogana delle tratte*). In the earlier part of the century, responsibility for the provisioning of Rome was shared between the Apostolic Chamber (which acted as Ministry of Home Affairs for the papal state) and the communal government of Rome. Main responsibility lay with the Apostolic Chamber, an arrangement against which the Roman Commune protested in vain to Leo X. The Council of the Commune still laid in its own grain stocks; in 1527 a reserve was held by the "captains" of the various regions of the city, and in 1531–1533 the Commune commissioned the banker Filippo Strozzi to buy 30,000 loads (*moggia*) of Sicilian grain, half (or at that moment of reduced population perhaps the whole) of the average annual supply of the city.

Most of the Roman granaries were in the port area of Ripa and Trastevere. But other granaries, many of them belonging to important Roman families, were spread out over the rest of the city. The families who were both bankers and estate-owners had the largest grain holdings; the Massimi, Mattei, Altoviti and Astalli all had their own granaries. The control of grain meant political power and responsibility, especially as breakdowns of public order were very often connected with dear or bad bread. At no time was this more evident than in the two or three weeks following the death of Clement VII on 25 September 1534, when the Roman governing classes for a few short days made what was virtually their only protest against the financial stranglehold of the Tuscan bankers on Rome. The large supplies of grain which they had ordered from Filippo Strozzi in 1533 had not been delivered in time, and when they were delivered were charged at far more than the agreed price. Strozzi was in many ways the symbol of Medici exploitation in Rome. He was the close relative by marriage of the Medici; he held the concession of the Roman customs, and had been papal banker or "depositary"; he owned the castle of Longhezza in the Roman Campagna, houses near the Vatican, and his banking house in Via de' Banchi.

In 1534, in the period of weak government which accompanied a papal vacancy, both the people and the magnates revolted against Strozzi. His granaries in Trastevere were sacked by the mob, and the Roman commune brought an action against him before the cardinals in conclave, demanding the huge sum of a hundred thousand florins in damages. But the sequel to the riots and the prosecution showed how powerless both the populace and the magistrates were against the great Tuscan bankers. The cardinals, while they were still in conclave, named arbitrators to deal with the case, but as soon as Pope Paul III was elected on 12 October 1534 the vendetta against Strozzi was as good as lost. Paul III as a young clerk had owed his first ecclesiastical promotion to the Medici; he was not anxious to disavow their client, nor to admit the protests of the Roman commune, whose orator had in the Strozzi affair complained that no modern city was "as outraged, as disdained, of so little credit as Rome", which had been taxed out of existence and "made to eat stinking earth instead of bread". Such language was unwelcome to Paul III, whose ideas about the dignity and grandeur of Rome were entirely theoretical, or, as it is now fashionable to say, "ideological". The prosecution against Strozzi was dropped, and after a few months the elections of the magistrates who had uttered these seditious sentiments were cancelled. Strozzi survived to enjoy for a short time the favour of Paul III. Four years later, when Strozzi was being tortured in the prisons of Cosimo de' Medici to make him avow his disloyalty to the Florentine government and to the Emperor, Paul III pleaded in vain with Charles V for his life.

Rome needed a government-directed grain supply not only for its stable population but for the floating population of pilgrims and visitors. On the whole the papal officials over-estimated need, probably because they were frightened of the political consequences of dearth. Government estimates of grain need seem to have run consistently at 50 per cent more than the population, at a moderate estimate of grain consumption (230 kg. annually per head), would have needed.* This kind of over-estimate was also made by Venetian governments, and was perhaps to be expected on the part of two rich cities that depended on foreign trade and visitors. It is possible, but unlikely, that the floating population would have consumed half as much as the stable population; such a situation only seems likely to have occurred in Rome in Jubilee years. In any case it is clear from the huge rises in grain prices in Rome in the bad years that government buying did *not* keep prices down when there was serious dearth. It is possible that while one papal official was buying corn to keep prices down, another was granting licenses *(tratte)* for the export of grain.

---

*Delumeau, *Vie économique et sociale*, pp. 122, 535–536; F. Braudel, *The Mediterranean and the Mediterranean World in the Age of Philip II*, I, pp. 420–422, 570–571. The difficulties of the calculations are considerable, particularly because of the varying densities of various kinds and qualities of grain.

IV

With the single exception of building construction, Rome was a city of service industries. Perhaps the most important of these was domestic service, though it is hard now to find more than fragments of information about the way servants lived. Hordes of domestics must have been housed in the five hundred or so inns, boarding houses, taverns and wineshops, and in the fifty-odd households containing more than fifty persons. The popes of the servants' halls were the *spenditori*, the male housekeepers responsible for running and provisioning the big households. The butlers, the *credenzieri*, were the other dignified domestic officers. Aretino in *La cortegiana* placed his naive social climber in the world of the *spenditori*, from whom he sought the recipe of the pill which would make him a proper courtier. Aretino also records in nasty detail the life of the *tinello*, the servants' hall, frozen in winter and grilled in summer, where in some foul basement dirty scraps and left-overs were gobbled in half-lit squalor. This world was far removed from the dignified life of the papal court, where even a "secret sweeper" was a person of some consequence.

Romans owned but did not manage inns. A notable investor in hotel property was Vanozza Catanei, the ex-mistress of Alexander Borgia. The innkeepers themselves were a heterogeneous lot: Germans, French, Flemish Belgians, Piedmontese and Spaniards. Most were men. A score or so of the inns were large and comfortable enough to house gentlemen and their suites. Such inns were known at the time of Frederick III's visit to Rome in 1469, and one of them was the "Albergo dell'Orso" visited by Montaigne. By the late seventeenth century the registration books of the "Donzello" record English and other gentlemen travellers. In the early sixteenth century the freedom conferred on Rome by the right of every Catholic to visit the holy places meant that, almost alone among Italian cities of the time, there was in Rome no strict regime by which foreigners were reported at the gates or by innkeepers (though innkeepers were made to report guests after the mid-century). The obligation on the inns was, typically, the financial one of reporting the goods of their guests to the customs officers. Innkeepers in Rome did not all enjoy a savoury reputation, but they were also liable to be defrauded by unscrupulous customers. A papal ruling of 1564 enacts for the benefit of

Roman innkeepers the immortal principle that the management takes no responsibility for valuables not deposited at the desk.

There were at least twice as many wineshops as inns in Rome, and the wine trade was one of the most important in the city. At the end of the sixteenth century over seven million litres of wine entered Rome annually by the Roman port alone, and the value of the wine tax was in the region of 180,000 scudi annually. Earlier in the century these figures were lower, but to them has to be added the large quantities of wine which came in from the Roman Campagna. The wine dealers in the Roman port, the *mercanti di Ripa*, were prosperous people. The intermediaries between the importers and the retail distributors, the *sensali di Ripa*, were another guild specially licensed and controlled by the government; altogether seven or eight separate craft guilds, wine depositers, coopers and others were involved in the wine trade.

Inns would normally offer their clients beds and some sort of bed-covers and sheets. But there were also large numbers of taverns and dossing houses which accepted poor folk who slept on straw palias-ses. The straw might be provided by the host, or might be bought by the pilgrim direct from the strawsellers in the outer atrium of St Peter's. There were forty-one of these strawsellers in the church in 1501. In Jubilee years the numbers of pilgrims accommodated in this primitive way could run into hundreds of thousands. Food was cheaper in this humble accommodation: in the doss-houses the poor would eat tripe and pigs' trotters.

The food-supply crafts had a central place. Bakers were numerous in all regions of the city. Frequently they were "foreigners", often Germans. Butchers, fishmongers, salame grocers *(pizzicaroli)* were important traders; the *pizzicaroli* got Clement VII to sanction their high prices. Fruitsellers were numerous; olive oil and soap vendors often obtained monopolies. But one soon reaches the divide between modern and Renaissance ideas of "shops". The ownership of booths *(botteghe)* was, it is true, profitable, and some owners of great palaces like the Altoviti rented to tradesmen shops in a row of wooden booths in the square in which the palace stood. But in food and other dis-tributive trades the small business was done either by itinerant ven-dors or from stalls or benches set up in the streets. The *Historia nova e piacevole, dove si racconta tutte le cose che si vanno vendendo dagli artigiani a Roma* is a verse anthology of street cries whose number runs into hundreds. Its pictorial equivalent is the *Ritratto di tutti quelli che vanno vendendo per Roma*, an engraving of the same period showing 260 different street vendors.

The millers were an essential link in the chain of food production. The cumbersome water mills, clustering round the Tiber island, are one of the most unfamiliar elements to the modern eye in contemporary drawings of the Tiber. In time of flood they were particularly vulnerable, and more than one Roman miller was carried away for ever on the yellow waters of the flood tide.

It is hard to say that, apart from building, Rome had any major industries at all. It would be nearer the mark to call most of them crafts. There had been a minor cloth industry in the city since the early Middle Ages; to protect her cloth industry Rome had struggled with and destroyed the neighboring town of Tuscolo in the twelfth century The clothiers' guild (*arte della lana*) had been quite powerful in Rome as late as the fourteenth century. But in the sixteenth century, especially since the political power was in the hands of the Tuscan merchants, the Roman cloth industry was in decline. Florentine clothiers reckoned to satisfy the bulk of Roman demand for common and fine cloths, and Roman local production was small. Rome had a small craft industry of gold lace embroiderers (*ricamatori*) who adorned garments with gold trimmings, and who were as much jewellers as textile workers. Attempts were made by both Leo X and Sixtus V to launch a silk industry in Rome, but neither succeeded. However, the Roman cloth industry did still exist in the Renaissance, as the 1526–1527 census attests, and as the survival of the Via dei Pettinari (wool combers' street) shows.

Butchers, tanners and curriers, many of whom were Lombards, were grouped in a flourishing quarter in the artisan region of Arenula; there was also a big shambles called the Scortecchiara near the present Piazza Navona. The great herds of cattle in the Roman Campagna, and the big demand for meat in Rome, meant that plenty of beasts and their hides were available. Tanning is a smelly and nasty business, and the butchers and tanners can hardly have added to the convenience of life in central Rome. One of the less pleasing habits of butchers was to throw animal guts into the street; equally unpleasing was the tanners' habit of spreading hides to dry on the façade of the local church.

There was far more money to be made in the luxury trades, especially those selling in the commercial and banking areas of Borgo and Ponte. The tailors were numerous and prosperous, as were the embroiderers and the makers of church vestments. In these opulent areas the fine shoemakers were usually Florentines. The Jews were often tailors, but also second-hand dealers and old-clothes-men. Mercers and drapers, pharmacists, druggists and perfumers had their shops in these zones. Barbers and bonesetters had pitches all over Rome; traditionally the barbers for working men pitched in Piazza de' Cenci, and gave their clients an apple to hold in their mouths while they shaved off a fortnight's growth of beard.

The vendors of religious objects (*paternostari*), including rosaries (*coronari*) and reproductions of the Veronica handkerchief (*il volto santo*), have an especial right to inclusion in a list of Roman trades, since they are to be found in the precincts of St Peter's from the earliest medieval times. With them in the outer atrium (*paradiso*) of St Peter's were not only the strawsellers but the copyists, the Jewish booksellers, and the moneychangers (*banchieri* and also, pejoratively, *bancherotti*), the last of whom had operated in the precincts of the church since the twelfth century and earlier. The later history of these tradesmen reflects that of the church. In 1515 the rights of the Vatican clergy over the square of St Peter had to be confirmed because of the abuse of the great wooden constructions constantly erected there for public spectacles. As the reconstruction of the main church advanced, the stalls of the tradesmen were gradually pushed out into Borgo and to Piazza Rusticucci, where they were to be found in the second half of the century. The rosary makers were also to be found in the region of Ponte, where their name survives in the Via dei Coronari, formerly Via Recta.

The junk dealers (*rigattieri*) had always dealt in ancient objects, cameos, sculptures. Ulisse Aldovrandi in the 1550s refers to a certain Francesco, a French junk dealer, who held a hundred or so ancient sculptures in his shop and vineyard. But antiques from the 1530s onwards were dealt in not only by junk dealers but by specialized antique dealers who excavated for profit, and called themselves *antiquari*, though they had more in common with twentieth-century Etruscan tomb robbers than with modern "antique dealers". The papal government never seriously attempted to control the rifling of ancient sites, but confined itself to making a profit on them. In the second half of the century it attempted to control the export of antiquities from Rome by a system of licenses.

The jewellers' and goldsmiths' crafts, typically exercised by Lombards, were among the most important in Rome. They satisfied a huge demand from rich clerks, of whom the pope was the most important. The papal court asked for the great objects of symbolic clerical use like the papal tiara itself, reliquaries, or the papal chalice about which the dilatory Benvenuto Cellini had a shouting match with Clement VII. The court also needed a steady supply of beautiful objects for presentation, particularly the "papal rose" and "papal sword" given to favoured rulers. Cardinals and magnates invested enormous sums in plate and jewellery, the indispensable pompous apparatus for the life of clerical diplomacy. There was also an industry of medallists and of workers for the papal mint. Many of the medals struck for Renaissance popes were masterpieces of the art, and they also played quite an important part in papal propaganda. The curialists and curial humanists commissioned medals; even the historian Paolo Giovio could afford to commission a fine one.

For the services of a Cellini or a Caradosso there was fierce competition, a competition which allowed Cellini to get one of his homicides pardoned. Cellini was a raffish individualist who employed few journeymen and acquired no property in Rome. Other jewellers were more solid citizens; there is still in existence, for example, a rather pleasant house in Piazza di Pasquino which was rebuilt in 1540 by a Roman jeweller called Antonio Alessandro. The distinguished Milanese jeweller Gian Pietro Crivelli was also a banker; he gave an earlier house to be the seat of the first municipal pawnshop (Monte di Pietà), and built himself a fine new one which still remains in Via dei Banchi Vecchi.

The booksellers were established in Rome at the beginning of the century, and so were the printers. Booksellers were located mostly near the papal palace in Borgo; many printers worked in Campo dei Fiori. Printers were not mere artisans, but often highly educated men who fulfilled the functions not only of publisher but of learned author. There was no official papal printer in the first half of the century, but Francesco Calvo tended to fulfil this role. Antonio Blado, who was active in Rome by the time of Leo X, was to become papal printer later in the century. The demand for reproductions of papal bulls and legal formulae gave employment to the German printer Silber, who also co-operated with the engraver Columba and the musician Andrea Antico in the publication of music. Other printers fulfilled yet more specialised needs. Jacopo Mazzocchi, who was himself a distinguished humanist, published for the Roman Academy, and also published the first and more learned phase of "Pasquino". Ludovico degli Arrighi, the master of early modern calligraphy, printed his book in Rome. There was a printing press of Zacharias Callierges of Crete, which under the patronage of Agostino Chigi published in Greek. Cardinal Giles of Viterbo, the General of the Augustinian Order, was the patron of a Hebrew press, and in the late 1540s the Ethiopian Tasfa Sion with the support of Cardinal Sirleto was printing books in Chaldean.

The art of line engraving, which was developed in Rome in the 1520s by Marcantonio Raimondi, was to be of immense importance in spreading the styles and the iconography of Roman art. Marcantonio was the first engraver to popularise the drawings and paintings of Raphael, which he began to do through close co-operation with the painter's studio during Raphael's lifetime. Another enterprise of Marcantonio was the engraving of Giulio Romano's sexual "Positions", which were subsequently illustrated by poems written to fit the engravings by Aretino. Judging by what is known of them these engravings were more quaint than indecent by modern standards, but the strait-laced datary, Gian Matteo Giberti, sent Marcantonio to prison for them. The print-seller and engraver Antonio Salamanca, "orbis et urbis antiquitatum imitator", was another key person for the diffusion of the iconography of Rome. The heyday of Salamanca was from 1538 to 1549. His young competitor Antonio Laffréry, later to be the publisher of the finest collection of views of Renaissance Rome, entered into partnership with Salamanca in 1553.

Artists, in the sense of painters, sculptors and miniaturists, were quite an important element in the Roman working population. In 1534, when Roman population was at its lowest ebb of the century, the guild of "Pittori, Miniatori, Ricamatori" numbered some 220 members. By no means all these would be considered "artists", nor to belong to what has been in our own time called a "creative elite". The embroiderers (*ricamatori*) were members, and so was "Antonio who makes the masks [*maschere*] in Borgo". Some artists at the top of their profession were socially accepted by the magnates of Medicean Rome, and very well paid. Five or six architects, one of whom was Raphael, were rich enough to build themselves "palaces": there were two Sangallo palaces in Via Giulia by the 1550s.

The artists at the top of the tree were rich businessmen, many of whom were deeply involved in the housing speculations which made fortunes in the Roman court from Julius II's time onwards. Raphael, the San Galli and other architects invested heavily in the development of Via Giulia and Via della Lungara. Another area in which Lombard and other masons and architects invested in new housing was the Medici-sponsored development in Campo Marzio. Artists also invested in the papal venal offices: Michelangelo, Bandinelli and Salviati were such investors, and Sebastiano del Piombo may be presumed to have purchased his office of *magistro del piombo*, which was valued at 5,000 ducats. Artists of this kind of wealth and distinction often led a Bohemian life in the company of courtesans and *bons viveurs*; this was especially true of the congenial ambience of the artists patronised by the Chigi and by the other great figures of Leo X's court. Cellini relates that the sculptor, Michelangelo of Siena, organised an artists' dining club to which members sometimes had to bring women of the town.

The social status of artists was very ambiguous. One particularly swashbuckling figure, Baccio Bandinelli, went to immense and rather absurd pains to claim for himself the status of a gentleman: he secured knighthoods from Charles V and Clement VII, but was mocked by the lampoonists as a shoemaker-turned-nobleman. Raphael, at the height of his reputation, was affianced to the niece of Cardinal Bernardo Dovizi of Bibbiena: but the alliance was less brilliant than it sounds, as Bibbiena was a promoted humanist of no very distinguished family. Bandinelli set up an "Academy" to train artists in the 1540s, and this was in one sense an attempt to professionalise and dignify the artistic calling, but Bandinelli was not a learned man, and his Academy was really only another variety of apprenticeship. Only at mid-century, with the appearance of numbers of genuinely learned artists like Pirro Ligorio, did artists begin to call for a properly educated profession. In the third decade of the century "artist" was a word which could comprehend all artisans, including "artists" in our sense. In 1525 the Papal Chamber made an order that "all the artists" should be made to pay a special tax to defray the expenses of the urban dustcarts. The Roman commune intervened with the pope to ask that the "poverty-struck artists" should be exempted, and submitted that they gave rise to no more street refuse than anyone else.* "Artists" in this sense were clearly not what we would term a "cultural elite". But it is also arguable that in the easy-going social atmosphere of Medicean Rome the successful artist was accepted with less question in curial society than in the more professionally stratified society of the Counter-Reformation period; the social malaise of a Caravaggio, at the turn of the sixteenth century, might have been less acute had he been a contemporary of Benvenuto Cellini.

The building industry, the one true industry of Rome, can be divided into suppliers and constructors. The oddest suppliers were the "excavators" (cavatori) who dug in the sites of ancient buildings for marble and for anything else they could find. They used the ancient materials either, if they were especially fine, for re-use as columns and so on, or else for reducing to lime to make mortar. In this way most of ancient Rome, in the Renaissance period, went into the lime kilns. The lime producers were another important craft, with their headquarters in the zone known as the "Calcararia" in the Circus Flaminius and the surroundings (between the Forum and Piazza della Torre Argentina). The constructors were organised into guilds of masons, carpenters and ironworkers. There was no separate class of "architect" but certain great entrepreneurs fulfilled this function. Architects such as Baldassare Peruzzi and the Sangalli generally worked in teams in a construction group or fabbrica. Most of the greater enterprises, St Peter's above all, required such teams. Additional labour was provided by the seasonal immigration of Lombard building workers.

The most notable capitalist of the Roman building industry was the so-called architect, the Roman Giuliano Leno. Leno dominated the building boom of Leo X's pontificate, and continued to be the greatest man in his field up to the Sack of 1527. He belonged to a Roman

---

*Delumeau, Vie économique et sociale, p. 244. The document is in the Archivio del Comune di Roma, Cred. I, tom. 36, fol. 180v, dated 3 May 1525.

family that can be traced back easily to the fourteenth century. He began his career working for Julius II, for whom he constructed the palace of S. Pietro in Vincoli, and for whom he would have perhaps built the great Julian Palace in Via Giulia, on the plans of Bramante, if the pope had lived to finish the work. Leno was the trusted servant of both Medici popes; he began working for Leo X immediately after the pope's election by constructing wooden edifices for the extravagant ceremonies of the papal *possesso* (the solemn episcopal taking possession of the see). From this point Leno did not look back. He worked on the strengthening of Old St Peter's for Raphael, and also on the foundations for the new church, where he continued to work for Pope Clement VII. He worked at the Vatican for Leo and Clement, on Leo's hunting lodge outside Rome at La Magliana, and on the fortifications which so signally failed to save Rome in 1527. He speculated widely, and not only in building and renting houses. Near his main workshops in the "Botteghe Oscure" he had Jews manufacturing cloth for him. He was intensely unpopular, and in pasquinades was named as the "spy" of the even more unpopular Cardinal Armellino. In 1523 he was denounced by the humanist Gianbattista Casale as a "diligent amasser of monopolies", and as the villain of the speculation in grain carried out by government officials. After the Sack Leno was used as a diplomatic agent by Clement VII, but the time of his greatness in Rome was over.

The time was a century past when, after the return of the popes to Rome following the end of the Great Schism, the Florentine Vespasiano da Bisticci had been able to say that the Romans dressed in skins like cowherds, and that their flocks wandered as far as the precincts of St Peter's. Yet the flavour of the countryside clung to Rome. Almost all the occupations described here so far were practised in the regions near the Tiber which housed three-quarters of Roman population. Large areas of Rome within the walls, particularly the region of Monti which was far the largest, were in effect open countryside. In Leo X's pontificate the Pincio, Quirinal and Esquiline were to some extent opened up for "villas" and "vineyards", and also for the excavation of antiquities. By mid-century this development had gone much further. But much of the rest was agricultural land. Shepherds still wandered in Rome with their flocks, and the sound of bells on the sheep was a typical one as they were driven by night through the streets. Vineyard workers and gardeners were numerous in the city. On the Tiber island herds of buffalo were kept, to be used to tow boats down the Tiber along the Via Portuense. Some churches, such as the Hospital of S. Antony of Vienne at S. Maria Maggiore, or S. Agnese fuori le Mura, owed much of their revenue to the annual blessing of beasts driven through the church by the peasants.

One thing dominated Renaissance Rome even more than it had classical Rome: the horse. All the great houses of cardinals and magnates, not excluding that of the pope himself, possessed enormous stables. In the more old-fashioned palaces of the Roman families the stables were part of the main buildings. A great personage might maintain fifty mounts for gentlemen and a hundred others; forty horses were practically a minimum for a cardinal's stables. Courier services, whose point of departure was Monte Giordano, also demanded great stables, and inns had to harbour horses as well as their riders. There were great barns full of fodder in the middle of Rome, often sited in ruins of classical date; the great "grotto" of Girolamo Muti near San Marcello al Corso was an example. In the Stadium of Domitian, Piazza dell'Agone (now Piazza Navona), the dominating sounds were the chatter of Spanish prostitutes and the bustle of the horse market.

There is little wonder that the contrast between the splendour of Rome's past and its humble agricultural present was a commonplace of Renaissance poetry. "Aurea templa, bouum pascua facta vides": the sites of the golden temples are made into pasture for oxen—so the papal cypher clerk, Trifone Benci, saw the city. "The countryman hoes and reaps, and drives his plough among royal trees; flocks low—no, they grunt!—in those golden scenes where the songs of mortals were heard by the gods." This was how the sixteenth-century poet Chiabrera described the peasants as they worked their fields on the Esquiline and Coelian hills, under the shade of the great pine trees. Renaissance literary men felt that Rome had returned to its condition before Romulus and Remus founded the city. "Nostris temporibus Roma est, quod fuit ante Remum" (Benci). Flocks roamed the Roman hills as they had done before Rome existed, and Benci and du Bellay could ironically quote Ovid's treatment of a Rome more ancient than the Republic.

Ces grands moceaux pierreux, ces vieux murs que tu vois
Furent premierement
le cloz d'un lieu champestre:
Et ces braves palais dont le temps s'est
fait maistre,
Cassines de pasteurs ont esté quelquefois.

These blocks of stone you see, this ancient wall,
Were wattles once around a country mead;
These splendid palaces whose sides now fall
Were sheepcots where a rustic flock would feed.

V

The city of Christian charity had to be the city of beggars. There is, however, less indication in the first half of the century than in the second that mendicancy was an urgent social problem. The Roman hospitals and hospices founded specifically for beggars did not begin until the mid-sixteenth century, though most of the earlier hospitals did take in the destitute, and there had always been a weekly distribution of food to the poor by the papal almoner. The multiplication of beggars in the late century was connected with the high prices of basic foods, with the agricultural distress of the Roman Campagna, and with the population increase. But dearth always made beggars: when in 1538–1539 Ignatius Loyola set up his hostel for beggars in the house of Antonio Frangipane it was used by 3,000 destitute in the course of that one terrible winter. In the following winter the Mantuan envoy said that there were ten or twelve thousand begging their bread ("poveri mendicanti et bisognosi del pane"). Such figures would make one Roman in four a beggar, and they may be exaggerated. But the problem was real enough. In 1542 Pope Paul III forbade beggars to ask for alms in churches—a classic way of trying to sweep an unpleasant fact under the carpet which was not abandoned by the Counter-Reformation popes.

Prostitution was a serious problem; one would like to think that Renaissance popes thought it a problem, though there is not much sign of their concern about it, and the reforming cardinals in their memorial of 1537 complained bitterly that courtesans circulated freely in the streets as if they were honest women, and were attended openly by noblemen and clerks who were familiars of cardinals. Rome contained an abnormally high ratio of male to female population, partly because of the large number of clergy, but also because the immigrant nature of the population led to large numbers of immigrant males being present without their families. Aretino attributed to Pasquino the opinion that the invasion of Rome by Florentines under the Medici popes led to Florentine wives being abandoned by their husbands, and he suggested that the Florentine government should issue an order that no one could stay in Rome without his wife:

> Fate mettere un bando
> Che chi l'ha o non l'avesse o non toglie,
> Non possa stare a Roma senza moglie.

Another cause for prostitution was the high cost of dowries, for artisans no less than for gentlefolk, which was a standard cause for complaint in Italy and elsewhere in the sixteenth century.

The prostitutes of sixteenth-century Rome have been rather comically discussed by some scholars, whose protestations about the distastefulness of the subject are followed by lengthy accounts of it. The numbers of the prostitutes have been very differently estimated. Some scholars have wanted to treat as prostitutes all women without a qualifying description in the census returns, and also all washerwomen. This seems rather hard on washerwomen, whose occupation was thought by contemporaries to be one for ex-prostitutes rather than for those still on the game. It is perhaps legitimate to suppose that women described in the census with what looks like a *nom de guerre* were in fact prostitutes, though deciding what is a *nom de guerre* and what is not is difficult. Even more questionable is the notion that all women described by a forename only and their town or country of origin in the census return are therefore prostitutes. Perhaps all the women called "Isabetta yspana" were Spanish whores, but it seems rather a bold supposition. Estimated total numbers of several thousand Roman prostitutes have been conjectured by such means.

Some accounts of Roman prostitutes can also be criticised for their failure to distinguish between the *cortigiane honeste*, the well-to-do women of easy virtue who possessed the entrée into some parts of Roman society, who were able to play the lute and to recite poetry, from the humble and ordinary *cortigiane alla candela*, the whores whose duty stopped when the light went out. The tawdry splendours of the rich prostitutes impressed the tourist, especially during the Carnival. To be pelted with perfumed eggs by handsome and finely attired whores was an experience which remained in the mind. But the majority of prostitutes in Rome were common tarts who were the *meretrices publicae* of medieval life rather than the re-named "courtesans" of the Renaissance. They differed from their medieval predecessors in being allowed to solicit from their own houses instead of being confined in brothels; they would wolf-whistle and call for custom from their windows. They could circulate freely in the streets, in public places, and in churches. They would often dress as men, either for reasons of sexual provocation or to avoid the attentions of the police. The tradition of easy-going morals in Rome was strong, and even after the Counter-Reformation very little was done to reduce the numbers and social importance of Roman prostitutes. The seventeenth-century diarist John Evelyn was much struck by their boldness.

It seems likely that Medicean Rome contained between 750 and 1,000 prostitutes. Such a figure—lower than that usually surmised —still makes their occupation one of the most important in the city, and shows Rome to have been comparable in this respect to Venice, another "city of foreigners". But reckonings of their numbers will always be guesses. Prostitutes were not anxious to be tidily listed in government records, nor perhaps even to be identified by former clients. So they constantly changed their names, so that the Giulia, Altabella, Imperia of one day became the Lucrezia, Porzia, Pantasilea of the next.

A Roman underworld not unlike that of Tudor London can be found in the pages of Aretino and of the Castilian *Lozana Andalusa*. Aretino at one point puts into his tart's mouth the terrible remark, "Le putane non sono donne, ma sono putane" ("Tarts are tarts, not women"). But typically he allows her the feminine inconsistency of contradicting this renunciation of human status by stating its opposite: "Non siamo noi donne, se ben puttaniamo?" ("Aren't we women, even if we're tarts?"). *La Lozana Andalusa* is an altogether looser, more picaresque account of a sordid yet somehow rather idealised Rome in which Jews, loose-living priests, boardinghouse-keepers, prostitutes and pimps move in a rather harmonious society. Aretino had a much keener sense of the social injustice from which prostitution grew. His Nanna gives to the novice whore the advice to seek business among men of her own social class rather than among gentlemen, because gentlemen are going to be too sexually exigent and to want too much for their money. It is a remark which puts gentlemen in the same moral class as prostitutes, and men of the people in a higher one.

Prostitution was also practised in the *stufe*, the public baths, some of which were "dry", and would now be called "saunas". The connection between baths and prostitution was typical of the late Middle Ages and the Renaissance: such baths were the equivalent of certain modern "massage parlours". There were also some innkeepers who were landlords of prostitutes and pimped for them—a familiar situation at any period.

Prostitution brought with it an even greater extension of venereal diseases, the new epidemic scourge of the sixteenth century. The gentleman visiting Rome was prone to return home, as du Bellay observed, without either his money or his beard, for syphilis and its antidotes made the hair drop out. The disease spared few who exposed themselves to it, from cardinals to ne'er-do-wells like the poet Francesco Molza, who marked his approaching death from syphilis by a poem addressed to his friends which contains some of the most sensitive and touching Latin elegiacs to be composed in the Renaissance period. Syphilis was treated as an "incurable" disease, although some cures were obtained, but syphilitics were those mainly catered for by the new hospital of S. Giacomo for incurable diseases.

It seems severe to Jews to treat them as a class with social disabilities comparable with those of prostitutes, but contemporaries would have thought the classification proper. The Medicean popes passed for friends of Jewry, and the 1,700 Roman Jews enjoyed as favoured treatment from them as from any popes since the early Middle Ages. The great catastrophe of Roman Jewry in the Renaissance was the setting up of the Roman ghetto and the passing of harsh restrictions of every kind against the Jews by Pope Paul IV in 1555. But earlier in the century Jewish doctors and musicians were freely employed in the papal court, and Jewish bankers were allowed to operate freely and to lend at up to 20 per cent interest; in 1536 there were thirty Jewish banking firms in Rome. Jews followed the trades of tailor, dyer, clothier, vendor of old clothes, furniture and junk, soap seller, tripe merchant and small grocer. Paul IV excluded them from food retailing trades.

The Jewish quarter was in the low-lying area near the Portico of Octavian, which was subject to frequent flooding. There seems no reason to suppose the quarter to have been more of a slum than any other; the average Jewish household was of five persons, more or less the same as the Christian one. For the first half of the century a "ghetto" did not exist in a legal sense, though there was a Jewish quarter. In other areas Jews jostled Christians, and in some great palaces the ground floors were let to Jews, small Christian traders and artisans, and prostitutes. The Jews were treated as social and civic inferiors, as they were elsewhere in Europe. They were subject to special taxes; they were made by Julius II to attend an annual sermon; the best known of their disabilities was the obligation to provide runners for an annual footrace during the Roman Carnival, for which the course ran down the Via Lata (called the "Corso" from the horse races and not from these footraces) to Monte Testaccio. The obligation of old Jews as well as young to run stripped in this race now seems a degrading one. But the Jews were not the only people subjected to social sanctions by the annual Carnival games, which imposed quite heavy obligations on all the villages round Rome. Contemporary accounts seem to show that the Jewish population took the same sporting view of the annual Carnival race that the Christian population did.

All in all, the lot of the Jews in Medicean Rome was by sixteenth-century standards not a hard one. But what is social reform for one section of the population can be a harsh blow for another. One of the most unfavourable developments for Jewish money-lending in Italy in the period was the institution of the *Monte di Pietà*, the municipal pawnshop, which the Franciscans had introduced into central Italy in the early fifteenth century. Rome and Venice, the two great financial centres, had both resisted this institution. Under Paul III, perhaps because of the shrunken Roman economy, the papal government decided at last to follow the lead of the smaller Italian cities. In 1536 a conference of Jewish and Christian bankers failed to stave off the new competitor: the famine of 1538–1539 precipitated the setting up of a Roman *Monte di Pietà*. Florentine and Roman bankers participated in its government, though perhaps as much from the wish to supervise its activities as to further them. Loans by the *monte* were interest-free at first, but were charged with 5 per cent interest after 1552. The pledges were received twice-weekly from the borrowers, at sub-offices dispersed through the Roman regions; they were sold if not redeemed at the end of six months. The credit of the whole institution was underwritten partly by charitable contributions and legacies, and partly by the lands of the former Bohemian hospital, which the pope attached to the *monte*. Interest of 10 per cent seems to have been paid on money left on deposit.

In the long run the *Monte di Pietà* took its place among the great credit institutions of the city, and became important as an institution of government credit. At this early stage it was a modest charitable foundation which made only two or three thousand loans a year, and whose main social function was to alleviate the serious problem of imprisonment for petty debts. But the small Jewish money-lender must immediately have suffered from its operations.

The destitute, the prostitutes, the Jews were all socially disadvantaged in one way or another. The most severely socially disabled class was that of the slaves, most of whom had been acquired by war or trade with Muslim countries. They were especially prized in the boudoirs of great ladies and courtesans. There was a rather ill-defined right of the Capitoline officials to manumit baptised slaves who claimed sanctuary in their offices, and another custom of manumission after ten years; but Roman magnates were concerned to keep their slaves rather than to free them. In 1546 Paul III was successfully petitioned to decree that Romans could keep their slaves as such as long as the slaves lived.

VI

Roman sixteenth-century guilds were at once trade organisations, friendly (or loan) societies and religious sodalities. In none of these things were they unusual in their time, but their small average size, and close dependence on the papal and Capitoline organisations, meant that their social effect was fragmentary and their political power tiny. The only large and powerful guild was that of the *bovattieri*, the stock breeders' or agricultural guild, which was run by the great magnates of the Roman Campagna and had only an indirect relation to urban life. The effect of the guild organisations was further weakened by "foreign" sodalities and associations, of Lombards, Florentines, English, French, Germans and so on, which acted as alternative social centres to the various "foreign" elements of which three-quarters of the Roman population was composed. Few of the artisans in Rome had much part in civic government; the binding factor was not the urban administration but the Church. The Capitoline official Marcello Alberini complained that the Roman artisans failed to co-operate properly in the military organisation of the *caporioni* or regional leaders because most of them were "foreigners".

The origins of the Roman guilds go back to the late Empire, but there certainly was a remarkable revival and extension of guild life in the fifteenth and sixteenth centuries. But the trades, because of the very nature of Roman economic life, were separately weak in numbers, and collectively lacking in economic power. It is significant that the corporation of "bankers", which dated from the fourteenth century, was not the guild of the great Tuscan and Genovese bankers but that of the small moneychangers. The true bankers or financiers were known as "merchants", with the courtier status of "merchants following the Roman court". Thus the great financiers took no part in the guilds, which were left to the small tradesmen. It is also significant that the masons, one of the most important industrial occupations, founded a guild only under Clement VII, and then only for small masters. The list of trades which set up guilds in the sixteenth century is of small people: shoemakers, violin-string makers, butlers, pork butchers, chicken vendors, second-hand merchants and so on.

The friendly society element in Roman guilds was considerable. Most of them had charitable funds for financing the dowries of poverty-stricken members, and in this way they joined in the charitable methods of the orphanages and hospitals, which also gave dowries to the indigent. Only a few guilds, of which the masons were one, gave dowries outside their membership. Many guilds provided their members with medical help. But all this was in each guild on a small scale; the charitable work of the Roman guilds cannot be compared with that of the great Venetian charitable foundations, which were a major factor in Venetian social policy. Roman charity was too piecemeal and particular.

· The supervision of the exercise of each craft by guild regulation was extremely detailed, as was the case for most medieval guilds. The requirement for a particular trader to belong to the appropriate guild was also strict. The control of guilds lay in the last resort with papal officials, especially with the Cardinal Chamberlain and the officials of the Chamber, and with the Governor of Rome. There was also supervision of guilds and their statutes by the Roman municipal authorities.

The funds held by the richer guilds were not contemptible. One or two of the finest small churches of Renaissance Rome were built for them, notably S. Maria di Loreto (now off Piazza Venezia), which Bramante and Antonio da Sangallo the Younger built for the bakers, and S. Eligio degli Orefici, which Raphael designed for the jewellers.

The religious sodalities or confraternities are at times rather hard to distinguish from the trade guilds, and at other times from the hospitals and charities. Some confraternities confined their membership to priests, but most had a mixed membership of clerks and laymen. The religious aims of the confraternities were too various to be distinguished usefully. As with the other charitable organisations, while their expansion was most rapid in the post-Tridentine period after 1563, there had been a medieval basis and also a continuous history of foundations in the first half of the sixteenth century. Julius II, for example, had a devotion to the Sacrament whose artistic expression in Raphael's "Mass of Bolsena" is known to everyone, but which also led the pope to patronise the Company of the Sacrament in the church of San Lorenzo in Damaso.

The social aims of the confraternities were concerned with giving dowries to poor girls, with medical assistance, with prisons, and with the death rites and burial of the poor. Some confraternities provided for the poor in general, but most thought first of their own members, or else made extremely careful social distinctions about the objects of their charity. The Company of the Gonfalone was rich enough by mid-century to build an elegant and beautifully decorated church, which they filled with frescoes that are among the finest works of the Roman Mannerist style. Like many of the richer institutions, the Company could draw money from the preaching of indulgences, and possessed affiliated companies in other parts of Italy. But most of its charitable activities—dowries for poor spinsters, medical assistance, mortuary assistance—were carried out for the benefit of its own members. A similarly restricted policy was carried out by the Company of the Annunziata alla Minerva, much of whose finance was supplied directly by the pope. The Annunziata Company gave dowries to poor spinsters, but specified that they should not be domestic servants, peasants, maids in domestic service. In other words, it specified that they should be decayed gentlewomen. Such distinctions were also typical of the great Venetian charities of the same period: Pope Paul III himself used his privy purse to award dowries to "poor baronesses". It would be unjust to suggest that no Roman charity gave dowries to really poor girls, but even the new foundation of S. Ignatius Loyola at the Santi Apostoli seems to have given preference to the genteel poor in its awards of dowries. The social level of the dowries can be known from their amount: at the end of the century the Annunziata fund gave dowries of 80 to 100 scudi, while at the same period the Confraternity of S. Marcello gave dowries of only 25 scudi.

Only a rather shadowy distinction separated some of the confraternities from the "national" institutions. The Florentines, the most powerful of the "national" groups, had in the fifteenth century formed a pious sodality in Rome whose function was to attend on and help those condemned to death by the civic authorities. The place of execution was behind the Capitoline hill on Monte Caprino; it is possible that some scene of execution there may have influenced Taddeo Zuccaro's fresco of the Passion in the Mattei Chapel in the nearby church of S. Maria della Consolazione. Not far from the gibbet was the Florentine guild church of S. Giovanni Decollato, on whose walls are the agitated frescoes of Francesco Salviati and Pirro Ligorio.

The origins of the "national" hospices are to be found in the needs of pilgrims of particular groups. Long before the end of the Middle Ages some of these hospices had tended to be absorbed by Roman civic needs, as the English hospice of Santo Spirito had been absorbed by the hospital of Innocent III. But other national hospices maintained a strong and independent position. The German hospice of S.

Maria dell'Anima, which rested on the powerful alliance of German elements in the papal court with German bankers and artisans, grew and flourished. The Genovese hospital in Trastevere was also based on fifteenth-century immigration. The English College, which had been founded in the fourteenth century to replace the vanished hospital in the Borgo, stagnated in the early sixteenth century because of the complete absence of English immigrants; in the Counter-Reformation period it became a seminary. But the Lombard confraternity flourished, and indeed set the pattern for the "national" hospices of the sixteenth century, which had the interests of immigrant groups rather than of pilgrims in mind. The pilgrims tended more and more to be looked after by some central organisation like S. Spirito in Sassia or Trinità dei Pellegrini.

Some "national" groups built imposing churches and institutions. The German fraternity church of S. Maria dell'Anima was a striking building which combined elements of German gothic taste with the work of predominantly Italian architects. Nearby, S. Giacomo degli Spagnoli in Piazza dell'Agone (Piazza Navona) was another big fifteenth-century church which continued to be expanded and modified in the following century by Antonio da Sangallo the Younger. Spanish funds for churches were abundant in Rome in the earlier sixteenth century, to which S. Maria in Monserrato, the result of the fusion of two earlier Spanish churches, and also the work of Antonio da Sangallo, belongs. S. Pietro in Montorio was also Spanish; this was the site of the wonderful *tempietto* of Bramante, the pattern of the new classicizing style in Rome. French building of churches tended to be delayed until after the peace of Cateau-Cambrésis, when the churches of San Luigi dei Francesi and Trinità dei Monti were completed.

VII

The medieval hospitals and hostels of Rome were numerous and well endowed. There were some new foundations in the sixteenth century, particularly under Leo X and Clement VII. That the two Medicean popes should appear prominently as sponsors of new charities may be thought surprising. The new "Counter-Reformation" foundations of the later sixteenth century were not overwhelming in number; the most important were the orphanages, of which the first was founded by Ignatius Loyola in 1540, and the pilgrim hostel of S. Trinità dei Pellegrini, which was founded with the help of S. Filippo Neri in 1548–1549. But Counter-Reformation charity work in Rome was essentially the reorganisation and improvement of existing resources, rather than the foundation of new. The reconstruction of the great hospital of S. Spirito in Sassia by Sixtus V is a good example.

Two of the greatest and richest hospitals were connected with the big churches of St Peter's and the Lateran. S. Spirito in Sassia, in the Borgo, was the descendant of the Anglo-Saxon burgh, made by Innocent III in the early thirteenth century into a great charitable institution, and linked to the European hospitaller order of the Holy Spirit. In the early sixteenth century it housed up to five hundred persons; it received the sick and the destitute, including abandoned women and orphans. Its medical services needed reorganisation, but were not despicable. But it suffered, like all the well-endowed Roman churches, from the neglect and the financial exploitation of the Medici and Farnese popes. At the end of the preceptorship of Alessandro Guidiccioni, who was a member of a well-known Tuscan curial family, in 1552, the hospital's extensive lands were encumbered with debt. Some of this debt may have been incurred for the reconstruction of the church of S. Spirito in Sassia in the 1530s and 1540s. The artistic success of the new church made it one of the big influences on the evolution of early Roman Baroque style, but the bills had to be met. Paul IV's attempts to reform the hospital were unsuccessful, and its complete renewal took place only under Sixtus V, after whose rebuilding it seemed "like a great castle, containing many squares and palaces".

The Lateran basilica had next to it the Hospital of the Saviour (del Salvatore, or S. Giovanni), which in 1526–1527 harboured less than sixty sick persons, though by the end of the century it could receive three times that number. Like S. Spirito, it could supply drugs and had skilled medical help. A third ancient hospital, Della Consolazione, was connected with the churches surrounding the Campidoglio, and in 1526–1527 harboured a hundred sick.

(107)

Typical of the charitable organs set up to meet the social needs of the sixteenth century were the hospital for syphilitics (S. Giacomo degli Incurabili), the hospice for pilgrims and invalids (Trinità dei Pellegrini), the hospital for reclaimed prostitutes (Convertite della Maddalena), the institute for orphans (Santa Maria in Aquiro), and the brotherhood for prison visiting (Confraternità della Carità). The inspiration for the hospital for "incurables" came from parallel Genovese institutions, but also from Tuscans resident in Rome. A Florentine priest called Giuliano Dati was instrumental in taking over one of the old Roman hospitals, S. Giacomo in Augusta, and in re-endowing it to receive those suffering from incurable diseases which, as it was later described, "were unpleasant to the eyes and the nose". Plague and leprosy were excluded, but syphilis was specifically catered for. Support for the new hospital came from highly-placed Genovese and Tuscan curialists, and also from the small group of pietist clergy round Gian Pietro Carafa and Gaetano of Thiene, who in Leo's pontificate had formed the group known as the Oratory of Divine Love. Finance for the hospital also came from the lands of the earlier hospital and from the preaching of indulgences by mendicant agents. Medical assistance was good, and the hospital used to treat syphilis the decoction of "acqua del legno" (*guajacum officinale* from central America). This was a treatment tried by Benvenuto Cellini.

Later in the century the treatment of patients in the hospital of S. Giacomo by *acqua del legno* was an impressive phenomenon. Two or three hundred beds would be specially prepared, and when on an appointed day they had been filled, at a set hour surgeons would bleed the sick and begin the administration, from immense cauldrons, of the "water" and "syrup" of the concoction. The course lasted for over a month, and even where it was not directly medicinally effective, gave rest and a proper diet to a large number of sick people. In 1526–1527 S. Giacomo harboured some 170 souls. Sangallo the Younger and Peruzzi had co-operated in the plan of the hospital, which was an elegant and costly building. The associated little church of S. Maria in Porta Paradisi (also by Sangallo) still contains an inscription which 1 cords the plague of 1523.

The Trinità hospice was founded in 1548–1549 in anticipation of tl e needs of poor pilgrims in the approaching Jubilee year of 1550. Its moving spirit was the kindest and most thoughtful of Roman priests, S. Filippo Neri, who in co-operation with other priests founded a large "confraternity" of Roman clerks and laymen. The financing and staffing of the hospice was thus helped by rich and poor. Its aims were to give lodging to poor pilgrims for at least four days, to give them religious instruction, and to wash and care for their feet—no empty religious service for people who had walked the pilgrim roads. The beginnings of the Trinità hospice were modest, but in the Jubilee year of 1575 it entertained over 100,000 pilgrims, and in 1600 over 200,000. It was thus essentially a great central charitable institution, a phenomenon of the Counter-Reformation, whose inspiration went back to the pontificate of Paul III. The pilgrim hospice was the main part of the work of the Trinità, but Filippo Neri added to it the extremely touching duty of offering refuge to the convalescent poor, who on discharge from the Roman hospitals had no one to care for them. A similar extension of social conscience was the institution for the mad, especially for the destitute mad, set up in the mid-century as S. Maria dei Pazzarelli.

The role of the court and of courtiers in sixteenth-century Roman charity has to be acknowledged. It was especially important to the "Compagnia della Carità" which was founded in 1519 by Giulio de' Medici, cousin of Leo X and the future Pope Clement VII. This sodality, which was founded and financed by courtiers, set up and ran a monastery for converted prostitutes, the Convertite della Maddalena. It is possible that, as the English playwright John Webster implied in *The White Devil*, there was a strong element of police work in the way such a house was run. The other main activity of the Compagnia della Carità was prison visiting and the liberation of prisoners held for debt. The vast majority of denizens of Roman prisons were debtors, so there was a close link between prison work and the demand for facilities for cheap credit for the poor. The same impulse lay behind the Compagnia della Carità as behind the creation of the *Monte di Pietà* in 1538.

St Ignatius Loyola founded in 1542 a new hospice for "converted" women (S. Marta) which tried to fill the gap caused by the harsh rule of the Convertite della Maddalena, which would admit neither women who were too ugly to make a living any longer from prostitution, nor women who had separated from their husbands. This house for "mal maritate" was not a monastery, but a hospice, so women were not compelled to accept a religious rule in order to enter it.

With the orphanages of S. Maria in Aquiro (for boys) and of SS. Quattro on the Coelian (for girls), Ignatius Loyola and his followers attacked, though they could not solve, the problem of child beggars. There was also another orphanage at San Caterina ai Funari for the female children of prostitutes, the "Vergini miserabili". If Aretino is to be believed, prostitutes often took female infants from orphanages and brought them up as whores. Especially in their early stages in the 1540s, orphanages were too small to go far in tackling the immense problem of mendicancy, which grew rather than diminished as the century proceeded.

It is hard to see Roman charities in the second half of the sixteenth century as different in kind from those of the first half. In so far as there were new forms of charitable work, most of them were begun before mid-century, even if their full development did not come until later. Sixtus V's hostel for beggars perhaps represents a policy for mendicancy which cannot be found earlier. But the main changes brought by the Counter-Reformation clergy were increased zeal and superior organisation and use of resources. In one way Rome in the late sixteenth century had increasingly serious social problems be-cause of larger population. But late sixteenth-century governments could do more in the field of social welfare because they were richer, or at least because they taxed and borrowed more heavily, and because more money was in circulation. Sixtus V may not have resembled Leo X in many ways, but he did resemble him in his frenetic building activity, and in his recklessly spendthrift budget.

Though the price rise brought new social problems, papal and clerical income rose at least as fast as prices. The huge increase in pilgrim traffic during the Counter-Reformation brought Rome both advantages and problems. Rome fulfilled its true function in receiving the great influx of pilgrims; it was also compelled to carry out social reforms in order to house and care for them.

Many of the Roman charities were supported in part at least by the preaching of indulgences in Christian Europe. They thus relied on the same kind of international financial organisation which supported the rich Roman curialists. The administration expenses of gathering the proceeds of indulgences could be heavy; S. Spirito in Sassia allowed the preachers to keep a third of their takings. The administration of the Roman charities was in few cases known to have been corrupt. But when doctors, bursars, hospital staff, porters and so on are taken into consideration it has to be acknowledged that the administration of the Roman charities was itself an important Roman occupation. Like the *enti di assistenza*, the Italian charitable institutions of later centuries, the Roman charities existed to alleviate social suffering, but also to promote employment.

Chapter Four

THE
ROMAN COURT
AND THE
PAPAL PALACE

The Roman court differed from other Italian courts only in some respects. In Pietro Bembo's dialogue, *Della Volgar Lingua,* Vincenzo Calmeta is quoted as having written that "la cortigiana lingua" (by which he meant the Italian spoken in the Roman court) is to be preferred to all other varieties of Italian. But to this assertion the ironical reply was made: "Which court do you mean? The courtly tongue is that which is used in courts, and there are many courts: in Ferrara, Mantua, Urbino, Spain and France there are courts." The papal court was the only bishop's court to enjoy the same temporal splendour, the same political prestige, as the greatest princely courts in Italy, and indeed was the only court in Italy to be the equal of the ultramontane royal courts. But the papal court was one of a species well known to contemporaries and very much anatomised by them. Especially to men of literary and administrative gifts for whom the court was the obvious place for social advancement, it was like some fascinating and dangerous woman who promised riches and fine diversions, but who might end by degrading their persons and their talents. The distinguished humanist, Guglielmo Sirleto, when the suggestion came from the pope himself that he should enter the service of a Farnese prelate, refused because his disposition and habits were alien to the court ("la natura molto aliena dalla Corte . . . per non esser atto al star delle corti").

The reasons for the distrust with which sixteenth-century intellectuals regarded the court were diverse. Gian Matteo Giberti after a brilliant and lucrative tenure of office in the papal court as datary—a great papal office, as Bembo wrote in his letter of congratulation on the appointment—decided to leave it in order to reside in his bishopric of Verona. He felt the need to "leave the court and to come here to live for God in your midst" ("questa necessità di partirmi di Corte, et venir a vivere a Dio et in grembo vostro"). But if Giberti went to Verona to do his duty as a pastor, in the course of which he was to set the pattern for "Counter-Reformation" bishops, other humanists withdrew from the court for motives which, if not totally selfish, had more to do with the humanist ideal of learned leisure or *otium liberale* than with pastoral care. Jacopo Sadoleto, one of the most brilliant scholars of the Medicean court, withdrew from Rome to his episcopal see at Carpentras in Provence only a few days before the Sack. He felt that it was time, having given so much of his life to others, to withdraw into himself. He had been sent by his father to the Roman court in the hope, which he had justified, that he would make the family's fortune there. He felt now that he had given enough to princes and friends, and to public life, and that it was time he thought of himself.

Sadoleto's flight from the Roman court did not mean the end of his public career, nor the end of his connection with Rome, to which he returned nine years later to be made a cardinal. But the circumstances of his first withdrawal from Rome have much that is typical of the ideas and interests of the more idealistic of the curial humanists. In his retirement from business at Carpentras Sadoleto wrote a tract, the *Praise of Philosophy*, which was a humanist discourse on wisdom whose aim was to reconstruct the lost tract of Cicero called *Hortensius* which had been the indirect cause of the conversion of St Augustine. The first part of *De laudibus philosophiae* sets up in opposition to the true humane wisdom or *sapientia* the pretended wisdom of the man of business of the Roman court, who is represented in the dialogue by the person of Tommaso Inghirami, Leo X's librarian, the type of the material-minded curialist whose life is devoted to court business and self-advancement. The tract is a fastidious rejection of the life of the scholarly businessman which Inghirami certainly had led, and which is characterised more vividly in paint than Sadoleto achieved with the pen, in Raphael's brilliant Inghirami portrait, now in Boston (see Ill. 1.1).

The two great manuals of court life with which the later Renaissance begins and ends, the *Cortegiano* of Baldassare Castiglione and the *Galateo* of Giovanni della Casa, were both written by men who had lived much in the Roman court. But into both of these works the Roman court enters only incidentally. Pietro Aretino's dialogue *Delle Corti* (published in 1538) is far more specifically concerned with the Roman court, which it refers to as *"the* court". The dialogue reflects Aretino's own turbulent career in the Roman court in the 1520s, which ended with his being wounded at the hands of one of the servants of the papal datary, Gian Matteo Giberti. It also reflects Aretino's discovery that, unlike most men of letters, he had the ability to make his own way outside the courts by living in Venice and exploiting the power of the printing press. Aretino knew only too well the dependence of most writers, artists and humanists on the court, and he compares those among them who had not lived in the courts to soldiers who have never been to war. Aretino acknowledges that without the Roman court Raphael would never have produced the marvels of the Stanze nor Michelangelo those of the Sistine Chapel; he acknowledges too that after the great promotions of Contarini, Sadoleto and others to the cardinalate in 1535–1536 it is clear that the papal court *can* reward ability and merit. But he also enunciates the venerable platitude that the court is the figure of Fortune, who neglects thousands of worthy men for the one or two whom she promotes. Aretino denounces the callousness of the court, whose nobles will encourage some attractive adolescent and indulge him for a couple of days, and then throw him back into the squalor of menial court life like some apple from which only a single bite has been taken. He attacks the barbarism and ignorance of courtiers and tells the story of a "marvellous intellect" (often taken to have been Raphael, but more likely to have been the humanist Fabio Calvo) who explained his archaeological plan of Rome to the inattentive and skylarking courtiers, who at the end of the lecture allowed the burning wax of the candles to set fire to the plan.

Aretino's satire is the product of a society in which civic office in a free city-state was no longer an established way of promotion for the able, and in which the princely patron and his court were supreme. Educated men disliked the venality and the insecurity of court life, and the humiliating progress up the stairs of the great. But how many other paths of advancement lay open to them? The distinguished scholar, Carlo Dionisotti, has suggested that as the sixteenth century progressed the opportunities offered by Italian society to clever and ambitious laymen diminished, and that clerical preferment became once more, as it had been in the Middle Ages, the best trodden of all roads to a good position and a fat retirement.* For humanistically trained men who did not come from the greatest families, the papal court was a more attractive option than the withering political life of the Italian communes. Francesco Guicciardini, the greatest Florentine in public life of his generation if we except the great secretary Machiavelli, reflected with irony and perhaps with regret that his father had refused to make him a clerk. Guicciardini spent most of his talents not on behalf of his native city but on that of the popes. Pietro Bembo's action in abandoning political life in Venice in favour of a career in the Roman court was remarkable for a Venetian patrician. Gasparo Contarini, the former Venetian ambassador created a cardinal in 1535, is a different but equally striking case. Dionisotti pointed out that of the participants of the dialogues in Castiglione's *Cortegiano*, Sadoleto, Bembo and Frederigo Fregoso were cardinals by 1540, and that the Portuguese bishop to whom the book was dedicated (Michel de Silva of Viseu) also entered the Sacred College, as would Castiglione himself probably have done had he not died relatively young. The careerist humanist was more and more a clerk in orders. Two families of humanists in papal service were those of Biondo and Ardinghelli. The descendants of the famous Flavio Biondo, the fifteenth-century archaeologist, remained laymen in papal service as their founder had been. But while Pietro Ardinghelli, a key figure in the secretariat of Leo X, was a layman, his son Nicola Ardinghelli became a clerk, served Paul III as secretary and datary, and was created cardinal in 1544.

Castiglione found it necessary in the *Cortegiano* to make the conventional deprecatory noises about the corruption of the Italian courts

---

*In a lecture, "Chierici e laici nella letteratura italiana del primo Cinquecento", republished in his *Geografia e Storia della letteratura italiana* (Turin, 1967).

of his day, but he did so extremely briefly and in the context of *de senectute*, a discussion of the way in which old men criticise the decadence of new times. The rest of his book is an idealisation of court life, though little of it refers directly to the papal court. Castiglione's suppression of the nastier facets of court life is notorious.

Humanist administrators like Sadoleto might quite sincerely complain of the strains and stains of curial life, of the life of *negotium*. But not until the end of their careers could they normally hope to retire from the court to the villa, and to enjoy the cultivated repose, the *otium liberale*, which they had hankered for at the time of their curial servitude. Paolo Giovio, bishop of the small south Italian diocese of Nocera dei Pagani, eventually found quiet and discreet luxury in retirement in his villa at Como. But he found this only after thirty-seven years of literary and political activity in the Roman court, and even then he was disgusted by the papal refusal to make him Bishop of Como. Only the very greatest churchmen, of the blood and eminence of an Ippolito d'Este or an Alessandro Farnese, could afford the construction of great country villas which they would use while still engaged in the business of the Roman court, like Villa d'Este at Tivoli or Caprarola, and these were in any case great palaces for the transaction of business rather than country retreats.

II

The Roman court was an appellation which came into use in the eleventh and twelfth centuries to describe the domestic and administrative offices which had grown up since the earlier Middle Ages in the papal "palace". The court included the College of Cardinals and the pope's domestic prelates; it excluded the Roman parish clergy and the religious of the Roman monasteries, and was separate from the papal chapel. The heart of the Roman court in the sixteenth century was the papal household or *famiglia palatina*, the pope's domestic officials and certain sections of his administrative offices, especially those of the datary and the Chamber. Outside this category was a large number of officials who enjoyed the title of "familiars" or "permanent members of the household" ("continui commensales"), whose familiars might in turn enjoy the same technical privileges. But these officials, even if they possessed certain rights at the papal table, were not part of the pope's true "family", and even the greatest of them such as the referendaries and the judges of the Rota had no part in the "parte del palazzo".

The numbers of the papal *famiglia* rose very steeply during the Renaissance period. The total number of papal "familiars" (then divided into "lords" and "ministers") under Pope Pius II (1458–1464) was about 150, and that of their servants about eighty. By Leo X these numbers had risen to 418 familiars and 265 servants, a total approaching 700 persons. The reformer Vincenzo Quirini recommended to Leo X that the number of the papal *famiglia* should be halved, but the words fell on deaf ears. Paul IV in the mid-sixteenth century had rather more familiars than Leo X, and in 1562 the *famiglia* of Pius IV numbered over a thousand. With some difficulty Pius IV managed to reduce the *famiglia* to 600 persons, a reduction which was maintained in the following pontificate. The pressure on the pope to expand his court and to increase its expenses was the same as that on all great lords of the Renaissance period. In the papal case it was due only partly to ostentation; the main cause was the claiming of rights by papal officials. Cardinal Alfonso Carafa, for example, of right maintained fourteen familiars in the Apostolic Palace and five horses in the Vatican stables. Even if such rights were possessed only by the palatine cardinals, they still produced an army of followers whom the pope had to feed.

The palace which contained the papal court was probably the most splendid of any government in Europe. The core of the palace on the Vatican hill dated from the time of the popes of the high Middle Ages, of Innocent III and Nicholas III. But the Renaissance popes expanded it on a vast scale. The improvements of Sixtus IV, of Innocent VIII, of Alexander VI, were in themselves piecemeal and modest, though the decorations of the Sistine Chapel and the Borgia Rooms were rich and beautiful. But the Belvedere villa built by Innocent VIII, on the hill facing Monte Mario and at a distance from the main palace, was to be, under Sixtus's nephew Julius II, the occasion for the greatest single extension to the Vatican Palace. Julius caused Bramante to plan, though only partly to execute, a great courtyard to be created by the building of two immensely long loggias from the main Vatican palace to the "Belvedere" of Innocent VIII. That the Belvedere was much higher than the main palace meant that not one but three great *piazze* were enclosed by the project, the first on the level of the main palace, the second on an intermediate level, and the third on the level of the Belvedere villa. The octagonal intermediate *piazza* was connected with the lower one by a ramp, and with the upper one by two external ramps and also by a fine internal spiral staircase. The Belvedere villa was reconstructed, and a great hemispherical apse or nymphaeum was built (though after Bramante's time) at the central point facing the main palace. The exterior wall of the whole project was in effect the external wall of a fortress, an effect which was heightened later in the sixteenth century by the construction of a great bastion of the Belvedere by Paul III.

The construction of the urban quarter of Prati has deprived our century of a viewpoint from which it is possible to appreciate the immense bulk of the Belvedere, though in certain lights some idea of it may be had from the Pincio. Sixtus V brutally cut the Belvedere in two, destroying the unity of Bramante's plan, by the construction of the new Vatican Library. But it was still the greatest single architectural project executed in Rome since the end of the Roman Empire. It was at once a circus for tournaments, bull fights and military displays, a theatre, a system of hanging gardens, and a fortress; while the great three-storied loggias were an enormous extension to the main palace. The harmony of Bramante's design made something which might have been oppressively huge into something light and airy, softened by fountains and gardens and extended and opened by the artful use of perspective. The area involved was enormous, and it was a very long time before the whole was enclosed by buildings: Bramante built only the eastern side. Under Paul III the gardens of the Belvedere were constantly infested by wild animals, especially by foxes, from the adjoining wood. The gardens were nonetheless remarkable; in them the popes placed some of the finest Hellenistic statues to have been recovered from antiquity.

Thus the most grandiose transformation of the Vatican Palace in the Renaissance was something essentially of this world, which provided for recreation, for art, for display, but not for the religious functions of the popes. Tournaments and bullfights were held in the

Belvedere well into the Counter-Reformation period. But the traditional religious and political functions of the Vatican Palace were not neglected by the Renaissance popes.

The popes dwelt uneasily in the uncomfortable rabbit-warren of state rooms in the Vatican Palace, each aware that his time there was unlikely to be long, yet anxious to impress the marks of his personality and his family on the palace. Julius II lived from his accession in 1503 until 1507 in the Borgia Rooms, with their strange friezes of pseudo-Egyptian decorations and Borgia bulls, before opening up on the higher level a new series of rooms whose decoration was assigned to, among others, Raphael. The Stanze, as the new rooms were currently called, were typical of the sumptuous and inconvenient interconnecting rooms in which sixteenth-century princes did their business, and where they kept their courtiers and suitors waiting. It is our good fortune that Julius II and Leo X should have commissioned for their decoration some of the great masterpieces of western art, normative for the civilisation to which they belonged and to which we precariously cling. The biggest of this set of rooms, in fact the only ones of really imposing size, were the Sala di Costantino and the Sala dei Palafrenieri, or "secret" Consistory room. The Stanze led into other rooms of a less formal nature, the "Logge" of the Cortile di San Damaso, which under Leo X were decorated by Raphael's workshop with a light-heartedness which was clearly meant for relaxation rather than for business.

Much of the Vatican Palace was cramped, short of light, and hampered by differences of level. Most of the improvements made by individual popes consisted of re-modelling and re-building. Paul III renovated the state rooms of the south-west part of the palace, notably the Sala Regia and the Sala Ducale; the architect responsible was Antonio da Sangallo. The Sala Regia gave directly into the staircase of access from St Peter's and also into the Sistine Chapel, and was used for the more strictly formal audiences of sovereigns and their representatives.

The Vatican Palace, although huge, did not provide living quarters for the whole papal court. Among the cardinals only those classified as "curial" or "palatine" had apartments in the Vatican Palace, a convenient right which Adrian VI tried to deny them. Essentially these were cardinals concerned with the papal secretariat, such as the humanist Bernardo Dovizi da Bibbiena, whose titillating bathroom decorations by Raphael have been the source of mild scandal. But most of the great curial churchmen, even such key figures in the papal household as the datary, had their own houses or palaces in Rome. The curial cardinals, even if they did not live in the Vatican, had the right to maintain a given number of their own familiars there.

The personnel of the papal court varied widely from one pope and one period to another. From Julius II's quarrel with the Romans in 1511 until the accession of Paul III in 1534 a whole generation elapsed in which virtually no Romans were employed in offices which brought them personally close to the pope. Only when the Farnese pope, who was himself a "Roman baron", succeeded to the tiara, did the chamberlains, secretaries and masters of the household of the pope once more include members of Roman families. Leo X employed large numbers of Germans in his *famiglia*, as had Julius II. Theirs are among the faces of the papal grooms in the "Mass of Bolsena" by Raphael in the Stanze. But for most of the first half of the sixteenth century the Roman baronage, which had so often roughly dominated the papacy, was held by the popes at arm's length or further. Roman baronial power was held by Guicciardini to have been inimical to papal power and peace of mind. Only Paul III's Farnese relatives achieved for a few years the sort of position which had been commonly held by Roman noble relatives of the popes at earlier periods. One may contrast the Raphael portrait of Leo X, with the tonsured Giulio de' Medici standing with another cardinal behind his cousin's chair, with the equally unforgettable portrait of Paul III by Titian, in which his two grandsons, the layman Ottavio and the Cardinal Alessandro, stand with him, and the layman slyly steals the picture from both the churchmen.

The head of the papal household was the official called the *maestro di casa*; under his administration were chamberlains, masters of the wardrobe, almoners, grooms, gendarmes or beadles (*servientes armorum*) and the rest of the elaborate household staff. A description of the dining room and kitchen staff may give some idea of the scale on which the pope lived. His establishment was princely but not gargantuan; it was larger but not greatly more complex than the parallel arrangements suggested by Paolo Cortese or Francesco Priscianese for cardinals, or by Cola da Benevento for great nobles. The staff of the two dining halls (*tinelli*) was supervised by two *maîtres d'hotel*, by their officials, and by the chief butler (*credenziere*) and male housekeeper (*spenditore*), and by three clerks with the duty of checking household expenses. There were two stewards (*dispensieri*), a chief wine butler (one of whom published a tract on Paul III's tastes in wine), a chief wine steward (*canevaro* or sommelier) and four sub-stewards; two chief bakers, a secret baker, eight sub-bakers; two chief cooks, two secret cooks, one common cook for the second kitchen, sub-cooks in abundance. The list is long but not endless, and one wonders whether a modern hotel manager would be content to provide with this staff the hundreds of daily meals which the Vatican certainly provided. Some of these officers received more distinctions than their titles suggest; one of the butlers held a canonry in Lübeck under Paul III, and one of the wine butlers held knighthoods from both Paul III and Charles V. One of Clement VII's cooks was an educated Frenchman who was the friend of the poet Francesco Berni.

III

The papal chapel was entirely separate from the papal household. The singers did not normally eat in the papal dining hall with the *famiglia*, and recorded it as a special privilege when they were allowed to do so. Under Leo X the boy singers ate in the *tinello*. The Sistine Chapel was staffed by a sacristan (usually an Augustinian friar), one or more Masters of Ceremonies, a Dean and Sub-Dean, two clerks, two writers and a librarian. The chief musician, the "Master of the Chapel", occupied a favoured post which could lead to bishoprics and fat benefices. The adult singers reached a maximum number of thirty-six under Leo X, whose passion for music was dominating. Under his successors this number sank by a third. The *castrati* singers, whose self-mutilation for money gain was against the spirit of Church law, did not appear in the papal choirs until the Counter-Reformation period.

The music of the Sistine Chapel was the heart of papal interest in music. Among the popes, the favours accorded to his musicians by Leo X were legendary. Leo's chapel master Elzéar Genet of Carpentras recruited singers from the Low Countries, and encouraged the

Flemish element in Roman church music, though this policy was no innovation, and was to continue under Leo's successors. Contrary to what is sometimes said, Leo X was not only an aesthete but a religious aesthete. His chapel master wrote that no music enthralled Leo as did the chant of the religious offices, which often moved him to tears of emotion. Leo did not admit to the ranks of the truly great composers those who were unskilled in the art of writing masses.

Leo X, as the son of Lorenzo de' Medici and the pupil of the composer Heinrich Isaac, was far from indifferent to *frottole* and to other secular chamber music, especially at Carnival time. His "secret musicians" (*musici segreti*), who were not members of the papal chapel, numbered as many as sixteen. He also liked the folk tunes played by the dancers of the *moresco*. Many of the *frottole* played for him had a political content, like the *Palle, palle!* which Heinrich Isaac based on the "cry" of the Medici, and which Leo X had copied into a sumptuous manuscript. Other popes encouraged political songs, like the song composed by Filippo da Luprano and sung at the wedding of Julius II's niece Lucrezia Gora to Marcantonio Colonna in 1506. The union of the houses of Colonna and Della Rovere was celebrated in a text which referred to the oak of the Della Rovere, the column of the Colonna, and to the titular church held by Julius II when a cardinal, S. Pietro in Vincoli (St Peter in Chains). "The oak is joined to the column; chains bind the oak" ("Quercus iuncta columna est, nectunt vincula quercum").

Leo X rewarded musicians richly, though this also has been misunderstood. He paid the converted Jewish lutanist Gian Maria lavishly, and allowed him to adopt the name of Medici. The Spanish clerk Stefan Gabriel Merino was a skilful musician at the courts of Julius II and Leo X who also excelled in organising papal hunting parties. Unwary musical historians have attributed Leo's conferment on Merino of the archbishopric of Bari to his musical abilities alone. But in reality Merino, far from being an over-rewarded musician, was typical of those able men of his period who used their social talents to advance themselves in a princely *famiglia*. Once given office he showed his abilities to be more than those of an entertainer; he had a distinguished career as papal *nunzio* in France, imperial ambassador and Grand Almoner of the Order of the Golden Fleece, and first Patriarch of the Indies; in 1535 he died a cardinal.

Under Leo X secular musicians played at the end of papal meals, as well as at the theatrical performances which took place in the Vatican. The small organ, *tanto variato di voce*, which Cardinal Luigi d'Aragona had given to Leo X, was used for secular music. The same kind of balance between secular and sacred music seems to have obtained in the court of Pope Paul III. Paul was the patron of the composer and lutanist Francesco Canova da Milano, whom he took with him to his meeting with Francis I at Nice in 1538. Both Clement VII and Paul III maintained a wind band in Castel Sant'Angelo; this was the band in which Benvenuto Cellini on one occasion played.

IV

The papal chapels were the setting not only for the finest music in Europe but for some of the greatest works of art. When Sixtus IV founded the chapel subsequently known as the "Sistine" he organised a programme for its decoration by which great artists illustrated the main aspects of his temporal and church policies. The programme was continued and extended by his nephew Julius II, who changed the course of western art by commissioning the sculptor Michelangelo to paint the Sistine ceiling.

To trace the theology and the politics which lie behind these and other great works of art which were carried out for the popes has proved extremely difficult. It is hard partly because we are still ignorant about the theologians in the courts of the Renaissance popes, but also because of the sheer complexity of the task, and because of the protean nature of Renaissance symbolism. Art historians have sometimes concluded too hastily that they have found the theologian whose doctrine fits certain works of art executed for the popes. But the theologians who may have been involved are many, and long periods of time are in question, particularly for Michelangelo, who began work in the Sistine Chapel in 1508, and returned (although unwillingly) to the chapel to begin the "Last Judgement" almost thirty years later in 1536.

The "programmatic" nature of almost all the works executed in the public rooms and the papal chapels of the Vatican Palace is beyond doubt, even if its exact nature is sometimes hard to establish. Sixteenth-century patrons did not leave their artists to compose their works according to the dictates of inspiration. Even the greatest artists had to accept detailed instructions as to the subject, content and imagery of their work. Michelangelo's claim that he was allowed liberty in painting the Sistine ceiling for Julius II refers to the interpretation and not to the substance of the scheme. That a pope of the temper of Julius would allow a young and uninstructed layman to dictate the theological plan of the decoration of his own private chapel is something which only a very naive art historian could believe. It is reasonable to call Raphael and Michelangelo "painter-intellectuals", but the limits of their knowledge must be remembered. Raphael did not know any Latin: any attempt to represent his culture as equal to that of the humanists surrounding him breaks down on this fact. Michelangelo's literary culture was much superior to that of Raphael, who was literate only in a rather primitive way even in Italian. But even if Michelangelo was a cultivated man, a poet and a deeply religious thinker, he was not a theologian. His work and that of Raphael were impregnated by taste, sensibility and intelligence. But not until the 1530s, when the stature of Michelangelo was god-like, can there have been any question of his having a voice in the subject rather than in the treatment of his paintings; and even when he planned the Sistine "Last Judgement" and the frescoes in the Cappella Paolina the papal theologians kept a wary eye on the work which this wayward genius was executing at the very centre of the Catholic world. We do not know whether Michelangelo refused to execute the "Delivery of the Keys to St Peter" which seems to have been projected for the Cappella Paolina, or whether the idea was dropped in favour of a more devotional formula.

Though the Sistine Chapel was the pope's private chapel, it was not so in the sense that the pope performed his private devotions there; this was the function of the chapel of Nicholas V, which stood next to the pope's bedroom. The pope and his cardinals celebrated the holy rites in state in the Sistine, attended when the occasion required by the ambassadors and the Roman nobles. On occasions specified by the Roman liturgy the pope celebrated mass in St Peter's or St John Lateran, but no longer, as in the past, in the other Roman churches where the "station" was to be held. St Peter's and the other churches had their own chapters, endowments and administrations which were quite separate from the central papal government. The Roman court found its normal ecclesiastical expression in the Sistine Chapel, and it was appropriate that this chapel should be splendidly adorned.

When Michelangelo was commissioned in 1506 by Julius II to paint the vaults of the Sistine Chapel, the upper side walls were already covered by the plan of decoration commissioned by the pope's uncle, Sixtus IV. How Michelangelo's mighty enterprise was planned is beyond the scope of this book. What is relevant here is its relation to the Roman Court. The view that Michelangelo was encouraged by the pope to make his own decisions about the theological content of the frescoes seems to me, as I have written above, untenable. Julius II may well have, on Michelangelo's advice, abandoned the earlier decision to paint the twelve apostles in the vaults, but the main scheme of decoration, which was located in the centre of the pope's liturgical life, must have been planned with the advice of the court theologians. A persuasive view was put forward by the late Professor Wind, who said that "there is no doubt that the Roman theologians who planned the programme of the Sistine ceiling for Michelangelo conceived the cycle as a hymn to the spirit that confers divine gifts by effusion".* The more exact identification of these theologians has escaped even the most learned, but it seems possible that responsibility was divided between the circle of Augustinian friars and secular humanists connected with the Augustinian General, Giles of Viterbo, and the Dominican theologians whose main patron was the elderly Cardinal Oliviero Carafa—another cardinal whose clients included both orthodox theologians and humanist scholars. The doctrines of the executed Florentine Dominican friar, Savonarola, seem to have made themselves felt, whether directly or indirectly, in the work.

The theological origins of Michelangelo's Sistine masterpiece are hard to determine exactly, but it seems to represent a fusion between late-medieval orthodox views and those of the learned humanist clerks who tended to go back to the church fathers of late antiquity for their theology. The fresco is also influenced by the vocabulary and

*E. Wind, "Michelangelo's Prophets and Sibyls", *Proceedings of the British Academy*, 1965 (1967), p. 82. Wind's view of the "untenable theory that Julius gave Michelangelo *carte blanche* to invent his own program" is in his article, "Sante Pagnini and Michelangelo", *Gazette des Beaux Arts*, 6th ser., XXVI, 1944.

religious symbolism of Tuscan Neo-Platonism. The humanist clerks were important for the powerful people they knew rather than for the offices they occupied; with certain important exceptions such as Giles of Viterbo they were of the evanescent breed of courtiers. But their imprint was placed on the Roman Renaissance in a permanent and unforgettable way, allowing the visual symbolism of great artists to express itself with perfect confidence and balance. The calm and the complete assurance of the culture of the Roman court in the first two decades of the sixteenth century, expressed in a series of great works which will last as long as our civilisation, were very different from the tension and uncertainty of Roman culture after the Sack of 1527; to see this we have only to let our gaze travel from Michelangelo's Sistine vault to his "Last Judgement" on the west wall of the chapel.

Typically, the contribution made by Leo X to the decoration of the Sistine Chapel was much more expensive than that of anyone else. Tapestry was as a decorative medium many times more expensive than fresco, and the series of tapestries which Raphael began to design in 1514 to cover the lower walls of the Sistine Chapel was a gorgeous luxury, woven in Flanders in cloth in which gold thread was lavishly used in the design. These tapestries treated traditional topics of the Roman Church in what was thought to be the idiom of classical antiquity. The themes may well have been drawn from the decoration of the ancient churches of St Peter and of S. Paolo fuori le Mura, but their classicizing treatment by Raphael was based on the latest archaeological discoveries.

V

Raphael, Michelangelo and the other artists employed in the Vatican Palace were not painting pictures for a museum, nor were they putting humanist culture on record for the benefit of succeeding generations. They were commissioned to create visual symbols of what were thought to be the truths of theology and the lessons of papal policy. Their employers were not cultivated dilettanti, but great masters of a millennial tradition which had always known how to express the Petrine primacy in symbols as well as in words. The function of the artists could be called political propaganda, if we took the phrase in its original meaning of *de propaganda fidei*. They could also be given programmes of decoration which were cultural rather than political. Thus the Stanza della Segnatura of Raphael seems basically to be an illustration of conventional academic doctrine of the liberal arts, a programme which would fit better with the identification of this room as Julius II's Library than as the room in which he signed papal petitions.

Glorification of the papacy's political role can be found at every turn in the Vatican state rooms. The link between the four frescoes of Raphael in the Stanza d'Eliodoro is the politics of Julius II's reign. Attila's halt before the gates of Rome would seem to be the deliverance of the papacy after the catastrophe of the French victory at the battle of Ravenna in 1512. The "Expulsion of Heliodorus from the temple" is likely to refer to the measures against simony taken by the Lateran Council; similar references are intended in the "Death of Ananias" in the Sistine Tapestries. The "Liberation of St Peter from Prison" probably also refers to the delivery of the papacy from danger, and refers too to Pope Julius having been the Cardinal of the Church of St Peter in Chains (S. Pietro in Vincoli). The "Miracle of Bolsena" refers to the personal devotion of Julius II to the Sacrament, and also to his voyage through the papal state.

An equally political decoration was executed by Raphael and his pupils in the Stanza dell'Incendio. The "Fire in the Borgo" represents the extinction of a fire in the Borgo by its builder, Pope Leo IV; this was an allegory of the role of the other Leo, Pope Leo X, as the bringer of peace and concord to Christian Europe. In the same room the "Coronation of Charlemagne by Pope Leo III" probably refers to the Concordat concluded in 1515 between Leo X and Francis I of France. The "Victory of Leo IV over the Saracens at Ostia" refers to Leo X's attempts to unite the Catholic powers of Europe in a crusade against the Turks. The "Oath of Leo III" refers to the oath taken by Pope Leo III to the Council summoned by Charlemagne in 800, and may be an allegory either of Leo X's Lateran Council, or (less probably) of the oath he took to the cardinals during the conclave of his election. The whole room is a panegyric of the political wisdom and success of Leo X.

Perhaps the most remarkable theme of the Vatican decorative programmes is that of the Emperor Constantine. The Renaissance popes were not shy of asserting the temporal power of the papacy. The panegyric of Julius II delivered by Giles of Viterbo at the opening of the Lateran Council praised him for recovering the papal state from its enemies, and for his making the papal armies into a force to be feared. Julius II and his successor Leo X occupied the cities of Parma and Piacenza which had not even formed part of the medieval papal state. Julius's uncle, Sixtus IV, had also been an exceptionally warlike pope; of the aggressive wars waged by Cesare Borgia in the papal state during Alexander VI's pontificate it is hardly necessary to speak. It was therefore entirely natural that the legend of the "Donation" by the Emperor Constantine to Pope Silvester I of (among many other rights) "the city of Rome and all provinces of Italy and the western regions" should have been maintained and propagated by the Renaissance popes. Papal imperialism in Italy was condemned by Erasmus, and even by Italian intellectuals like Guicciardini who worked as its agents. But this papal imperialism was a political fact, and the popes were not going to abandon its theoretical basis, even if a part of that basis had been undermined by scholarly criticism. The so-called Donation of Constantine was a forgery of the eighth or ninth centuries. Its falsity was denounced in the fifteenth century not only by the anti-papal humanist Lorenzo Valla, but by Cardinal Nicholas of Cusa who was one of the most distinguished intellects of the Roman court. But Renaissance popes found no difficulty in ignoring denunciations of the forged Donation, and Alexander VI even employed the Donation as the basis for arguments for imposing a division between Portuguese and Castilian interests in the New World. The Donation was also one of the justifications alleged for papal occupation of Parma and Piacenza.

From the time of the frescoes executed for Sixtus IV in the Sistine Chapel in the 1480s, the Emperor Constantine or his associations were frequent themes in the decoration of the Vatican Palace. Raphael was not the first artist to depict the great twisted pillars in St Peter's which were thought to be those of the Emperor Constantine. But Raphael's use of the pillars in the "Healing of the Lame Man in the Temple" turned out to be one of the most influential inventions of his art.

The Sala di Constantino in the Vatican contains a series of large decorative paintings *all'antica*, executed largely by Giulio Romano and his co-heir of Raphael's workshop, Francesco Penni. The paintings were executed in the last part of Leo X's pontificate and the first part of that of Clement VII, and they reflect the gloomy and magnificent *romanità* typical of Giulio Romano, who was brought up in the shadow of the Forum of Trajan. The whole aim of the Sala di Constantino is to impress on the beholder the worldly power and empire of the Church. On one wall Constantine, surrounded by the elaborately researched panoply of Roman arms and armour so dear to Renaissance antiquarians, harangues his troops. On the main wall an enormous panoramic painting shows the battle of the Milvian Bridge, the feat of arms which in the traditional view imposed Christianity on the Roman Empire. This painting, wrote Vasari, became a guiding light for all who had to paint similar kinds of battles after him, and it has been hailed in our own time as a masterpiece of assimilation of ancient motifs. The third wall shows the baptism of Constantine in the Lateran Baptistery by Pope Silvester, who according to the legendary "Acts of Silvester" had freed the emperor from leprosy. Over the window Constantine is depicted in St Peter's, offering to Silvester the silver model of "Rome" which symbolises his donation of Italy, the west and the islands to the pope. Between these large paintings are others of great popes, each of whom sits under the papal umbrella and holds the keys: the umbrella and the keys together formed the feudal coat-of-arms of the papacy.

Some have thought the continued preoccupation of Renaissance popes with a document like the Donation of Constantine which had been "proved" false, to be politically inept. But to propagandists nothing can be proved false or true. The papacy which had just seized important new lands in Emilia needed all the evidence of title it could get, and the citation of the Donation was far from inept. As late as the end of the sixteenth century the great Catholic historian, Cardinal Baronius, though he reluctantly passed over the Donation in his history, still asserted the genuineness of the "Acts of Silvester" which are the Donation's origin. Pope Pius V ingenuously told the Venetian ambassador in the late sixteenth century that Constantine did not need to donate rule over the western Empire to the Church, since it possessed it already!

Under Adrian VI decoration of the papal palace came to an abrupt halt. For the first three years of Clement VII work was resumed, and artists and architects poured back to work under the clear skies of Medicean Rome. Those skies were darkened by the plague, then the Colonna raid of 1526 brought vandals and looters into the Vatican Palace, and presaged the greater darkness of the Sack of 1527. In that year a German soldier scrawled "Martin Luther" on one of the Raphael frescoes in the Stanze, and seemed to pronounce a death sentence on the luminous and balanced view of the Christian faith which they spelled out. But before twelve years had elapsed Paul III, that great Renaissance courtier, had resumed the embellishment of the Vatican Palace. The two great halls for public consistories leading off the Sistine Chapel, the "Sala Regia" and the "Sala Ducale", were reconstructed by Sangallo. In the same part of the palace the same architect built a new chapel, the Cappella Paolina. Architecturally these are all fine rooms, superior to the box-like apartments decorated by Raphael for Julius II and Leo X. The decoration of the Pauline Chapel is oppressively rich. Its treasure is the two frescoes which Michelangelo began there in 1542, and did not complete until after mid-century. In these frescoes, the "Conversion of St Paul" and "Crucifixion of St Peter", Michelangelo expressed his feelings on the problem of justifying faith, which engaged the most sensitive Catholic minds of that decade. The topics were suitable devotional ones for the pope's private chapel, far removed in conception from the complex programmes of the Sistine. They show how the "evangelical" school of Catholic devotion could get its theological iconography accepted in the heart of the papal household.

The continuity of purpose which is so typical of the papacy as an institution can be seen with especial clarity in the history of the Sistine Chapel, whose decoration began under Sixtus IV in the 1480s and was pursued by both Julius and Leo. The final great fresco above the high altar was commissioned from Michelangelo by Clement VII, probably in 1533. Paul III renewed the commission, which Michelangelo was reluctant to execute, but which he began to paint in 1536 and finished in 1541. Michelangelo's "Last Judgement", whose tragic pessimism sums up the disasters which had overtaken the Medicean papacy and its Tuscan servants, was thus the completion of a decorative series whose execution was begun when both Michelangelo and Paul III were small children. There is no doubt that Paul III was pleased with the work, since he immediately proceeded to commission the frescoes of the Cappella Paolina. But the inconvenient envious, vulgar Aretino wrote from Venice in a way which showed how the wind of taste was blowing. Aretino had lived outside the Roman court for twenty years by this time, and he could see that the individualist emotionalism of the "Last Judgement" was just as out of touch with contemporary taste as its background of Tuscan Neo-Platonism. Aretino criticized both the nudity of the figures and the taste of the whole fresco, "as impious by its irreligion as it is perfect as a painting". As Aretino's own new religious writings were beginning to imply, the future of Catholic religious propaganda lay in a formula of decorous academic statement of received orthodox truths. Pius IV showed his acceptance of zealot criticism by commissioning the absurd additions of "breeches" to Michelangelo's nude figures. But the "Last Judgement" remained, a monument to the overwhelming power of genius and also to the conservative taste of the late Renaissance popes.

Chapter Five

THE
NOBLE
LIFE

"Cardinals of the Roman Church," wrote Guicciardini, "[are] accustomed to being honoured and virtually worshipped." The College of Cardinals, however, was not at the very height of its power in the Renaissance period. These parish priests and deacons of some of the Roman basilicas and churches, united with some of the local bishops of the Roman area, had during the late Middle Ages reached a point where it seemed just possible that their corporate control might modify or even supersede the ancient autocracy of the Bishop of Rome. By the late fifteenth century that possibility, if it had ever really existed, was closed. The conciliar constitutionalists had been repulsed by the popes, and their defeat was repeated by the failure of the Council of Pisa in 1511–1512. The attempts of the cardinals to impose "electoral capitulations" on the pope whom they elected, though reiterated as late as the election of Leo X, were ineffective. The great expansion of the number of cardinals which began under Sixtus IV and was maintained right through the Renaissance period, had the effect of weakening the corporate power and the financial strength of the College of Cardinals. The Renaissance papal secretariat also weakened the consultative functions of the cardinals. The Counter-Reformation period saw a final blow dealt to the corporate power of the cardinals by the setting up of the "Congregations".

But even if their political power was enfeebled, the cardinals remained, as they always had been, the centre of the Roman court. Renaissance humanist writers, affected by classical models and also by the senatorial trappings assigned to Roman clerks in the forged Donation of Constantine, described the College of Cardinals as the "Senate" of the pope. In the papal consistory, whose history went back to the Roman councils of the eleventh-century Reform popes, the most important papal decisions and pronouncements were made, embassies received and answered, the more important benefices conferred, all in the presence of the cardinals. The consistory was analogous to the feudal council of the pope; the cardinals were not the only papal officials to attend it, but they were the most important. A distinction was made between secret and public consistories, which were held in different papal halls, the former in the "Sala del Papagallo" (of the Parrot) or "dei Palafrenieri" (of the Grooms); and the latter in the Sala Ducale; embassies were also heard in the "Sala Regia". The "Sala del Papagallo" was no mere name: the parrot was a princely pet, and from the early Middle Ages the popes had kept their parrots in an audience chamber. The "secret consistory" did most of the administrative work; in these consistories the cardinals operated the lucrative business of "proposing" clerks for bishoprics or abbeys which were to be conferred by papal provision, for which the cardinal responsible received a gratuity, or *propina*.

Whether a cardinal was of noble birth or not, his office imposed on him the role of leading a "noble life". The minimum required of a cardinal was that he should entertain liberally and keep learned clerks in his household, besides offering hospitality to genteel poor persons. The dress and ceremonies of the Roman court were extremely expensive, and although cardinals received grants in aid when they went on legations, they could not accept such commissions without ready money of their own. There was therefore a decent minimum below which no cardinal, however pious or economical, could live. Adrian VI himself said that as a cardinal he had lived *outside* the Roman court at the rate of 3,000 ducats a year. It is doubtful if a cardinal in Rome could easily have lived on an income of less than 4,000 ducats a year, and a figure of 6,000 ducats was often proposed as the minimum below which a cardinal should be able to ask for a subsidy from the pope. These were considerable sums. An ordinary priest or schoolmaster could live on twenty-five to thirty ducats a year.

The household of a great man was an entirely personal thing which depended completely upon him, and which broke up immediately upon his death. Its officials, majordomo (*maestro di casa*), stewards, wardrobe officials, chamberlains and so on were organised on the same pattern as that of the Vatican household of the popes. The obligation on all members of a great man's *famiglia* was to ride with him and attend him when he rode out. This obligation (to *cavalcare*) was very strictly interpreted. There was a bell rung to summon the familiars to accompany their lord; failure to come to the signal of the bell could entail the loss of dining rights at the lord's table. Aretino tells a story of a prelate who was so pressed by financial need that he had to get out of the obligation of feeding his familiars. So he stole in the middle of the night to the stables and hid the harnesses and staffs of office of the familiars; then he sounded the bell to move off while the household were breaking their fast early the next morning. As the familiars could not harness their horses to accompany him he rode off without them, and hence after eight days had the right to refuse to feed them at his table.

Between cardinals of great families and those of modest extraction there was a great gulf. The cardinals of the houses of Gonzaga, Colonna, Trivulzio, Este, Farnese and Medici were great nobles who lived like feudal lords. In 1533, at a moment when papal fortunes were low, Clement VII looked into the household of his nephew, Cardinal Ippolito de' Medici (then aged twenty-two), and found that it contained over 500 persons, many of whom were troops (*bravi et capitani*). Even for a papal nephew such a household was exceptional, but several cardinals, almost invariably of great noble family, maintained households which were at least half the size of the papal household of 700. The average size of a cardinal's household in Rome in 1527 was about 150 persons, which conforms with the recommendation of Paolo Cortese's treatise on the Cardinalate, written at the beginning of the century. There were a few cardinals in Rome with households numbering between forty and eighty. In 1564–1565 Cardinal Carlo Borromeo, a papal nephew who would normally have been expected to keep up a greater state than this, cut his household from 150 persons to 100, with the intention of reducing their numbers finally to about eighty persons and twenty horses in the stable. At the Council of Trent in 1562 Cardinal Ercole Gonzaga had a train of 160 persons, and the other four cardinal legates some fifty or sixty each.

Cardinals were each the centre of a system of patronage. One of the main aims of any cardinal was to secure the advancement of his relations and there were scores of clerical dynasties connected with the Tuscan cardinals alone. A cardinal could get papal permission to "resign" benefices either in favour of the hungrier members of his family or of his circle of clients, or as a means of alienating the benefices to make a capital gain. In this way Cardinal Pietro Accolti, the head of a family remarkable for avarice and corruption even in Rome, transferred the bishoprics of Ancona, Cadiz and Cremona to his nephews. A much poorer cardinal like Jacopo Sadoleto exercised this privilege in order to endow the clerical members of his family, though its exercise made him "poorer" than ever. But patronage was not reserved for relatives alone. Many other clients, either with claims on the cardinal because they were his countrymen, or with some recommendation from a great man on the score of ability, or merely because they were well-born hangers-on or parasites, lived in a cardinal's *famiglia*. Able men like Sadoleto, who was trained in the household of Cardinal Oliviero Carafa, or the future Cardinal Giovanni Ricci, trained by the elder Cardinal Del Monte, began their careers in the Roman court as hardly more than children. The presence of students and unruly young men in the households of cardinals led to trouble, and it was necessary to legislate against the disorder caused by rowdies (*facinorosi*) in the palaces of the cardinals and in the streets. From the point of view of these young men, the households of some cardinals could be described as boarding schools with a low moral tone. Pedro Ribadaneira, who left his post as a page in Cardinal Farnese's household to join St Ignatius Loyola, described Palazzo Farnese as a bottomless pit of filth and uncleanness, where arrogance and violence were encouraged among the young instead of reproved.

To finance these huge households and to support these clientage networks was difficult even for men who could tap the golden rivulets of the papal court. Cardinals drew their monies from many sources. They had a communal financial organisation of the College of Cardinals, whose revenues from the taxes on benefices ("common service" taxes) bestowed by papal provision in the early sixteenth century provided a corporate revenue of about 20,000 florins annually, which was shared out between twenty to thirty cardinals resident in Rome. Individual cardinals drew sums which could be quite large from the *propina* on benefices which they "proposed" in consistory; the amount any cardinal received from this source depended on his position as "cardinal protector" to one national interest or another. Cardinals could also gain appreciable sums from the revenues of their titular church in Rome. But the nerve of any cardinal's monies came from the income he drew from benefices occupied by him as an absentee pluralist. By contrast with curial offices, which he had to purchase for large sums and which were a form of capital investment, income from benefices was largely unearned and untaxed. A cardinal might if he chose visit the bishoprics or abbeys which he "administered", and might decide to spend a part of their revenues on the fabric of the churches concerned or for similar purposes, but such expenditure was entirely discretionary. His only compulsory expenditure was on the official he paid to administer the diocese or abbey on his behalf. Cardinals might be said to have performed a useful social function in the central administration of the church, but so far as most of the cures of souls they administered were concerned, they were merely drones.

The revenues of individual cardinals varied widely. Only a few had incomes below 3,000 ducats or above 20,000. The total number of cardinals varied between forty and seventy, but the number resident in Rome was usually between twenty-five and thirty. An income of 12,000 ducats made a cardinal rich; in 1501 only one in six of the cardinals possessed this income or more. Not only did the revenues of individual cardinals vary, but the revenue of an individual cardinal varied from one period of his career to another. Benefices came and went with political favour or disgrace. Most cardinals were either "French" or "Imperial" in sympathy, and the fortunes of European politics influenced their benefices, pensions and incomes. Nor did riches protect cardinals—any more than they protect anyone else —from the effects of extravagance. Cardinal Giulio de' Medici at the very peak of his career as a cardinal in 1521 had an income of 20,000 florins and debts which more than matched his income. No doubt he had been caught with the rest of the close relations and clients of Leo X in the financial collapse of the last two or three years of the pontificate. Cardinal Luigi d'Aragona, who was one of the great figures of the papal court in the first two decades of the century, died heavily in debt, though he had been rich at some points of his career. The same is true of some cardinals from great noble houses—for example, Sanseverino, Trivulzio and Della Rovere. These were problems of the rich. Some "poor" cardinals were granted papal pensions to help them maintain their status. Under Leo X, not surprisingly, such pensions went to greedy scoundrels like Accolti, but under Paul III the recipients were more likely to be scholars and theologians such as Sadoleto or Cardinal Pole of England.

There is some evidence about the cost of day-to-day maintenance of a cardinal's household. Cardinal Armellini, the financial expert of Leo X, drew in cash from his bankers about 3,200 ducats annually (266 ducats monthly), and it may be assumed that this was the estimated expenditure on his household of 100 persons and his stables. Francesco Priscianese, who was a humanist in the household of Cardinal Niccolò Ridolfi in the 1540s, reckoned the annual expenses for a cardinal's household of just over a hundred persons at the huge sum of 6,500 scudi, of which 4,000 scudi were for food, and the rest for salaries and stables. Priscianese is at pains to emphasise that he is describing a household in which no expense is spared to do things properly!

The price of accommodation for a cardinal and his household was naturally high. In the early sixteenth century the rent paid by a cardinal for a palace of moderate size was between 200 and 400 ducats annually. The price of a palace under Julius II or Leo X was about 5,000 or 6,000 ducats, double the prices before the great building boom under Sixtus IV. After the Sack, building values naturally tumbled; the palace of the Franciscan Cardinal Numai, which had been sold to his nephew for 4,000 ducats in 1526, was resold in 1531 for only 2,450 scudi. But prices picked up again at the time of the great street improvements of Paul III. The palaces built by artists were sold for large sums; Raphael's palace, which had passed into the hands of the Accolti, was sold for 6,000 scudi in 1540, and Cardinal Giovanni Ricci of Montepulciano paid very large sums indeed to buy the palaces of the Sangallo family in Via Giulia. All these transactions, however, pale into insignificance beside the construction of Palazzo Farnese, on which 243,000 ducats had been spent by 1549.

Some cardinals could not afford a palace at all; this was often the lot of humanist cardinals such as Bibbiena, for whose lying in state after his death a palace had to be "begged", or of Bembo or Pole (who seems to have used the English College to accommodate his "family") or Sadoleto. But these poor cardinals were a minority. Francesco Albertini's description of Rome at the time of Julius II mentions over twenty palaces inhabited by cardinals which he found worthy of note because of their external splendour or the magnificence of their contents. About thirty cardinals' palaces are identifiable in the Roman census of 1526–1527, and a similar number is identifiable in Aldovrandi's book on the sculpture of Rome in the mid-century. Almost all these palaces were owned or rented by the cardinal concerned; only in one or two cases, such as those of the palace of S. Marco or the Cancelleria, does the cardinal's palace seem to have come to him with his title or with an office.

II

The cardinals were the top layer of a society of rich clerical bureaucrats; poor cardinals were indeed poorer than rich officials. Not all the curial posts were lucrative in themselves, but that of datary, not normally given to a cardinal, was the key to the whole patronage apparatus. Clerical curialists below the rank of cardinal depended for their main source of income on the pluralist absentee occupation of benefices, as their red-hatted betters did. More important curialists could receive the revenues of benefices in the form of pensions from lay princes. Henry VIII of England granted a pension of 2,000 florins a year from the revenues of the diocese of Worcester, which was shared by the datary, Gian Matteo Giberti, and the Bishop of Castello. But these were the perquisites of great men.

The fees of curial office were not unimportant. During the first two decades of the sixteenth century they constantly tended to rise. From the late fifteenth century onwards some influential clerks had been conscious of the acute moral problem which fees in the papal court represented for the Church. Indeed, the problem was not unknown to St Bernard in the twelfth century. Renaissance popes from Alexander VI onwards made some attempt to respond to these uneasy consciences by enquiring into the system. These enquiries produced no effective reforms, and a glance at the membership of the reform commissions under Julius II and Leo X explains their failure: they contained just those clerical politicians such as Riario, Della Rovere, Pucci, d'Aragona and Accolti, who were among the most shameless exploiters of the curial system. Far from reducing curial fees, the reform bull of Leo X in 1513 legalised a number of sharp practices which had hitherto been doubtful, and authorised a heavy increase in the level of fees charged to supplicants and litigants in the Roman court. In making these increases the pope was no doubt influenced by the need to provide curialists with incomes commensurate with the amounts he was making them pay for their offices. This big rise in fees might be compared with an issue of free stock to its shareholders by a modern company, but it still could not keep pace with the level of government borrowing initiated by Leo. By Clement VII's time, even before the Sack, curialists were looking back wistfully to the "golden days" of Leo's pontificate. The first crisis of curial officeholders had already occurred, during the pontificate of the puritanical Adrian VI, who examined plans to reduce the venal offices. The poet Francesco Berni cynically advised Adrian VI's curialists to let the curial offices go: they were poor investments. According to Berni a curialist did better to invest his money in benefices bought for cash down. At this moment of papal financial need he purported to think that the return on investment in benefices could be as much as 60 per cent.

> Keep the money and let the offices go!
> Benefices are better if you've cash.
> Sixty per cent is what you ought to show.
> A sound investment; nothing rash!

Another poet, Ludovico Ariosto, had in Leo X's pontificate given directly contrary advice. He took in his Second Satire the example of a curialist who mistakenly sold his offices in order to become a bishop, and so to wear a green-trimmed headgear instead of the ordinary black one. According to Ariosto the new-made bishop was likely to find that by the time he had compensated the previous owner of the bishopric and paid the "first-fruits" tax to the papal offices, he had no money left to support his inflated *famiglia*, and was indeed likely to be publicly denounced for his unpaid debts! His "family" was so re-

duced that he could not ride to the Vatican Palace accompanied by the
train of followers which a bishop's dignity made obligatory.

> His clergyman's black cap with green made gay,
> He's left his well-lined offices, and found
> More worry, more expenses, and less pay!
> He has a flock of folk to feed, and not a pound
> To spend: the first fruits are already pledged:
> The old debt must be paid: it's overdue:
> Though for two terms' non-payment he has hedged,
> The third will post his name in public view.
> To St Peter's Church in haste he now should go,
> But can't: his majordomo and his cook
> Aren't there to ride behind him in a row.
> His mule is out, or sick; its haunches look
> Quite fallen-in: and girth and saddle are broke.
> Or, back from Ripa, it's tired, and has cast a shoe.
> The poor chap can't go out unless all his folk
> Are trotting just behind him: it won't do
> Unless down to the kitchen-boy they're present.
> Not in Matthew or in Mark does he seek the founts
> Of knowledge: all the study he finds pleasant
> Is how he's going to balance his accounts!

That the pope himself sold benefices for cash, in flagrant defiance
of canon law, cannot be proved from the accounts. But there was certainly a big open market for benefices bought and sold by individual
clerks, a traffic which could not take place without papal consent to
their "resignation", nor without payment of substantial taxes oc-
casioned by the transfer.

With the appointment of a reform commission by Paul III in 1536
the system of fees charged by the datary and the market in benefices
came under fire for the first time from critics within the Roman court.
The point at issue was the delicate one whether, by authorising these
practices, the pope was not himself committing the sin of Simon
Magus (Acts 8:18–25). The matter was examined by further commissions under Paul III and Julius III, but no clear ruling was made,
and the matter was never seriously discussed at the Council of Trent.

Papal finances had slid into a position which allowed little scope for economies, and in which it was hard to make drastic changes in the Roman Curia. The markets in offices and in benefices continued, and theologians were still discussing the moral issues in a desultory and inconclusive way in the early seventeenth century. Urban VIII's theologians in 1642 got no further with these questions than the curial theologians of the 1540s and 1550s.

Yet even at the very summit of curial office the financial position of office-holders could be insecure. Baldassare Turini of Pescia, the cultivated Tuscan correspondent of Lorenzo de' Medici, and a personal dependent of the Medici family, was one of the most prominent clerks of Leo X's court. In 1517 he was in such financial straits that he pledged his offices of *cubicularius* (chamberlain) and papal secretary to the banking firm of Strozzi against a loan of 5,300 florins. In 1518 he was made papal datary, an office which might have been expected to solve his financial problems. But it clearly did not, perhaps because the loans which Turini had been obliged to make to the pope were bigger than the profits of his office. He also failed to hold the office long enough, being replaced by Adrian VI after Leo X's death in 1521, at a time when the Medici pope owed him 16,000 scudi. Turini had by Leo's death undertaken the building of one of the most beautiful villas of Renaissance Rome, the villa on the slopes of the Janiculum which from its subsequent purchasers became known as Villa Lante. In 1523 Baldassare Castiglione evidently knew that Turini was in money trouble, since he offered to buy a fountain in the form of a satyr holding a goose, which he thought Turini wanted to sell to help finance the villa. But in the long term Turini's career justified the stability of employment in the Roman court and the investment he had made in Villa Lante. Turini managed to retain the villa after the Sack of Rome and to repair the damage done there by the imperialist troops who had scrawled on the walls: "A di maggio 1527 fo la presa di Roma". Turini went on as a clerk of the Apostolic Chamber until his death in 1542, and kept his villa and his two palaces in Rome until the end.

III

Most successful careerists in the Roman court of the Renaissance period were "humanist"-trained in the sense that they had followed the liberal arts or *studia humanitatis*, and that their culture was literary rather than theological. Raphael's great allegories of the liberal arts in the Stanza della Segnatura assign a pride of place to theology which it did not really at that time possess in the culture of the papal court. Most curialists had at some point been educated by lay schoolmasters, sometimes in the households of older curialists. Greek and Latin of a high standard were taught in the Italian universities, but curialists who had attended the universities were likely to have followed courses of civil and canon law as their main studies. The "Academies" of humanists which were established in the late fifteenth century were schools which trained some future curialists. Some curialists, like Flaminio, Beroaldo the Younger, Sadoleto, were themselves sons of humanist teachers. Sons of noblemen would be taken privately by distinguished teachers; Paolo Cortese, the author of the handbook on the Cardinalate, mentions a reading party of young Roman nobles which he took in the 1480s to one of the islands on Lake Bolsena, and which included Alessandro Farnese, the future Paul III. Such instruction might be far more important than that received in the universities, where the teachers tended to teach different doctrines in their private circles to those which they professed in their university chairs. There is no mention of the university in the educational programme for Castiglione's *Cortegiano*, but Paolo Cortese's ideal cardinal is required to be learned in canon law as well as in the humanities, a requirement which presupposes the university. But theology had no formal place in any of these educational courses. Few of the Italian bishops who attended the Council of Trent had received formal training in theology.

The education of the Italian upper classes at this period, though brilliant in some ways, was unsystematic in others, and this fact lies behind the uncertain and groping nature of the response of the clerks in the papal court to the moral and ideological crisis of the Lutheran Schism. If a papal clerk had been professionally trained for his post, it was most likely to have been as a lawyer. But even the lawyers of the Roman Rota received only rather cursory examination of their professional qualifications, and most papal clerks seem to have taken up their offices without any enquiry at all into their training. It is significant that little is known of the formal education of one of the most brilliant of the reforming curialists, Gian Matteo Giberti. Some of the other reformers at Rome, notably Pole and Contarini, had studied at the University of Padua. But very few of them had received formal instruction in theology, and in this they resembled most ordinary curialists. The religious orders supplied the few professional theologians in the Roman court; secular clerks were likely to be without theological training. The ideal clerk, as described by Gian Matteo Giberti after he had retired to his diocese at Verona, would have a good moral formation and the power to set a good example; he would be well versed in Greek and Latin, and would have some knowledge of Scripture, but not of "disputational" theology (*cognitione de letere sacre, et non disputative*).

Latino Giovenale Manetti, the domestic secretary of Paul III, the administrator of the reconstruction of Rome after the Sack, and the learned humanist who showed Charles V the antiquities of Rome on the occasion of the emperor's visit in 1536, was described by a contemporary as "l'homo molto fattivo", the hard-working man of business. This phrase singles out the characteristic which might be said to split the humanists in the Roman court into two groups, the willing horses and the decorative swans. The papal court had an enormous appetite for good administrators—the Manettis, Inghiramis, Della Casas and Bibbienas of that world, who besides great literary ability had the instincts and the powers of the good civil servant. They were in a sense the traditional type of the medieval churchman; behind them stretched a long line of predecessors which went back to that distinguished *praefectus urbi*, Pope Gregory the Great. It is not very profitable to contrast these industrious bureaucrats with men of letters like Francesco Molza who were fundamentally court writers and not court officials. But it does seem possible, and more interesting, to contrast with the real men of business a figure like Monsignor Angelo Colocci, the possessor of numerous venal offices under Julius and Leo, but given after the death of his wife in 1518 the "expectation" of the diocese of Nocera, which he eventually and by none too creditable methods occupied as an absentee bishop. Colocci's real interests, like those of Goritz, were his archaeological collections and his literary circle; the curial business he had to do was the tedious necessity which financed his academic and literary life.

If Manetti and Colocci were the opposite poles of humanism, other humanists in the Roman court did not fall into such definite categories. The work of Paolo Giovio in his long life in the court was fundamentally literary and propagandist. Giovio was a Roman who had been rather sketchily trained in medicine; under Leo X he became the official papal historiographer, though he had critics during his lifetime and afterwards who implied that his real function was that of chief papal gossip writer. There was a certain frivolity about Giovio, but he was an able and well-informed man, the depth of whose intelligence can be tested, for example, by his grasp of Turkish and Muslim affairs of his day. There were other humanists in the papal court who, while of great ability, did not succeed as Giovio did in finding a political function which brought them success. The poet Annibal Caro was a man of great talent, whose Italian translation of Virgil is still read by Italian schoolchildren. But Caro, while being the secretarial maid of all work for great churchmen, never attained a position of importance in the curial hierarchy. Much was explained by family connection: the poet Giovanni Guidiccioni was perhaps no more able an administrator than many others, and so far from anxious for great responsibility that he dodged the difficult post of datary when it was offered him, but he still occupied the row of distinguished curial posts to which his family's solid place at the Roman court entitled him. The elderly and distinguished Greek man of letters John Lascaris, on the other hand, had to write a begging letter to Angelo Colocci asking for a gold coin to pay his bill at the inn, and a little more to see him through the approaching week.

The lot of literary men in the court who were without curial office was precarious. In Leo's court some of the "poets" were entertainers rather than men of letters. A great deal of importance was attached to the ability to improvise songs in Italian or Latin to the lute: Bernardo Accolti, who arrogantly styled himself "l'unico Aretino", was one of these improvisers, and the one-eyed Marone of Brescia another. The line between a literary man and a court buffoon was sometimes thin. Leo X made cruel fun of the self-styled poet Baraballo, for whom he organised a mock Roman triumph in which Baraballo was placed on an elephant and led towards the Campidoglio to the sound of drums and trumpets. The uneducated buffoon-friar, Mariano Fetti, was famous in Leo's court for gluttony and uncouth wit. Cultivated and able a poet as Francesco Molza was, he found himself a down-at-heel and dissolute hanger-on of great men such as Ippolito d'Este or Alessandro Farnese. The poet Francesco Berni became secretary to Gian Matteo Giberti when he was datary, but found himself in a humble and penniless position; though Berni admired horseflesh he could not afford a horse.

Yet there were compensations for hard-up literary men in the Roman court. One of the most typical manifestations of humanism in Renaissance Rome was the gathering of humanists in the garden, vineyard or villa of some curialist patron who was rich enough to entertain them but not so rich as to overawe or bully them. The Luxemburger curialist, John Goritz, entertained his literary friends on St Anne's Day in his vineyard near the Forum of Trajan, and from this circle came in 1524 the anniversary volume *Coryciana*, one of the most elegant collections of occasional neo-Latin poetry to be brought together in the Renaissance. Similar meetings were held by Monsignor Angelo Colocci, whose villa was in the new archaeological zone on the Pincio which he and other speculators had opened up during Leo's pontificate. The grounds of such villas were re-planted with trees and vines, and decorated with antique statues and sarcophagi. In Colocci's house in the region of Colonna there was another garden of this sort, and a "grotto" in the antique manner which housed the press of the Greek faculty founded by Leo X. The Sack put a temporary stop to these earlier groups, but similar ones appeared with the "Vignaiuoli", "Sdegnati" and "Virtuosi" of the 1530s and 1540s, in which the literary dining club was gradually moving in the direction of the Literary Academy. But the drift to high seriousness in these gatherings was not so swift. When Giovanni della Casa and his friends met as the Vignaiuoli it was under the protection of the Mantuan curialist Uberto Strozzi, who was also the protector of the courtesan Isabella de Luna. This circle composed Italian "Capitoli" of the type of "La Fava", "Priapo", "Il mal francese", or Latin compositions like Della Casa's "Formica", whose subject is an ant which penetrated the pudenda of Venus. Such exercises (whose revived memory was to cost Della Casa his chance of a cardinal's hat) would have been pursued by the Inquisition in the 1550s.

IV

The bankers of Rome were both socially and legally a part of the Roman court. As "merchants following the Roman court" they were technically courtiers who were subject to the jurisdiction of the Papal Chamber and not to that of the senator on the Capitoline Hill. They were also the hinge on which the whole cumbersome apparatus of curial finance turned. The composition of the Roman financial world changed according to the political regime. From the time of the Borgia pope Alexander VI to the end of Julius II's pontificate in 1513, the dominant banking firm was that of the German Fugger family, who used their Roman branch as a *point d'appui* for their growth into a European financial power. But though the Fugger remained important in Rome until the end of Adrian VI's pontificate in 1523, and were connected with the prominent positions held by Germans in Rome in the period, they left curiously little permanent mark on the city. There was no great Fugger palace, no Fugger literary circle, and the Fugger record of patronage of the arts is curiously fugitive. With the papal break with the Empire in the mid-twenties the Fugger family faded out of the Roman picture, to return only fleetingly later in the century. Nor did the other German bankers, the Welser, remain in Rome.

The Italian bankers, who like all bankers of their time were traders as well as financiers, had never been driven from their powerful positions at the papal court. With the withdrawal of the Fugger family they resumed the dominance of Roman society which was practically theirs by right. They fell into regional groups of Genovese, Florentine, Sienese and Roman bankers; there were few Milanese early in the century, but the Odescalchi and the Olgiati of Como made a modest appearance in Rome in the 1530s. Papal policy was usually to balance one firm against another, so that although a single banker like the Sienese Agostino Chigi could accumulate immense wealth in the first two decades of the century, he never drove his competitors out of business. The popes tended to farm out different parts of their revenues to different banking firms; a typical situation was revealed in the papal budget of 1525, which shows the Roman customs taxes farmed out to the Roman firm of Della Valle, the Roman salt monopoly to the other Roman firm of Bernardo Bracci, the Umbrian revenues to Pietro del Bene and the Sienese firm of Sauli, the alum mines at Tolfa north of Rome to the Chigi, the Treasury of the March of Ancona to the Florentine Luigi Gaddi, that of Romagna to the other Florentine Giacomo Salviati. In 1529 the papal commissioner for taxation was yet another Florentine, Bindo Altoviti. "Spiritual" revenues were also farmed to bankers, like the 3 per cent interest in church "annates" held by Luigi Gaddi, the relative of Benvenuto Cellini's patron, Monsignor Giovanni Gaddi. The powerful position in Rome held by Filippo Strozzi, the close relative of the Medici popes, has already been explained. The bankers were locked into the central papal organisation with cardinals and curialists: the main financial agent of the Medici popes, Cardinal Armellini, banked personally with Filippo Strozzi and Luigi Gaddi. The whole banking system possessed great strength and coherence, which were further increased later in the century by the system of floating papal loans through *monti* which were each handled by a banker or group of bankers. Popes, cardinals, curialists, bankers were connected in a web which could never be untangled. An Italian historian has described Roman banking as a "leprosy": it was a leprosy which did not kill Rome, but gave it life.

That members of the great banking families were rich and powerful clerks in the papal court is scarcely surprising. The Florentine bankers alone (even excluding the Medici) could claim Strozzi, Salviati, Ridolfi and two Gaddi cardinals in the first half of the century. But the great banking families did not have a monopoly: there were many smaller firms. There was a whole street of bankers in the region of Ponte, and another area in Borgo where bankers congregated. There can seldom have been less than forty or fifty Christian banking firms operating in Rome at any one time. Members of the lesser known banking firms also reached distinction in the curial hierarchy: Giovanni della Casa was the son of one of the smaller bankers, and Marcello Cervini, who became pope as Marcellus II, was the son of a Tuscan bank manager who worked for the Sienese firm of Spannocchi.

But the power and magnificence of the great bankers cannot be overlooked. The palaces of the Chigi, Massimi, Della Valle, Gaddi and Altoviti were among the greatest in Rome. As patrons of the arts, as hosts, as powers in the world of diplomacy and in the specialised field of clerical politics, the bankers moved the cogs which made the great Roman machine rotate. Money was itself a scarce commodity in the sixteenth century; the beautiful gold coins in which the bankers worked were themselves a treasure which might be thought valuable independently of their money exchange value. Bankers traded in luxurious objects and in ancient and modern works of art. They bought and sold, many would have said, not only legitimate merchandise but the garments of Christ and Christ's poor. But no one moved, in spite of all that was said and done at that time in Germany and the rest of northern Europe, to drive the moneychangers from the temple.

V

The ideal style of life led by the Roman court may be summed up in the word "noble". The bishops' courts of the Middle Ages had always tended to imitate the courtly way of life of the lay nobles. In late medieval England it was not surprising that an aristocratic bishop like Cardinal Beaufort should adopt a nobleman's way of life; but the same noble way of life had been led by his predecessor as Bishop of Winchester, William of Wykeham, who was neither a cardinal nor a nobleman. The noble life had been led for so many centuries by the Roman bishops and their court that it was taken entirely for granted in the Renaissance that this should be so. It seemed normal that Cesare Borgia should marry the sister of the King of Navarre and become Duc de Valentinois, or that Ottavio Farnese should marry the emperor's natural daughter and become Duke of Parma and Piacenza. These were no inventions of a decadent Renaissance papacy, but part of the political tradition by which Roman bishops claimed personal parity with sovereigns; in the early thirteenth century Innocent III (1198–1216) had once planned to marry a papal nephew to the daughter of King Philip of Swabia and to make the nephew Duke of Tuscany.

Another element in the social situation of the Roman court was the tendency for Italian families which in the Middle Ages had been of merchant status to seek a noble style of life and, eventually, noble status, in the Renaissance period. In Rome many families which were merchant in the late medieval period appear as patricians in the sixteenth century. The political disadvantages of noble status which had existed in many Italian communes in the Middle Ages had largely disappeared. Everything tended, as it did in other parts of Europe, to make the merchant oligarch into the nobleman. But the clericalization of Roman society in the sixteenth century meant that the rich clerks

(149)

and the lay bankers intimately connected with them were the possessors of the greatest houses and the donors of the most sumptuous hospitality. As the Roman notable Marcantonio Altieri lamented early in the century, the great *conviti* or banquets could no longer be freely given by the many Roman families which had fallen upon hard times. Nor were the Roman feudal barons by any means as rich and powerful as they had been, and before the end of the century many of the feudal families were to slide into bankruptcy. However, the great feudal barons were the pope's vassals, and still possessed rights in the papal court as they continued to do until 1870.

The struggle of the great Roman nobles to control the papacy had been going on since the eighth century: it seems hardly an exaggeration to say that during the late Renaissance the nobility was finally defeated. There was no question of the great families paling into insignificance; the landed power of such groups as the Colonna, Caetani and Orsini was too great for this to be an immediate prospect, and such families were the more formidable in that they possessed great landed wealth through their branches in the kingdom of Naples. But the defeat of the Roman nobles by Julius II in 1511 marked the turning of a secular tide. The Colonna, who had been the inspiration of that revolt, dominated the Roman countryside for the last time during their revolt of 1526. The Sack of Rome seemed to mark the triumph of the Colonna, but no one can have been so deceived as to think that universal catastrophe a victory for a particular family. In the "salt war" of 1540–1541 Paul III finally broke the military power of the Colonna family in the Roman area. No other family arose to challenge papal despotism in the Roman countryside, unless we count the short-lived rising of the Farnese in the early seventeenth century. But though Paul III made the Farnese great, he was careful not to make them too great in Rome itself. To the disgust of the lay members of the Farnese family, the great palace in Rome was constructed for its priestly representatives and not for the lay noblemen.

The great Roman families continued to be rich, and continued also to ensure that at least one of their clerical members held a cardinal's dignity. Cardinal Savelli, for example, who like several Romans was made a cardinal at a disgracefully early age by his relative Paul III, lived to be a prominent figure in the application of the reform decrees of the Council of Trent to the Roman clergy. But the gradually weakening hold of the great families can be seen in the way they used their Roman palaces, which were very frequently let either to cardinals or to foreigners. The Savelli palace in the Theatre of Marcellus was usually let to diplomats; the Orsini let their great palace on Monte Giordano to Cardinal Ridolfi. Even the Colonna were unable at all times to retain full title to their huge palace at the Church of the Holy Apostles; under Pius IV they were compelled to grant a life interest in the palace to Cardinal Carlo Borromeo, the papal nephew, as the price of a marriage alliance with his family. The Roman families to build new palaces in the sixteenth century were mostly merchants and bankers like the Della Valle, Massimi and Mattei. Even if the great feudal families were not yet, in mid-century, as crushed by debt as they were to become at its end, they were failing to dominate urban life as they had done in the earlier Renaissance.

There was still, however, a common noble way of life shared, in different degrees and with differing emphases, by the Roman feudal baronage, by the Roman merchant aristocracy, and by the cardinals and the other rich clerks of the papal court. In Rome the clerical and the chivalrous orders tended to mix, and it is hard to make a clear distinction between the clerical humanist ideal presented in Paolo Cortese's book on the Cardinalate and the lay humanist ideal presented by Baldassare Castiglione in the *Cortegiano:* both schemes implied education, order and luxury.

VI

The ground floor of a Roman palace would be given over to offices, stables and kitchens; it might contain the owner's library; a part of it might be let to outsiders as dwelling rooms or shops. The entrance and the courtyard of the palace would be splendid. Their architectural form changed a great deal in the course of the century, and there is a great gulf between the undramatic and untidy entrance and courtyard of the Palazzo dei Penitenzieri at the beginning of the century and the vibrating rhythms of Palazzo Massimo in the 1530s. As the century advanced, the part played by classical statues and sarcophagi in the decoration of the entrance courts became more important. The state staircase to the formal upper rooms was always dignified. On the first or "noble" floor the main audience rooms and the bedrooms and study of the master of the house would be located. On the second floor there would be other state rooms in a great palace, and guest bedrooms. In the attics or the basements the servants lived. There was usually a large courtyard round which the rooms of the upper stories would be grouped; there might also be an arcaded loggia on the first floor round the courtyard. Gardens would usually lie adjacent to the palace, and, especially in palaces which gave onto the Tiber like Palazzo Farnese or Palazzo Sacchetti, the courtyard on the ground floor might look into the gardens through a decorated portal.

The luxurious and luxuriant decoration of the Roman palace interior was notorious. Rich effects were obtained with colour, either with marble pavements and frescoed walls and ceilings in the case of great rooms and halls, or with velvet or tapestry hangings in the case of small rooms or studies. The use of ancient marble and of ancient marble objects and statuary enabled the Renaissance palaces to re-create at least some of the decorative effects of the ancient Romans. The lights and colours of *giallo* and *rosso antico*, the common *breccia verde*, the sought-after porphyry and *lumachella*, either re-used to make new columns or objects, or shown in ancient statuary, vases and other marble artefacts, all served to create the illusion of old Rome in new Rome.

Published in 1556, Ulisse Aldovrandi's description of the ancient statues of Rome describes not only the statues but the palaces which housed them. He wrote at a time when the numerous small collections of ancient objects were beginning to give way to the few very great collections, but his booklet is still an extraordinary testimony to the wealth and taste of the Roman possessing classes. In the first of three similar rooms of Cardinal Pio da Carpi, Aldovrandi says that twenty Greek vases were placed on cornices round the room. Under these were shelves of Greek, Hebrew and Arabic manuscripts. On other shelves were a score or so of marble heads and ancient epitaph slabs. More manuscripts were kept in intarsia-work chests. Other rooms were decorated with statues and busts, with velvet hangings and with paintings by Raphael and other moderns. A small room was dedicated to vases, crystal objects, curiosities, surgical instruments and weapons. Other collectors possessed huge holdings of ancient cameos and jewels, and of modern medals, bronzes, sculptures and paintings. Rome was an immense museum, almost all of which a gentleman possessing the right credentials might visit.

Roman wealth could be displayed in the discreet and restrained luxury of the archaeological collections, or in the exuberant decoration of the great state rooms in the palaces, or in the vulgar ostentation of the banquets or *conviti*, with their endless courses from the kitchen or the sideboard, their musical and dramatic entertainments, and the expensive liveries of their retainers. The equipment of gold and silver plate for the *conviti* was particularly expensive. When Henry VIII of England presented Cardinal Lorenzo Campeggio with Palazzo Guiraud in 1518, the king added to his gift gold and silver vessels worth 6,000 scudi.

Roman luxury was not confined to the palaces. The "urban villa" with its flower parterres, groves, fruit trees, vines, fountains, ancient statues and grottoes was a civilised ambience whose object was to revive the "learned leisure" of the ancients, and also to conserve something which was essentially a transformation of the milieu of the courtly pastoral. In the villa the learned, the amorous and the frivolous all met. Some villas were hardly more than summer houses, but others were of great architectural distinction; the villa later known as the Farnesina, and built by Agostino Chigi early in the century, was a summer house worthy of a prince.

VII

The pleasures of the Roman court were consonant with the sixteenth-century concept of the "noble life". Not all were honest pleasures. It is not a tribute to the morality of the Roman court that the expression "an honest courtier" (*cortegiana honesta*) meant a high-class prostitute. The great women of pleasure played a far from retiring part in many of the entertainments in which the court delighted. Many of these women were educated and agreeable people, whose duties lay as much in providing social conviviality for the guests of great men as in anything else. Such women would recite poetry, play the lute, dance and sing. They are portrayed in innumerable paintings of the time, and it is especially likely that the subject is a courtesan if she is wearing a fantastic dress out of keeping with current fashion, or a luxurious parody of peasant dress. A few of the great courtesans would own their own house, and would like other persons of quality be accompanied in the street by a train of servants on horseback. The biggest change in the social habits of the great courtesan was made by the coach, which began to be common in Rome by mid-century.

There is little sign that the place of the courtesan in Roman society changed very much between the beginning of the century and the death of Paul IV in 1559. The admired mistress of the courtiers of Julius II was "Imperia", the daughter of a Roman prostitute, whose beauty and civilised qualities made her acceptable in the highest circles of the court. The banker Agostino Chigi recognised one of her daughters as his own. Imperia's other admirers—not all of whom necessarily shared her bed—included the painter Raphael, the humanists Sadoleto, Beroaldo, Inghirami and Colocci, and the clerk Giulio de' Medici who later became Pope Clement VII. Other great courtesans were bluestockings: Tullia D'Aragona, who was a prominent figure of the 1520s and 1530s, was a poetess; Camilla of Pisa in the same period published elegant letters to well-known literary figures; "Matrema-non-vuole" was known for her recitations of Latin and Italian poetry as well as for her charms. Nor did the great courtesan disappear under Julius III and Paul IV. Under Paul IV "Pantha" was one of the best-known women of Roman society, courted by cardinals as well as by others. The tragic scandal of the disgrace of the Carafa family at the hands of Paul IV began with a quarrel which took place on New Year's Day 1559 over a courtesan called "Martuccia", between a member of the Carafa family and a brother of Cardinal Pio da Carpi.

The Roman court was not devoted primarily to the pursuit of illicit pleasures. But these pleasures, like all the rest, took place in an atmosphere of polished luxury. The exterior was glittering, even if moral and physical squalor lay not far beneath the surface. In any case the social gatherings of the Roman court which were most typical and complete were not the discreet dinner parties of self-indulgent curialists, but the great religious and state ceremonies: the public papal consistories which the whole court attended, the Lenten ceremonies and stations, the great banquets to which the whole court and the Roman princes and foreign ambassadors were bid.

There were other social gatherings of the Roman court of a convivial and cultural kind, particularly during the pontificate of Leo X. For most of the first half of the century the theatre in Rome existed not as a public spectacle but as the private enterprise of great men whose servants would perform a theatrical entertainment as a part of a banquet or reception. The Inquisition and the attempt to tighten public morals in the 1560s finally made such performances difficult. But for a few brief years under Leo there was a court-inspired drama whose centre was the Vatican itself. There was not a single theatre under Leo, but three or arguably even four. On the one hand there were "comedies" performed by troupes of travelling actors, whose subject was peasant life, and who were in effect the predecessors of the Commedia dell'Arte. There were also *moresche* or *intermezzi* which were nearer to musical ballets. In 1521 Castiglione saw performed before the pope an entertainment in which, a maid having asked Venus for a lover, eight hermits in grey habits led Cupid in chains and danced a *moresca* round him. Cupid then charmed the hermits, who turned into armed youths who fought one another, the victor being chosen by the maiden as her lover. Fine entertainment for a bishop! Thirdly, there were performances in Latin of classical comedies: Tommaso Inghirami, who had got his byname Fedra from performing in a classical play, produced Plautus at the notoriously gorgeous celebrations of Roman citizenship being conferred on Giuliano de' Medici in 1513. Finally there were performances in Italian of sophisticated comedies. Cardinal Bernardo Dovizi da Bibbiena had a performance of his own play *Calandria* staged for Isabella d'Este in the Vatican in 1514 in Leo X's presence. In 1519 Cardinal Innocenzo Cibo staged for the pope a performance of Ariosto's *Suppositi*. For some of these plays Raphael or Baldassare Peruzzi had designed the scenery, which was some of the earliest perspective backdrop scenery ever painted. It will be remembered that such scenery was practically unknown in English Elizabethan theatres.

Many of the pleasures of the Roman court revolved round the

Roman Carnival, which is described below. But the Medici and Farnese popes patronised a further pleasure of secular courts: the hunt.
Hunting as a pursuit for bishops was contrary to canon law, but Leo
X and Paul III managed to ignore the prohibition—not surprisingly,
since they spent much of their lives in dispensing other people from
observing similar rules. Nor were the popes by any means the only
bishops in Europe to hunt: the chase was merely one of the many
ways in which episcopal courts followed chivalrous courts.

The papal hunt was organised by Leo X on a properly princely
scale. The territories over which he hunted were of enormous extent,
though not all were included in the *bandita*, the area which in 1514 he
declared as a hunting preserve. The Campagna Romana immediately north of Rome was the area most intensively hunted, but Leo X
hunted as far north as Castro in the very north of the papal state. In
this distant area, or in that of the Lake of Bolsena, he was the guest of
Cardinal Alessandro Farnese, the future Paul III. The hunt could be
for stag, for wild boar, for pheasant, for quail, for ortolan; in the Lake
of Bolsena the pope fished; in Campo dei Merli near his great hunting lodge of La Magliana he practised falconry. Between clerks and
noble hunters, huntsmen and mounted guards, the papal hunt would
number at least two or three hundred persons. The papal kennels
of seventy or eighty hounds was near the Vatican. Elegant Latin
poems were composed to celebrate the hunts of the Medici and
Farnese popes. The historian Paolo Giovio, while accompanying the
papal hunt near Tivoli, and wearing scarlet velvet clothes, was so concerned to amuse Cardinal Ippolito d'Este that he rode into a swamp.
The most charming memorial of papal hunting is the handbook composed by the chief huntsman of Leo X, Domenico Boccamazza, which
takes its reader on an elaborate tour of the hunting reserves of the
Roman Campagna, from one long forgotten and long deforested
covert to another, pausing at carefully chosen spots for the papal
open-air meal.

Hunting remained an acknowledged pursuit of Roman prelates far
into the sixteenth century. Not only did Paul III and his family, who
lived in the heart of the hunting country of the Campagna, continue
to hunt, but Saint Carlo Borromeo can be found enquiring of the
papal *nunzio* in Germany in 1561 whether he would kindly send him
some German hunting hounds for big game ("cani di caccia grossa").

VIII

There is no easy way of judging the Roman court. From that day to this it has staggered by its brilliance and shocked by its social injustice. A Luther or a Von Hutten found no difficulty in condemning it out of hand. But moderate and rational judgements falter. Erasmus, using that transfer of the humanistic doctrine of imitation to the moral sphere which gave his writings their characteristic flavour, wrote in 1510 in the *Praise of Folly* that the popes of Rome, who were Christ's vicars, ought to imitate Christ's exemplary life. How many of the pleasures in which the popes indulged would remain to them, he enquired, if they were endowed with a little wisdom or with a grain of that salt which Christ mentions in the Gospel? "All their riches, honours, victories, offices, dispensations, tolls, indulgences, horses, mules, familiars, pleasures see what a sea of their merchandizing," says Erasmus, "I have compressed into a few words!—all these would be forfeit." And, he goes on, we must remember that in the case of a return to the apostolic life on the part of the popes, how many scriptors, how many copyists, notaries, advocates, promoters, secretaries, grooms, ostlers, bankers, pimps, together with those concerned with yet more lustful matters which he forbears to mention—how many of all these gentry would lose their jobs and go hungry!

Erasmus, it seems, was for sweeping the moneychangers from the temple, for getting rid of the whole heap of officials and familiars, for abolishing the "noble life" of the Roman court and reducing it to a few famished preachers. Many of his contemporaries took it that this was precisely his opinion. When the Sack of Rome came in 1527, the Erasmian secretary of Charles V, Alfonso Valdès, brother of the great pietist Juan Valdès, wrote a "Dialogue of Lactancio and an Archdeacon" whose intention was to justify the policies of Charles V and the actions of his armies in sacking Rome. The "Dialogue" is consciously Erasmian, and quotes from the passage in the *Praise of Folly* which has been cited above. In an equally Erasmian spirit Valdès goes on to criticise as hypocritical the expressions of pious shock which so many people had used because in the course of the Sack the churches of Rome had been turned by the Imperialist soldiery into stables for their horses.

How blind all you people in Rome were, and how little you understood God! Every hour you met in the streets men who had already turned their souls into stables for vices, and yet you thought nothing of it. But when a stable was needed for horses and they were sheltered in the church of St Peter, you tell me that it was a great evil and that it breaks your heart to think about it. You weren't heartbroken at the sight of the many souls so full of ugly and abominable sins that God, their Creator, was shut out! A fine religion!*

Was this, then, the opinion of Erasmus himself? Did the old master share the feelings of his disciples that in the Sack of Rome the Roman court had met no more than its just desserts? The evidence does not point in this direction. Erasmus was too aware of the cultural heritage which Rome—corrupt, modern, clerical Rome—had preserved and transmitted to share the radicalism of young Valdès. He felt also, perhaps, that he himself belonged to the same clerical class as the clerks of the Roman court. The messages which went out from Erasmus to the survivors of the shipwreck of Roman humanism of 1527 were not severe, but solicitous, concerned and conservative. For Clement VII Erasmus expressed not contempt but sympathy. To Sadoleto Erasmus wrote that the disaster of Rome was the disaster of all nations, since Rome was "not only the fortress of the Christian religion and the kindly mother of literary talent, but the tranquil home of the Muses, and indeed the common mother of all peoples".

Were these the words of a declining and pessimistic old man, overwhelmed by the Lutheran crisis and anxious to keep in with the clerical authorities and to avoid the pain and the danger of a break with Rome? Or are they not rather the words of a man who can remember the splendour of Rome as he had known it twenty years earlier, who could recall the freedom of conversation with other humanists there, the ready entrance given him into learned libraries, and who was deeply pained by the irruption of the hated soldiery into the sanctuary of humanist culture? Erasmus in 1529 expressed sympathy not only for Rome, "the common parent of all nations", but for Italy which had formerly been so flourishing, and which was now in-

*J.E. Longhurst, *Alfonso de Valdès and the Sack of Rome. Dialogue of Lactancio and an Archdeacon* (Albuquerque, 1952), p. 72.

accessible because of the danger on the roads. In the hour of decision Erasmus's sympathies went out not to the Imperialist Erasmians who saw the Sack as the just reward of corruption, but to the Italian curialists who had lost their books and their jobs. Erasmus knew the Roman court to be corrupt and its pursuit of the noble life to be against apostolic tradition, and he had trenchantly said so. But his affection for the humanist shell which enveloped the kernel of the Roman court was too great for him to approve its being broken.

Chapter Six

THE
FACE OF
ROME

I

"The priestly city of Rome", as it was described by Pope Sixtus IV, was close to the hearts of the popes. The popes wanted Rome to be orderly and splendid. In theory their powers to legislate to this end were limitless. But the reality was different. As in so many other things, the popes were pitifully deficient in real power to make good their aims and claims. The development of Rome in the first half of the sixteenth century, though swift, was piecemeal. Most individual popes confined their attentions to the planning of only a relatively small area of the city. Capital was available in astonishingly large amounts for private and public construction at some times, but there were other long periods, especially that following the Sack, in which the improvement of the city lagged. There was never, before the time of Pope Sixtus V in the late sixteenth century, any urban plan which contemplated the whole city.

Nevertheless there did float before the minds of the popes and of the rich curialists a vision of classical urban style and decorum which placed a stamp on all that was built and planned in Rome at this time. This ideal, based on humanist ideas of style and iconography, was not confined to the very rich; even the smaller builders who had their houses painted with classical motifs, and the speculators who built terraced houses, subscribed to it. In order to put this vision into practice there was a tradition of urban planning and social control which in Rome, as in many other Italian cities, went back to the medieval period of the free communes. There was also the duty of the Roman bishops to look to the decent housing and care of the pilgrims, and to the welfare of the Roman people in general, especially in such things as water supply and defence works. These obligations went back to the remote past of late antiquity and to the post-Constantinian Church.

The number of buildings actually constructed by the Renaissance popes was tiny. The popes were far more remarkable for the number of buildings they knocked down during the Renaissance than for those they put up. Building and development in Renaissance Rome were carried out by subjects, not by the ruler. One asks oneself how, in such an authoritarian society, people were induced to invest and build on this scale. The mere establishment of peaceful and orderly government does not seem enough.

The most conspicuous buildings were the "palaces", whose constructors at one end of the scale were the very rich clergymen, bankers and nobles, and at the other the solid curial officials, jewellers, artists and architects whose imposing houses are termed small palaces or *palazzetti*. The most obvious motives for building palaces large or small were display, show, love of "glory", desire to be numbered among those who contributed to the adornment and splendour of the city. Such considerations were common to cardinals, nobles and also to the lesser curial officials who built large houses like the Palazzetto Turci or the "Farnesina ai Baullari" (Giovanni Pietro Turci, "Abbreviator of Apostolic Letters", and Thomas le Roy, who held various curial offices under Julius and Leo). Among many builders of great palaces, including clerks who came from rich families like the Farnese or Della Valle, a powerful motive in building was the wish to bequeath a proud family monument to relatives. Noble families such as the Savelli (who built a palace above the Theatre of Marcellus), Massimi, Mattei, Chigi and so on built with the same motives. The desire to modernise and make more comfortable as well as more splendid may have been present, though apart from a few baths the new palaces were no more comfortable than the old; the state rooms received too great an emphasis. Some architects like Raphael, Bra-

(162)

mante, Antonio da Sangallo the younger, may have built themselves palaces in order to attract commissions as well as to impress by evidence of success.

It is not very likely that palaces were built as speculations. The return from rent on building costs seems to have been well below 10 per cent, and so below the figure for the return on money invested in venal offices or in government funds. Well known speculators like Giuliano Leno or Giulio Alberini put their money into shops or into vineyards rather than into these large and expensive buildings. But the building of palaces may often have been the means by which clerks invested the profits of their operations in the Roman court. The movable property of clerks who died in the Roman court was technically liable to confiscation for the benefit of the papal fisc, under the name of "spoils" (*spolia*). Until Sixtus IV's time, if a clerk's money had been invested in immovable property and he died in the Roman court, there was some doubt whether this property also was not liable to confiscation. Sixtus IV's law to encourage building in Rome removed this doubt by specifically protecting the estates of clerks who invested money from benefices in real property in Rome. This law enabled a clerk to will such property to his heirs, knowing that it ran no risk of confiscation. Leo X extended this law to gardens and villas constructed outside the walls of Rome. Adrian VI's action in going back on Sixtus IV's legislation and in apparently starting to revive the papal right to take "spoils" from the estates of dead clerks caused a panic in Rome, and for a short time building stopped. But if Adrian VI did change this custom, his threat to the legal security of clerical property lasted only a couple of years, for the Sixtine law was reapplied after his death. Thus to some extent the great building boom of Renaissance Rome seems to have owed its existence to this legal loophole which allowed the rich clerk to invest the profits of his benefices in a form which could safely pass to his heirs.

There were humbler forms of profitable building speculation. Middle-class housing was built on a substantial scale, much of it by Roman hospitals or charities like those of the Salvatore or S. Giacomo, whose houses can still be identified from the external ownership marks, as well as from the archival documents. Terraced houses (*case in serie*) were built in Campo Marzio and Trastevere. Many inns were

(163)

built and rebuilt; this was a classic form of investment for native Romans. Rows of shops paid well, like those under the Theatre of Marcellus, or in the Botteghe Oscure, or in the square of the Pantheon, or in front of Piazza Altoviti (an important site for its situation facing Canale di Ponte). But some of these shops were merely wooden booths.

If the popes did not build many churches, they spent much on defence works. Papal responsibility for the walls of Rome went back to Pope Gregory the Great in the seventh century. Pope Alexander VI, advised perhaps by his son Cesare Borgia, commissioned important defence works in Rome and the papal state, notably, in the former, the rebuilding of the towers of Castel Sant'Angelo, which he surrounded by the new-style septagonal bastions. The bellicose Julius II improved the walls of Rome, but the great military builder of Renaissance Rome was not Julius but Paul III. His determination not to allow the Sack of Rome to recur persuaded Paul III to spend large sums on the city's defence, particularly on the fortification of the Vatican and the adjoining Janiculum hill.

The most remarkable thing about Renaissance building in the "priestly city" of Rome is the small number of new churches. The bulk of building between 1500 and 1559 was secular. Apart from the single great enterprise of St Peter's, few churches of note were built during these sixty years. The construction of the churches which were built, unlike that of most of the palaces, tended to be very slow. St Peter's itself was unfinished at the end of the century; S. Giovanni dei Fiorentini, S. Luigi dei Francesi, S. Marcello and S. Caterina ai Funari were all started long before, but unfinished at mid-century. Compared with the huge investments made in secular buildings, the amount of church building seems paltry. Such churches as were built tended to be commissioned either by "national" interests such as the French, Germans, Florentines or Spaniards, or by devout congregations or hospitals (S. Spirito, S. Marcello). It is true that the maintenance of the hundreds of existing Roman churches was very heavy, and must have swallowed up many of the rents belonging to clerical foundations in Rome. But the rebuilding of the Roman churches was the triumph of Counter-Reformation Rome, not of Rome of the Renaissance.

(164)

II

There was a formidable legal machinery for the improvement of Roman urban conditions. Important administrative officials of the Roman Commune, under the pope, were the *maestri di strada* or street controllers. Their duties were to clean and improve the streets, and to stop the Romans from clogging up the streets with outbuildings, balconies, stairways and galleries built out from their houses—to see, in fact, that the streets were genuine highways and not tracks which wandered in and out of the built-up areas, frequently stopping entirely when someone had extended his outbuildings across the road. They were supposed to pave the streets where they could, though the expense meant that only major streets would be paved. They had to discipline the Romans in order to stop them from throwing their manure, sewage and refuse into the street, or to clear the street, especially in the summer months, when this had occurred. They had to discourage the butchers and tanners from holding their shambles in the roadway and throwing the guts and refuse down there. They possessed some kind of urban dustcart service, which was supposed to dump the refuse in the Tiber. They also were responsible for the proper functioning of water supply, which primarily meant the water of the Acqua Vergine which issued at the Fontana di Trevi.

Some idea of the way in which old-fashioned houses were organised can be had from a description of the Boccapaduli houses near S. Angelo in Pescheria in 1428. The property was described as a "house or palace" with a well and a bath or pond beneath the house, the pond opening into the alley (*viculum*) which was the property of the owners. There was a main house of some size, and a dower house which was connected to it by two wooden bridges or galleries across the alley. Under the dower house was a stable. There was another house in the alley, let to a Jewish doctor, which was on two floors with a mezzanine, and stood by a courtyard in which there was a barn for hay and fodder, and another shack of one storey. This cluster of buildings, more like a farm than a "palace", was a typical dwelling house of a well-to-do Roman family. There was far to go before such clusters of rustic buildings could be turned into the dwellings of a well-ordered early modern city.

(165)

The first step in ordering the streets was the abolition of "porticoes" or outjutting outbuildings of all kinds; this was initiated by Sixtus IV and carried on by his successors. But the widening and the rationalisation of streets brought new needs, first for the compulsory purchase and demolition of houses which were in the way of the improvement, and second for funds to finance compensation for the owners of demolished houses and the cost of new road construction. The solution adopted was an improvement tax levied on the owners of property in the area affected. This was the tax known as the *gettito*, for the ruin or casting down of buildings; it was assessed and levied by the *maestri di strada* with the help of the local official or *caporione*. When the improvement was decided upon there was a meeting between the *maestri di strada* and the property owners at which the project was discussed and decided, and the apportionment of the cost worked out. Householders were treated differently if they were freeholders or lessees; the latter were liable only for a proportion of the cost of improvement. The dispositions in favour of developers were very radical, and under certain circumstances a speculator who proposed to build in a way which would "embellish the city" could get compulsory purchase orders for the demolition of inhabited houses to enable him to build. No body of law better illustrates the plutocratic principles on which Rome was run.

The drainage of the city was also a concern of the *maestri di strada*, though not one which they fulfilled very efficiently. The destruction of the ancient sewage system in the early Middle Ages meant that in the Forum of Nerva, for example, a swamp formed (known as the Pantano di San Basilio), which no attempt was made to drain before the late sixteenth century. There were other swampy areas in the Velabrum on the other side of the Palatine, which probably drained into a stream called the Marrana which passed through the Circus Maximus. The job of the *maestri di strada* was also to keep the street drains clear during heavy rain and flooding. They also had to keep the markets clear of refuse, especially Piazza Navona, Campo dei Fiori and the market by the Campidoglio (Macel de' Corvi).

III

In the early Renaissance period the densely inhabited areas of Rome were limited to the low-lying areas on either side of the river.

On the left bank the inhabited area went from the ancient Campo
Marzio to the Campidoglio and the Tiber Island, with the ancient Via
Lata (Via del Corso) as the main boundary between the inhabited zone
and the hills. On the right bank there were the two nuclei of St
Peter's, the Vatican and the Leonine Borgo to the north, and Trastevere and the port of Ripa to the south. In the rest of Rome, both within and without the Aurelian walls, small isolated centres clustered
round the main ancient basilicas and the main city gates. On the left
bank the main network of streets was based on three roads converg-
ing on Ponte Elio (Ponte Sant'Angelo), leaving Canale di Ponte. One
of these routes was the ancient processional Via Papale whose terminus was the Campidoglio. Another was the route passing through
the market of Campo dei Fiori to S. Angelo in Pescheria near the
Tiber island bridges. The third, the most difficult to follow by modern
landmarks, went by the route of the present Via de Coronari (then Via
Recta) to S. Agostino and to the church of the Maddalena, so com-
municating with the quarter of Colonna. The most important thing
about all these routes was their terminus in Banchi, in the commercial
quarter which communicated over the river with Borgo and the Vatican Palace. Only one of them was a route of ancient religious ceremonial (Via Papale). The route through Campo dei Fiori was clearly
commercial.

Probably the best way to look at Roman urban growth is not to
consider it as a series of grandiose plans with wide urban aims, but as
a series of smaller developments, each of which was sponsored by
some powerful man or family, and each of which then produced new
requirements for urban communications and facilities. The other
great stimulus to urban planning was the needs of pilgrims, especially
in Jubilee years. The zone of S. Agostino, for example, acquired importance from the powerful Cardinal Estouteville; the route to Campo
dei Fiori skirted the great palace of Cardinal Raffaele Riario (the
Cancelleria Nuova). The needs of the pilgrims of the Jubilee Year of
1500 and of defence dominated the urban plans of Pope Alexander
VI. By clearing the "Via Alessandrina", Alexander gave a decisive
push to the curial area between the Vatican and the river.

A surviving inscription of 1512 seeks, in the rather inflated humanist dialect of the court, to describe the urban policy of Pope Julius
II (1503–1513): "To Pope Julius II, who, after enlarging the boun-

daries of the papal state and freeing Italy, in the interests of imperial glory adorned the city of Rome, which had formerly been like a city under military occupation rather than one well-arranged, with fine streets which he measured and widened." As with everything else he attempted, Julius's urban policies were bold, expensive, and linked with what he considered to be the achievements of his uncle, Sixtus IV. Julius's projects proved bigger than either the length of his pontificate or the depth of his purse could permit. The new "Via Giulia" which he built in order to link his uncle's bridge, "Ponte Sisto", through Via di Banco S. Spirito with the commercial quarter of Ponte and the other bridge of S. Elio (Sant'Angelo) was a finely conceived street. But its centrepiece was never built. Julius planned not only a huge Palace of Justice in the centre of Via Giulia, but also a great new square in front of the Palace of Justice which would extend as far as the old Chancery Palace (now Palazzo Sforza-Cesarini) owned by Julius's nephew and papal vice-chancellor, Cardinal Galeotto Franciotto della Rovere. Neither the Palace of Justice nor its facing square were built. But on the other side of the Tiber Julius launched another new street which was perhaps even more interesting because of its new style of development. Via della Lungara was a new quarter of villas built partly outside the existing walls of the city. Its purpose was to link Trastevere, which historically was distinct from Rome and quasi-independent of Roman communal administration, with Borgo and the Vatican. A number of the main investors in land and property in both Via Giulia and Via della Lungara were painters and architects.

Like many popes, Leo X (1513–1521) hinged his urban development on the palaces of his own family. His main adjustment of the street plan was the opening of the Via Leonina (Via della Scrofa and Via di Ripetta), an important new artery which connected the commercial quarter and market in S. Eustachio with the slowly developing areas of Porta del Popolo and Campo Marzio. In Campo Marzio there came into existence a new centre of artisan and middle-class habitation, mostly either Lombard architects or masons, or Slavs. The two hospitals of S. Girolamo degli Schiavoni and S. Giacomo in Augusta (one for Slavs and the other the Medici-patronised hospital for syphilitics) took part in this movement as property owners and developers. The axis of the new development was Piazza Lombarda, the site of the main Medici palace which was later known as Palazzo

Madama. The location of this palace, contiguous with the Roman University, suited well with Medici cultural interests. Leo X and the Sangalli draw up very ambitious plans for the complete rebuilding of this palace, round which was to be cleared an immense square extending to Piazza Navona on one side and to the Roman University on the other. But, like the grandiose plans of Julius II for the square in front of his Palace of Justice, Leo X's scheme fell through.

The most original and influential contribution of the Medici popes to Roman architecture, if their part in St Peter's is excepted, was their villa (subsequently called Villa Madama) built outside the walls of Rome on the slopes of Monte Mario. The building of Villa Madama was an extraordinary act of faith in the peaceful future of Rome, since it was far outside the walls and entirely vulnerable to a hostile army, as was sadly shown in 1527. Villa Madama was incomplete when it was looted and badly damaged in the Sack, and of the ambitious plans drawn up for Leo X by Raphael and the Sangalli, only a part was ever executed. But it was influential, first, because it transferred in a different form to Rome the Tuscan idea of leisure in villas outside the city walls, and, secondly, because it was a particularly brilliant and imaginative attempt to translate the scenography of the classical Roman villa, and its peculiar interpenetration of garden and living space, into Renaissance terms. The Medici villa on Monte Mario was originally conceived, in a letter which has been attributed to Raphael, as placed in the centre of three sets of differentiated gardens, on the fourth side looking into a hemispherical theatre on the Greek model, carved out of the hill. Below the villa were to have been three *piazze* of varying forms, set out below the main entrance courtyard and descending down to the Tiber. The villa was for entertainment and not for habitation, and was thus a "suburban" villa linked with city life, like Chigi's Farnesina villa and the later villa of Pope Julius III. The decorative programme of "grotesques", both in the loggias and in the gardens, was inspired by the archaeological discoveries then being made in Rome, especially in the Golden House of Nero.

The complement of the Medici villa in Leonine Rome was the much smaller but delicately beautiful villa constructed for Agostino Chigi by the architect Baldassare Peruzzi on the new Via della Lungara; this villa was later known as the Farnesina. Chigi's villa used the same concept of loggias which opened into gardens running from the villa down to the banks of the Tiber. The decorative plans were influenced by classical models as in the Medici villa, though in the Farnesina *trompe l'oeil* plays a more important part; in both villas Giovanni da Udine, a painter famous for his treatment of flowers and fruits, was extensively employed. It is worth remarking that the exterior wall spaces of the Farnesina, which are now so bleak, were originally filled by decorative frescoes of this kind. Like the Medici villa, the Farnesina contained no living quarters but was designed for sumptuous entertainment in a pastoral vein. It encouraged the development of Via della Lungara, which was enabled to continue after the Sack when Paul III protected this zone by the construction of a new wall on the Janiculum.

IV

When we think of the destructive whirlwind of the Sack of 1527, of a Rome without doors or windows, with streets of houses and palaces ruined and burned, of a Rome hardly beginning to lift its head when it was again prostrated by the flood of 1530, Pope Paul III almost appears as a man who gave Rome a second "rebirth". Paul III had no single urban vision, no one grandiose plan, but the untiring old pope, with his archaeological adviser Latino Giovenale Manetti, and his architects Antonio da Sangallo and Michelangelo, by their labours between 1534 and 1549, gave Rome a new chance to re-emerge as one of the great cities of the West. Paul III was responsible for five great enterprises: for the resumption of work on St Peter's, for the building of Palazzo Farnese, for the rebuilding of the Campidoglio, for the revision of the Roman street plan, and for reconstructing the defences of the city. In Roman urban history he can be compared with Popes Sixtus IV and Sixtus V.

The first basic changes in the designs for St Peter's were made after the death of Raphael, when the Raphael-Bramante idea of a great nave was abandoned, and the architects returned to the idea of a centrally planned church. But the decisive period of change began in 1535 with the studies of Baldassare Peruzzi and Antonio da Sangallo for the preparation of a scale model *(modello)* from which the builders would work directly. It was then, also, that the narrow spatial proportions originally envisaged were transformed into wider ones by means of the elevation of the old floor level, and that radical changes were made in the Bramante design for the dome. A further decisive change was made, still by Paul III, by the appointment of the seventy-one-year-old Michelangelo to be in charge of the works at St Peter's in 1546, after the death of Antonio da Sangallo. Michelangelo was long in making final decisions, especially about the dome. But his appointment was crucial in determining the final form of a building which exerted immense influence over western architecture.

The history of Palazzo Farnese is that of a building planned by a great cardinal of a great Roman family, designed in a form which was only partly executed when the cardinal in 1534 became pope. The Farnese palace backed on Via Giulia, though slightly at an angle to the street alignment. It was designed in a manner which, far from incorporating the building in the urban surroundings, tended proudly to isolate it; Antonio da Sangallo planned it with four independent façades, the rear one of which was much later abandoned by Giacomo Della Porta in favour of the existing loggia. The palace was not of the immense proportions of the two great fifteenth-century palaces of San Marco and of the Cancelleria, but was nevertheless designed in a manner which seized every opportunity to suggest size, space and grandeur. The refinement of the design and the luxurious materials used are apparent in the great atrium, whose optical subtleties are due to Sangallo and not to his successor Michelangelo, and in which the twelve main columns, re-used from Roman buildings, are of the finest granites known to the ancients. When Paul III became Pope in 1534 it was decided greatly to enlarge the palace; the number of bays in the courtyard was increased from three to five. On the death of Sangallo in 1546 Michelangelo added the palace to his heavy list of commitments.

The urban setting of Piazza Farnese was revised after Cardinal Alessandro Farnese became Pope Paul III. The Via dei Baullari, begun by Leo X, was completed so as to connect Campo dei Fiori with the Massimi palaces and the main Roman arteries. If Michelangelo had had his way, a new bridge would have been built across the Tiber, so that from Piazza Campo dei Fiori the spectator would see through the courtyard of Piazza Farnese (where he planned to place the Farnese Hercules), across Via Giulia and the river, to another Farnese garden over the river in Trastevere. But like the great courtyards of Julius II and Leo X, this proposal also came to nought.

Pope Paul III's restoration of the Roman Capitol, the Campidoglio, and its area was inspired by the humanist idea of Romanism which he had acquired from his own classical education. The Renaissance Campidoglio is easily misunderstood by modern people, who are accustomed to seeing the Corso as the main axis of central Rome, and although knowing that the focal point of the Corso is the nineteenth-century monument of Vittorio Emanuele and not the ancient Capitol, they may still be inclined to think of the Campidoglio and the church of Aracoeli, which adjoin the modern monument, as natural focal points of Renaissance Rome. This was not the case. The Via Lata (the Corso) was not the main Renaissance artery, nor was that end of the Via Papale which terminated at the Campidoglio. The cluster of buildings defined by the Campidoglio, the church of Aracoeli, the palace of S. Marco, and the former market of Macel de' Corvi, was of some importance in sixteenth-century Rome, but not of central importance. The Roman Fora, on which the Campidoglio buildings turned their backs, were of no importance whatsoever. The decline of the importance of Roman communal government in the late Middle Ages and Renaissance further diminished that of the Campidoglio buildings, which were its headquarters. In the fifteenth century the archaeologist Antonio Loschi reversed, when on the Campidoglio, the sense of Virgil's verse about the hill, which he described as "golden once upon a time, but now covered with stunted shrubs and bushes" ("Aurea nunc, olim silvestribus horrida dumis").

Paul III was embarrassed by the poor state of the Campidoglio on the occasion of the ceremonial visit of the Emperor Charles V to Rome in 1536, when the imperial route passed through the Fora into the square of San Marco, and so alongside the Campidoglio buildings. He also spent much time in the Palace of San Marco, especially in the summer months, and he had a "corridor" constructed from the palace to the church of Aracoeli on the Capitol hill, next to which he built a "tower" intended as a summer villa. In 1537 he showed his intention of renovating the Capitol by moving there the ancient equestrian statue of Marcus Aurelius which had during the Middle Ages stood in front of the Church of St John Lateran. The pope and the Commune then commissioned Michelangelo to draw up plans not only for a pedestal for the statue but for a complete rebuilding of the Capitoline administrative buildings. Michelangelo's proposals were based on the idea of uniting the two lower communal towers by a new Senatorial palace; under the stairway of the palace would be the two river god statues given to the Commune by Leo X, and at the head of the stairs a statue of Jupiter. Michelangelo also designed not only an entirely new façade for the existing palace of the "Conservators" or councillors, but also an entirely new palace on the north side of the square, which would be a formal equivalent to the palace of the Conservators, but did not correspond to any existing administrative building, and had no real function at all except to give symmetry to the design. The square with the statue of Marcus Aurelius in the centre was planned by Michelangelo as a marked trapezoidal space, though his plan was not executed in this respect until modern times. The old medieval tower of the Roman Commune was to be replaced by a new belltower, centrally placed above the Senatorial Palace.

It has been pointed out how the new Campidoglio of Michelangelo and Paul III combined pagan and Christian symbolism, as for example in the figure of Jupiter, who could also be understood as the first person of the Trinity. The geometrical plan of the piazza contains zodiacal elements, and the pedestal of the Marcus Aurelius statue can be understood as the "umbilical point" of the Roman world (not too far anatomically from Aretino's oft-repeated description of Rome as *coda mundi*, the anus of the world). The inclusion of the Dioscuri in the decorative scheme is unintentionally ironical. The Dioscuri twins may have been intended to refer to the twin powers of the pope and emperor. But the Dioscuri were also the symbols of Roman liberty, a liberty which the whole scheme of the Campidoglio showed plainly that the Romans had lost for ever. Michelangelo's scheme was typical of the great decorative programmes imposed on their supine peoples by Renaissance despots. It paid no attention to the real administrative needs of the Roman communal government, which since the suppression of the Romans by Julius II in 1511 had been a helpless tool of the papal authorities.

The inscription (composed, inevitably, by Latino Giovenale Manetti) on the monument erected by the Romans to Paul III on the Capitol paid tribute to his activity as a road builder. Some of this road clearance was in the Florentine quarter of Rome, and showed the continued importance of Tuscan banking and commerce under Paul. The Via Paolina from the Florentine "national" church of S. Giovanni to Ponte Sant'Angelo, and the new Via del Panico, completed the three-pronged exits from Ponte Sant'Angelo into the commercial quarters. Two other roads were fundamental for the structure of later Renaissance and Baroque Rome. One was the Via Trinitatis (subsequently Via Condotti) leading from the French church and monastery being constructed on the folds of the Pincio to Piazza Nicosia and the commercial region of Ponte. The other was the continuation and development of the road later called Via del Babuino, from the same point of Trinità dei Monti, to Piazza del Popolo. Via del Babuino thus completed the Paolina Trifaria, the three-pronged road exits from Piazza del Popolo consisting of Via del Babuino, Via Lata (Via del Corso) and Via di Ripetta. The "trifaria", or three-pronged road development, was one of the most important planning concepts to take hold in Renaissance and Baroque Rome. Paul III's political sympathies were clearly shown in his road-building programme. The Tuscan bankers, many of them enemies of the imperialist Cosimo de' Medici, the French interest in Rome, the Venetians whose "national" church was San Marco—these were Paul III's political friends. Even the clearing of Piazza Santi Apostoli was in the interests of the French ambassador, whose palace overlooked the square.

Paul III was frightened of two external threats, of a repetition of the Sack of Rome in 1527 by the imperialists, and of a repetition of the Sack of Rome in 846 by the Muslim Turks. The second threat was the more immediate, but the first was arguably no less real. In 1537–1538 the whole papal state was placed on a war footing in order to counter the Turkish peril, which in 1534 had led to the sacking by Turkish bands of the Neapolitan countryside just south of the border of the papal state. Antonio da Sangallo on Paul III's instructions drew up an immense programme of fortification, which was not only to repair and reinforce the Aurelian and Leonine walls, but to add long new stretches of scientifically designed defences. These consisted, especially, of a line of curtain walls and bastions, running round the church of Santa Saba and along the Aventine hill down to the river, picked up again on the Trastevere side by a similar new line of defences which ran to Porta San Pancrazio, and thence along the Janiculum over Via delle Fornaci until they joined the main defences of the Vatican and the Leonine city. A further new curtain wall went from within Porta Latina to San Giovanni. The new fortifications round the Vatican were planned to command the high ground to the west of the church; thanks to this extension Vatican City is today the larger by the area which includes the Vatican radio station. The Vatican Belvedere was reinforced by a huge bastion. By these means Paul III and his successors were enabled to assume a defensive military posture which was politically credible, though the events of 1557 suggested that the new defences would have availed little to protect Rome against a determined army.

V

The 1540s were a time of hard work and reorganisation in Rome; the 1550s were a time of false starts and self-delusion. Pope Julius III (1550–1555) was a serious politician, but also in some respects an advocate of the *dolce vita*. He was the first pope since Leo X to return to the idea of the *villa suburbana*, though in doing so he was only following the trend of his period. Outside Porta del Popolo, a short distance from the Via Flaminia, Julius undertook and rapidly completed a great villa in a vast area of gardens and walks which extended (in the same way as the gardens of Villa Madama and the Farnesina) down to the Tiber. He employed a number of architects, some in a consultative capacity and some as principal executants, but his main agents were Vignola (Jacopo Barozzi), who built the main body of the villa, and, according to some architectural historians, Bartolomeo Ammanati. The true scenographic value of Villa Giulia has been lost for ever; its gardens meandering down to the river are occupied by a vile complex of buildings whose central point is the tramdrivers' kiosk; above it now lie the vulgarities of modern Parioli. The eclectic little church of S. Andrea on the Via Flaminia, which Vignola erected in connection with the villa, is also now lost in a sordid urban wilderness. It is hard now to imagine Julius III proceeding down the Tiber from the Vatican to his gardens and his villa, in a boat trimmed

(175)

with flowers and accompanied by musicians. Inside the villa some of the intentions of Vignola can still be recaptured, since they relate to a closed-in and private courtly life. Like Villa Madama, the villa was designed to provide a series of garden rooms, of which the most enchanting is the nymphaeum, which employs the same "grotesque" tradition as that of the Medici villa.

The villa of Pope Julius was part of a trend in mid-century for the very rich and the very powerful to build great palace-pleasaunces in the countryside. These were not country houses, nor even villas in the manner of the Florentine patriciate: they were huge palaces in great enclosures, so costly as to be possible only for the very greatest members of the Roman court. Julius III spent not less than a quarter of a million *scudi* on the construction of his villa and of Palazzo Firenze. They were not related to the agricultural life of the countryside in which they stood, and they descended from Roman imperial villas rather than from the senatorial villas described by Vitruvius and Pliny. They contained great decorative and iconographical programmes glorifying the political life of their builder and his family. The two most remarkable of these great constructions were the Farnese fortress-villa at Caprarola, and the villa of Cardinal Ippolito d'Este at Tivoli, of which he was papal governor. The Farnese constructions at Caprarola, in the Ciminian hills, were part of a vast family building programme in the papal patrimony, in the zone from which the Farnese came. The great lakeside castle at Capodimonte on Lake Bolsena, and the whole new town of Castro, in the very north of the papal state, have to be added to the Farnese building list. Villa d'Este at Tivoli was very much the personal creation of Cardinal Ippolito, who had no connection with the Roman countryside beyond his own office in the Roman court. Like Pope Julius's villa, both Villa d'Este and Caprarola were planned to integrate with huge and complex gardens. Like Villa Madama, they used the huge translucent expanses of the Campagna Romana as a part of their scenic effects.

Pope Paul IV (1555–1559) was also responsive to the trends of his time, but his projects were more modest and discreet than those of his predecessor. Perhaps because the Belvedere, which had originally been a rustic arbour, was now in effect a part of the Vatican palace, he planned the erection in the Vatican enceinte of a new small villa to the west of the palace, which would domesticate the landscape, formerly wood and scrub, and provide a new area of gardens. Though the villa was not completed until the following pontificate of Pius IV, and is known as Villa Pia, it was designed by Pirro Ligorio for Paul IV, even if changes were later made in the plan. It certainly suggests nothing of the Inquisition, nor of a new dogmatic theology. Far from being a break with the tradition of humanist architecture and scenography, Villa Pia is its fine flower. Ligorio was a learned humanist and a practical architect who had so thoroughly absorbed the lessons of classical architecture and landscape that he could manipulate and transform them in a perfectly harmonious concept whose architectural language was his own. The most original thing in Villa Pia is the oval marble-bottomed sunken basin which is its focal and unifying point, and which also gives spatial meaning to the hill on which the villa is built. The basin has aedicules at the two extremities, a casino or *diaeta* for leisurely and learned talk on one side, and on the other the atrium and main façade of the villa. The basin may well have been intended for *Naumachia* or water spectacles such as those which were frequent on the Tiber during Carnival time; there may be some connection in the iconography of the villa with the barque of Peter. Villa Pia is one of the most exquisitely delicate compositions of the Roman Renaissance, and a proof that as the Counter-Reformation dawned, the popes did not abandon the old traditions of a papacy permeated by humanism.

VI

Classical Rome was in one sense immediate to sixteenth-century men, in another very remote. Even when sixteenth-century archaeological knowledge was based on a competent acquaintance with classical texts, it was knowledge apprehended in a quite different way to that in which such things have been known in the nineteenth and twentieth centuries. The predominant philosophy of Platonism of sixteenth-century men made them see Roman art and architecture as symbols of hidden realities, not as designs connected with social patterns. The most ambitious poems which the humanist poet Joachim du Bellay wrote in connection with Roman ruins were called *Un*

Songe, a dream. The most beautiful learned book of the Renaissance, a book soaked in knowledge of the ruins and their inscriptions, was the *Hypnerotomachia Poliphili*, the strife of love in a dream. Men saw the classical past not as a mass of facts awaiting organisation, but as a self-sustaining reality which manifested itself in ways which were indifferent to what we would call scientifically verified truth. Not only the *Hypnerotomachia* mixed fact with fantasy; its period was also that of Annius of Viterbo, the great forger of classical remains, and when the first book of classical inscriptions was published there was a similar reluctance to separate what was from what might have been. Most sixteenth-century students of the classical past mixed observed fact with learned and imaginative conjecture. If this had not been so the great archaeological fantasies in the paintings of Raphael, Peruzzi and Giulio Romano could not have been conceived. Raphael was typical in sometimes painting imaginative classical ruins (as in the 'Meeting of Leo I with Attila') and in sometimes designing complete imaginary classical buildings (as in the Sistine Tapestries).

At the beginning of the century the humanistically learned artist or architect was an exception—not for nothing did Leonardo da Vinci call himself "uomo sanza lettere", an unlearned person, in the sense that he had no knowledge of classical literature. Fra Giocondo (Giovanni of Verona) was an elderly religious with technical and artistic ability who assisted Raphael in the works on St Peter's, and was a man of extensive classical culture, including Greek. Andrew Coner, of whom we know little save that he was a German clerk in the circle of Raphael and Bramante who drew or sponsored a book of architectural drawings from the modern and the antique, was also a learned humanist with a fine collection of books. But Raphael himself, ignorant of the Latin tongue, read classical books only in the translations made for him by learned friends like Fabio Calvo or Andrea Fulvio. The other way in which artists and architects learned from the antique was by direct observation, measuring and drawing. Hundreds of such drawings were made from Roman monuments: the Sangalli, Peruzzi and Bramante were prolific in sketches of this kind. Raphael, in spite of the position given him by Leo X as Commissioner of Antiquities, and in spite of his evident enthusiasm for the antique, did not make such studies, or if he did they have been lost. Only four drawings by Raphael exist which can be called archaeological, all of

Renaissance
R·O·M·E
1500-1559

St Peter's Square in the mid-1530s.
Drawing by Marten van Heemskerck.

A papal benediction in St Peter's Square during the latter part of the sixteenth century. In the background can be seen the drum of the new St Peter's.

Chryfiecle laue alacres concurrite fepe fideles

Hic Deus in terris numinis alta iubet

dicis amici

Pix fili

Hac

The interior of St Peter's in the mid-1530s.
In the centre is the temporary structure
built by Bramante to protect the
Confession of St Peter during the rebuilding.
Drawing by Marten van Heemskerck.

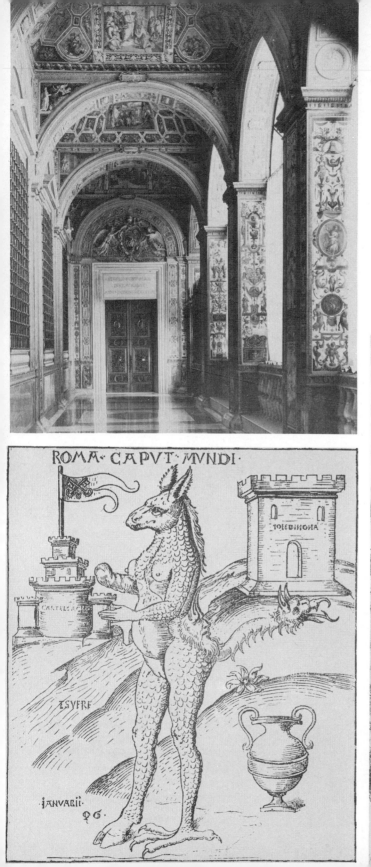

ROMA · CAPVT · MVNDI ·

LEFT: *The "Logge" of Raphael in the Vatican Palace.*

LOWER LEFT: Roma Caput Mundi. *Engraving by Wenzel von Olmutz inspired by the story that after the great Tiber flood of 1495 a monster was found on the banks of the Tiber with the head of an ass and the body of a woman. The picture was used by Luther and Melanchthon in their pamphlet on the pope-ass published in 1523.*

BELOW: *Detail from Marcantonio Raimondi's engraving of Raphael's Massacre of the Innocents. Ponte Cestio and some of the buildings of Trastevere.*

ABOVE: *Raphael's* Philosophy *in the Stanza della Segnatura of the Vatican Palace.*

UPPER RIGHT: *Detail from G.A. Dosio's plan of Rome (1561). St Peter's Square is in the right lower foreground, marked "R".*

RIGHT: *St Peter's Square and the Borgo. Engraving by Hendrick van Cleve.*

BELOW: Portrait of the papal librarian Tommaso Inghirami by Raphael.

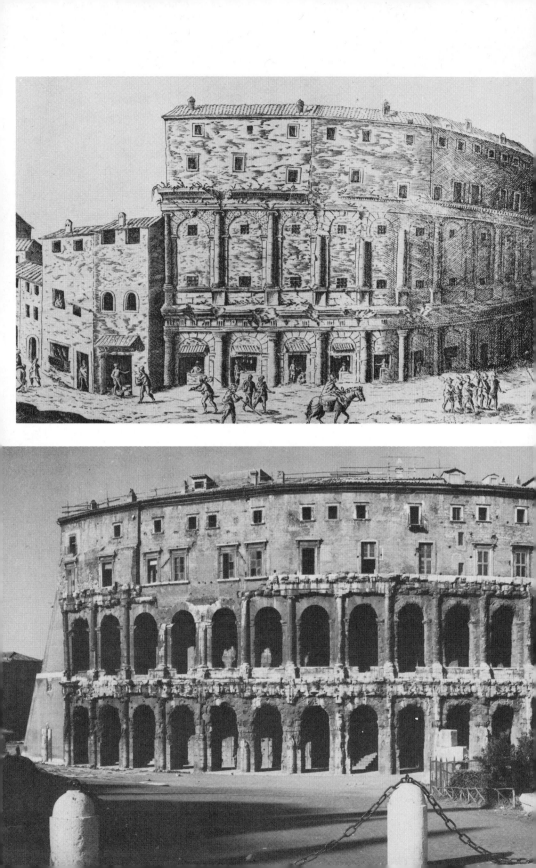

ABOVE LEFT: The Theatre of Marcellus
(Palazzo Savelli) in the sixteenth century.

ABOVE CENTER: The atrium of the Palazzo Farnese
with trompe l'oeil
vaulting in the right foreground.

ABOVE RIGHT: The portico of the Palazzo
Massimo alle Colonne.

LEFT: The Theatre of Marcellus.

Veduta del giardino del Card.l Cesi.

LEFT: *The antiquarium of Cardinal Cesi. Engraving by Marten van Heemskerck.*

BELOW LEFT: *The casino and basin of the Villa Pia in the Vatican Gardens.*

BELOW: *Villa Farnesina alla Lungara.*

ROMA

ANTONIVS SALAMANCA, ORBIS,
ET VRBIS ANTIQVITATVM
IMITATOR

FACING PAGE: *The engraver
and antiquarian Antonio
Salamanca. Engraving
by Nicholas Beatrizet.*

LEFT: *Detail of the stucco
decoration in the loggia
of the Villa Madama.*

BELOW: *The courtyard and garden
of the Palazzo della
Valle-Capranica. Engraving
by Hieronymus Cock.*

LEFT: *The nymphaeum in the Villa di Papa Giulio.*

BELOW LEFT: *Relief stucco of an elephant-drawn chariot by B. Peruzzi in the Palazzo Massimo alle Colonne.*

BELOW: *The "elephant fountain" at the Villa Madama. Drawing by Marten van Heemskerck.*

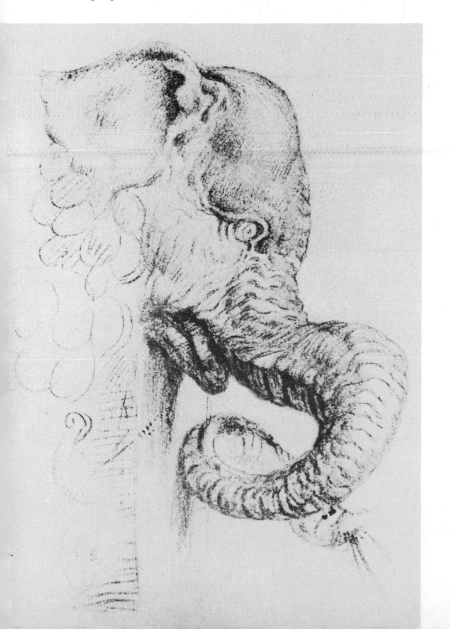

ᴛ: *The ruins of the Forum as seen through the Arch of Titus.*
rawing by Marten van Heemskerck.

ʟᴏᴡ: *The ruins of the imperial palaces on the Palatine.*
ngraving by Du Pérac.

FACING PAGE: *The* tempietto
in the Church of S. Pietro in Montorio, by Bramante.

BELOW: *S. Maria di Loreto,*
designed by Bramante and Antonio da Sangallo the Younger.

Henri. Cluen. inuen.   Mons Testaceus.   Philipp. Gall. excud

LEFT: *The games on the Testaccio hill during the papacy of Paul III.*

BELOW LEFT: *A bullfight in the Piazza Farnese.*

BELOW: *Part of the Du Perac plan of Rome [1577].*
Castel Sant'Angelo, leading over the bridge to Piazza di
Ponte, is top left. Piazza del Popolo, bottom right.

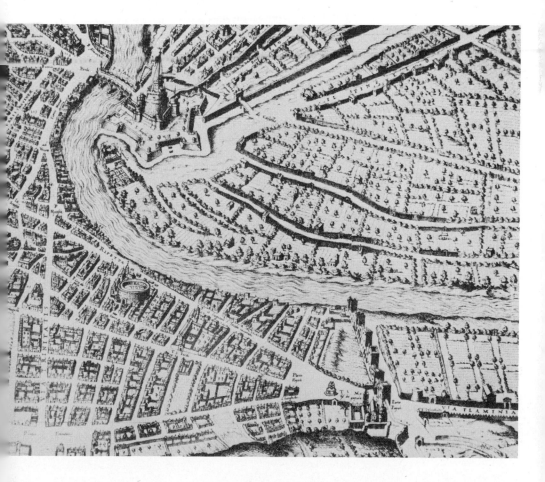

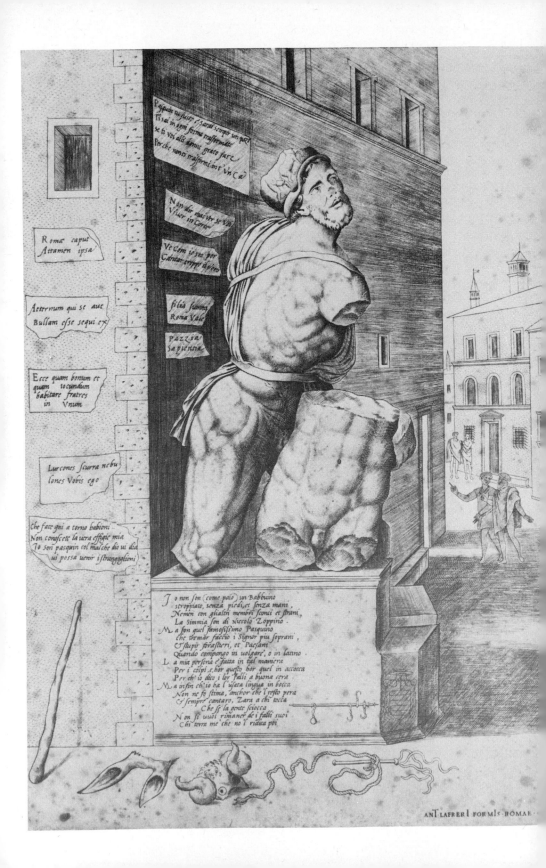

ANT. LAFRERI FORMIS ROMAE

ABOVE: The statue called Marforio. *Engraving by Nicholas Beatrizet.*

FACING PAGE: The statue called Pasquino. *Engraving by Nicholas Beatrizet.*

RIGHT: The Conversion of St Paul *by Michelangelo*

BELOW RIGHT: The Crucifixion of St Peter *by Michelangelo*

BELOW: The Seven Basilicas of Rome. *Engraving executed for the Holy Year of 157!*

NEXT PAGE: Pietà by Michelangelo.
Drawn for Vittoria Colonna.

them of the Pantheon. Like Michelangelo, he adapted and transformed classical idiom rather than copying it. The place of Raphael in
the *academic* investigation of classical Rome is fascinating and
elusive. He was said to have been preparing, during the latter part of
the pontificate of Leo X, an archaeological plan of ancient Rome. How
Raphael would have found time for such an enormous project, at a
period when he and his studio were furiously working on the
"Transfiguration" and other great enterprises, is hard to understand.
It seems that the eventual disappointing outcome of the archaeological
labours of Raphael and his circle on the plan was the mediocre little
sketch published by Fabio Calvo, seven years after Raphael's death,
in 1527.

Raphael's direct responsibility for a famous letter of 1519, which
Baldassare Castiglione seems to have prepared for him, is uncertain.
But the letter expresses principles to which Raphael, "the emulator of
the ancients" as the memorial inscription in the Pantheon calls him,
certainly subscribed—which were, in fact, already the principles of
most of the most successful artists of his time. The distinction which
that letter makes between the lack of grace in "Gothic" art principles
and the "maniera" of the modern imitators of classic style is fundamental for Renaissance art theory. But when the letter comes to attack the modern destroyers of classical Roman monuments, and to
condemn them as worse than Goths or Vandals, Raphael (if the part-
author was Raphael) is on slippery ground. Though everyone in
Renaissance Rome paid lip service to the principle of conserving the
ancient monuments, when it came to expediency or profit no one,
from the pope down, hesitated to exploit or destroy them. Raphael's
own office of "Commissioner" for antiquities in 1515, made principally with the idea of protecting the ancient inscriptions, was barren of
result. Raphael himself tried to lay greedy hands on the Diana of
Ephesus belonging to the Rossi family. When in 1520 the Roman
civic authorities tried to stop an agent of Cardinal Scaramuccia
Trivulzio from looting the Forum of Nerva of its antiquities, and used
the same metaphor of "Goths and Vandals" that the Castiglione letter
had used a year earlier, they failed entirely. The benign Leo X would
not stop a cardinal from making a decent profit.

One good reason why the papal government was not going to stop
the digging up and burning or disposing of ancient marble was that it

took a tax of a third part on all such operations, the so-called *cave di preti*. The whole area from the Forum to the present Piazza della Torre Argentina was filled with the kilns of the lime-burners, and known as the *Calcararia*. Nor were the *cavatori* or excavators ignorant of the value of the antique objects they found, whether for collectors or as specialised building material. Pope Paul III gave the impression in 1534 when he appointed Latino Giovenale Manetti as Commissioner of Antiquities that at last a halt was going to be called to the destroyers of the ancient city. The bull of appointment speaks eloquently of the trees and the ivy pushing their way through the ruins, deplores the burning of the marble for lime, and foresees a time when ancient Rome will only be visible in the buildings of modern Rome. But it was only a bull. Not only did everything go on as before, but in 1535–1536 Manetti carried out clearances in the Forum in order to let Charles V see the ruins clearly in his visit to Rome. In 1540 Paul III took action more disastrous for the Roman monuments than anything yet deliberately done by his predecessors: in order to finance the prosecution of the works at St Peter's he granted to the Fabbrica of the new church the monopoly on all the profits of excavation and exploitation of the ancient monuments, together with permission to sell licences to third parties. The agents of St Peter's sawed and burned their way through mountains of marble, especially in the whole zone of the Forum. This vandalism was new not in kind but in scale. Add to it the insatiable demands for the Farnese palace, and for all the other works set in motion by Paul III, and the demand for ancient material either for lime or for re-use was immense. The foundations of whole temples disappeared in the Forum. The destroying *cavatori* followed one another, as du Bellay remarks in one of his sonnets, like gleaners after the harvest.

VII

The most notable act of Renaissance vandalism in Rome was the destruction of old St Peter's, a deed which did not go unnoticed by contemporaries. It is unlikely that Julius II took this decision for the pragmatic reason that the old basilica was collapsing, though this was the excuse that he used on some occasions. It is more likely that he seized the occasion to build the new church as a symbolic statement of the achievements and aims of the Roman Church as he saw them, and also to give his own tomb a principal place in the new centre of Christendom. The custody of the tombs of the apostles (as contrasted with the tombs of the later popes) was one of the objects for which the Roman bishopric existed. It was therefore impossible for Julius to accept the suggestion of Bramante that the church should be re-orientated in order to face the obelisk from Nero's Circus to the south of the church, which would have meant displacing the Confession of St Peter. But Bramante was nevertheless allowed almost complete freedom to demolish the old basilica, including the great columns at the end of the nave which Raphael pointed out could well have been individually saved. Over the Confession Bramante erected a temporary doric structure to protect the holy memorials after the roof of the nave had been removed; this structure remained in position until almost the end of the century.

New St Peter's was like a symbol of Roman urban progress. When St Peter's grew, Rome grew; when the great church halted, so did the city. The original plan of Bramante was for a huge church, almost a third bigger than that eventually planned by Michelangelo. The Bramante plan imposed itself on all successors in one respect, since the main piers for the crossing, and the coffered arches which connected them, were complete by 1512, thus determining that something like Bramante's centrally planned structure, with its great dome which was perhaps modelled on that of Santa Sophia, must come into existence. The great worry about this immense church, naturally enough, was money. Bramante's design was too big, and his successors spent half a century in reducing it. Under Leo X, Raphael and other architects, including Antonio da Sangallo, did little more than strengthen and extend the foundations of Bramante, though basic changes in the design were discussed. From the death of Raphael in 1520 activity slowed down even further, to come entirely to a halt in 1527. Rethinking of the whole building plan began after Raphael's death, but was not intensively pursued until 1535, when the serious work for the preparation of a new scale model began. The new work was planned by a team of architects, but especially by Baldassare Peruzzi and Antonio da Sangallo the Younger. Work was not properly resumed on the church until 1542, and some of this was in vain, since Michelangelo, on succeeding Antonio da Sangallo in 1546, caused the terminal hemicycle of the apse which had been started by his predecessor to be razed.

From the mid-1530s, artists in Rome began to produce sketches which were no longer merely directed to recording archaeological and architectural material, but which were compositions for a later painting or—more often—engraving. Of these artists Martin van Heemskerck is the most interesting and vivid, and the survival of his sketchbook is a piece of great good fortune. New St Peter's appears in his drawings of 1535–1536. On the tops of Bramante's huge piers, which had been erected for over twenty years, bushes may be seen growing. There is no sign of building activity, and anyone ignorant of the subject of these drawings might easily suppose themselves to be looking at the ruins of ancient Rome, and not at the workshop for the greatest building of modern Rome.

No doubt one of the reasons for the dictatorial powers over the works at St Peter's given to Michelangelo by Paul III was the approaching Jubilee of 1550. The Sangallo partnership of architects had been thorough but very slow; the seventy-one-year-old Michelangelo was thought to have the ability to re-design and complete the work both faster and cheaper. By 1550 all that Michelangelo had in fact completed were the apses of the northern and southern transept arms; work on the drum to support the cupola had not started, or hardly so. But at least the pilgrims of 1550—who were less numerous than had been hoped—could see that a noble structure had not only been planned but was actually being built. Throughout the 1550s building continued, not always at a great rate, but the troubles of Paul IV did not halt construction for more than a very short time. By Michelangelo's death in 1564 the exterior and interior facing of the south transept was complete as far as the attic, and the drum was complete up to the level of pilaster- and buttress-capitals. The cupola, which was the solution to the whole building, had not been begun, though Michelangelo's influence in lowering it was to prove decisive. A sketch of 1559–1561 shows Bramante's shrine over the Confession no longer standing under the open sky. The drum above it is almost finished; on the other hand the western apse of Bramante and Rossellino stands untouched behind the altar. The eastern half of the nave of the old basilica, its façade, and its atrium, were all still standing in 1559. Adjoining the exterior doors of the atrium, the fifteenth-century benediction loggia of Pope Pius II still looked out over the square of St Peter. Beside the loggia was the main entrance to the Vatican Palace. The atrium extended much further east than the façade of the present church; beneath the atrium steps was the great tetragonal square, with a single fountain in its centre. The obelisk from the Circus of Nero still stood in its old place on the south side of the church; after Bramante's suggestion of re-orientating the church to face it had been rejected, Michelangelo had thirty-odd years later considered the idea of moving the obelisk, only to pronounce it impractical.

Thus in 1559, as the Roman Church stumbled towards the final session of the Council of Trent, the works at St Peter's bore the marks of purposeful restorative genius. The apparently moribund condition of Rome in the decade following the Sack had been succeeded by signs of powerfully reviving life. Five years later Michelangelo died (18 February 1564). Two months before his death the papal legate at Trent had told the conciliar fathers at the last session to "go in peace" (4 December 1563) and set the Church on a new course.

No great church was completed in Rome during the Renaissance period. Like St Peter's, S. Giovanni dei Fiorentini was incomplete when Michelangelo died. S. Maria degli Angeli was only an indistinct Michelangelo sketch on the surface of the ancient Baths of Diocletian. The façade of S. Spirito in Sassia, which was the influential part of the church, may have been planned by Antonio da Sangallo but by 1559 had not been executed. The great art of Roman Renaissance churches lies essentially in their private chapels: the Chigi chapels at S. Maria del Popolo and S. Maria della Pace, which contain some of the greatest art of the Medicean period; the Mattei chapel in S. Maria della Consolazione, which Taddeo Zuccaro made into a pattern for the developed Mannerist style; the Cesi chapel in S. Maria della Pace which Rosso had in the 1520s made one of the earliest Mannerist compositions. But these chapels are socially just an extension of the same courtly society which produced the great villas and palaces. The guilds and "national" sodalities produced fine small churches, some of which contained important works of art. But the bulk of Roman investment went into secular building.

VIII

By no means all the well-to-do of Renaissance Rome lived in Renaissance palaces. In spite of the long building boom, most of Rome in 1559 was still a rabbit-warren of medieval houses of a sort which now exists in the Roman area only in the medieval quarter of Viterbo. In modern Rome one or two courtyards off Via del Pellegrino or Vicolo Savelli can still give a faint idea of this earlier city. The towers of medieval Rome have also disappeared or been altered drastically. Tor dei Mellini or the tower in Via Margana offer some suggestion of these old houses; in Trastevere the Torre degli Anguillara is a much restored survival in a quarter once packed with towers; Torre dei Conti and Torre delle Milizie look out over the wilderness made in the Roman Fora by Mussolini's archaeologists. On the other side of the Campidoglio the Vittorio Emanuele Monument and Mussolini's other clearings have emptied a quarter once densely filled with medieval houses.

Apart from Castel Sant'Angelo the only classical monument in Renaissance Rome still to be used as a notable dwelling house was the Theatre of Marcellus, which was the palace of the feudal family of Savelli. It is probable that the Theatre was occupied by the Portuguese ambassador at the time of the Sack, and that it was taken by storm by imperial troops using artillery. Perhaps before, but more likely after the Sack, the palace was rebuilt by Baldassare Peruzzi, so that the exterior side facing Piazza Montanara had a dignified appearance which preserved two of the original three orders of the earlier Theatre. But a view of the other side of the palace shows that it still included the medieval fortress of the Pierleoni. Under it in Piazza Montanara was a quarter of butchers' shops.

Many great families continued in the Renaissance to live in the unchanged palaces of their ancestors, or at most to renovate them. The great Orsini palace on Monte Giordano had been the seat of some of the splendours of fifteenth-century Rome. It was particularly brutally sacked in 1527, but twenty years later was so far restored as to be worthy to be leased to the munificent Cardinal Ippolito d'Este. The Colonna palace at the Santi Apostoli was restored at the beginning of the century; it was one of the greatest palaces of Rome, but also one of the oldest. Lesser but still rich families like the Cesarini, who set up one of the first museums of antiques in Rome, still remained in their ancestral towers and palaces. Ancient families like the Astalli, Jacobacci and de Velis, stayed in the buildings they had inherited.

The great Roman mercantile families were able to build themselves splendid new palaces. The Massimo family possessed houses on the ancient Via Papale; after the disastrous fires of the Sack the sons of Domenico Massimo proceeded to build two independent palaces on the site, one on the curved alignment of Via Papale, the Palazzo Massimo alle Colonne designed by Baldassare Peruzzi, and the other, backing onto it and facing the square of S. Pantaleo, by Giovanni Mangone. The haphazard arrangement of the two buildings shows clearly how far were the architects of the time from "town planning"; a third palace of the Massimi adjoined these two. The Peruzzi palace is probably the finest and most imaginative work of this great architect; the curved façade and the restricted ground plan are turned to advantage in an ingenious relationship between atrium, internal courtyard and loggia which uses the lighting effects of the antique cryptoporticus.

The Della Valle family, also bankers, and just as rich as their neighbours on the Via Papale, the Massimi, built a fine palace early in the century. Its builder, Cardinal Andrea della Valle, was also responsible for a second palace which he constructed after the Sack, in 1530 (Palazzo Della Valle-Capranica). The great glory of the Della Valle palaces was their archaeological collections, which in one palace were in a sort of hanging garden on a terrace, and in the other in an elaborately arranged courtyard. Cardinal Della Valle also prided himself on the possession of a painted and decorated bathroom like those in Castel Sant'Angelo and the Vatican. The branch of the Mattei family living in the Calcararia rebuilt their fifteenth-century palaces to make two new ones (Palazzo Mattei and Palazzo Mattei-Paganica). The Mattei group of palaces had by the end of the century become three. Already by 1559 the Della Valle and the Massimi each occupied a group of three adjoining palaces. The palace of the Cenci, which in the second half of the century was the scene of one of the bloodiest family tragedies of noble Roman life, was another case of adaptation. A Renaissance façade and courtyard were built, but medieval towers continued to form part of the palaces, which were on two opposite sides of a square, and were connected by bridges.

The small palace built by the successful prelate or courtier was an essential element of the fabric of the Roman streets. Some of these were modest in size, like the *palazzetto* of Giovanni Pietro Turci built at the beginning of the century, which was narrow and shallow (about 9m x 11m), and above which (invisible from the street) is the pleasingly rustic embellishment of a tall dovecote. Other curialist palaces were more ambitious. Palazzo Gaddi presents a narrow façade to the street (about fourteen metres) but goes back over sixty metres, and includes a fine little courtyard. The palace built by Antonio da Sangallo the Younger for the canon lawyer Melchiore Baldassini under Leo X was a large building (about 24m x 30m), with a fine atrium and a courtyard with an arcaded loggia on the first floor. Equally imposing is the palace built in Parione for the French curialist bishop Thomas Le Roy (the "Farnesina ai Baullari", on the Corso Vittorio Emanuele). The small palace in Borgo (now demolished, but recorded in a fine prospective sketch by Antonio da Sangallo the Younger), built for the Protonotary Guglielmo del Pozzo in Borgo, is one more indication of the luxury in which Leo X's curialists could live. Also in Borgo is the house of Leo X's doctor, Bartolomeo da Brescia, which may have been designed by Raphael; its plan is curiously shaped because it stood on an awkward corner site, but the façade is elegant and impressive. Well-built smaller houses which could not be called palaces belonged to other papal doctors who lived in Borgo or Parione. Successful artists also built, besides architect-speculators like Raphael or the Sangalli. The painter, Giulio Romano, had a beautiful small house in Campitelli, with a fine rusticated façade. The merchants of Parione could build more extravagantly; the beautiful little palace now called the house of Cassiano del Pozzo is of a size and elegance which made it, in the seventeenth century, a fit habitation for the patron of Nicholas Poussin.

IX

The humbler dwelling-houses of Rome underwent a change in the Renaissance period no less radical than that of the houses of the rich. The typical Roman dwelling of the workman, artisan or small trader in the early Renaissance was a small detached unit. The poor lived in one-roomed brick cabins. In mid-century such a rustic little cabin stood next to S. Maria della Febbre, within a few paces of new St Peter's. Small traders or artisans inhabited detached two-storey houses with the workshop or counter and storeroom on the ground floor and the living quarters in a single room on the first floor; the stairway could be internal or external. The frontage on the street was only irregularly aligned with the frontages of neighbouring houses. In the larger units with more than one room on the first floor, access from one room to another was often by a covered external balcony (*ballatoio, vallatorium*); or alternatively the first-floor rooms left space for a loggia which was covered by the roof of the building. Larger houses might include a brick or brick-and-stone portico whose function was to support the first storey; the destruction of the portico would therefore mean the destruction of the house!

Such houses survived in large numbers right through the Renaissance period; the butchers' shops in Piazza Montanara, facing and adjoining the Theatre of Marcellus, may serve as an example. But the great development schemes of Medicean Rome brought a new urban pattern with them. They were often carried out by a Roman hospital or clerical corporation in conjunction with a capitalist speculator or a group. They might involve the re-development of areas already built-up or partly built-up, as in Borgo or Arenula, or the development of formerly open or agricultural land, as in Via di Ripetta in Campo Marzio. In either case, though particularly in built-up areas, the speculator's urge to get maximum use from the land and the government's wish to have orderly streets combined to impose a new uniform street alignment, in which houses and shops gave directly onto the street. The terraced house or block, usually with a series of shops or workshops on the ground floor, and with two storeys of dwelling quarters above each shop, made its appearance. Alternatively, houses or pairs of houses were built on a single street alignment, separated by short intervals. The building components for these small houses appear to have been standardised, and the width of the individual unit could be as narrow as 4.14 metres. Behind the street frontage, shop and dwelling quarters, the pattern tended to be that of a small courtyard, with outbuildings sited across the courtyard. The development areas were sometimes very large, as in the cases of the central zone of Borgo Nuovo, which belonged to the Hospital of S. Spirito, or of the large area in Campo Marzio which was developed by Lombard architects and masons in combination with the hospitals of S. Girolamo and S. Giacomo. Typical streets of this area were those traversing the roads bordering the Tiber, Via di Ripetta and Via Tor di Nona (e.g., Via della Frezza, Via dei Pontefici, Via dell'Arco di Parma).

The destruction of the porticoes and the construction of these new rows of houses and shops produced the first examples of the uniform street alignments which became typical of Baroque Rome. These new streets were easier to clean, to pave and to police than their predecessors, and they also lent themselves to the precursor of modern traffic problems, the coach. By Paul IV's time the coach had become a source of concern to the government, especially when either furiously driven or used by prostitutes.

The new building developments were aimed at several social classes. In Arenula and Campo Marzio artisans with small counters or workshops occupied many of the new houses. But other more ambitious houses, even those of cardinals, were placed among these humbler ones; the cheap land in Campo Marzio must have encouraged richer folk who were deterred by high prices in the centre of the densely inhabited areas. It is clear that Palazzetto Turci, for example, in Parione, was cramped by a very small site which compelled the builder to place the well within the house. But there was plenty of middle-class development in Parione and in the quarter round Campo dei Fiori, such as the block of shops on the corner of Via del Pellegrino and Via Monserrato, which has two storeys of living accommodation and an attic loggia above the shops. A building such as the last was of stone construction with travertine or rusticated facing, expensive materials. Less pretentious middle-class housing was built of brick or tufa, perhaps faced with plaster.

X

One way of imparting a dignified and antiquarian flavour to the façades of modest houses in Borgo or Tor di Nona was the use of monochrome drawings, executed by drawing through a white plaster facing onto a darkened foundation (*sgraffito*), or else by fresco. These decorated façades were invariably in what was thought to be classical taste. Dolce's *Dialogue on Painting* praised this decorative method as superior to the use of travertine or coloured marbles. It was certainly much cheaper, and it enjoyed a great vogue in the first three decades of the century, because it allowed the constructor of modest means to participate in the fashionable movement of classical antiquarianism. Most of the scenes in these decorations were from Roman history or mythology, though some Biblical subjects exist. It was a cheap and effective way of giving not only palaces but houses a decoration inspired by the classical fantasies of courtly culture. These decorations were sometimes commissioned by great families like the Massimi, or the Mattei, who gave Taddeo Zuccaro the commission to decorate Jacopo Mattei's palace which effectively launched Zuccaro's career as an artist. But so also did relatively modest persons like Giovanni Antonio Milesi, whose house was an important example of the style. The numbers of painted façades must have run into many hundreds; forty façades are known to have been executed by Polidoro da Caravaggio alone, and those between 1520 and 1527. The vogue for these painted walls was not confined to the outer façades of palaces; Perino del Vaga was said by Vasari to have decorated the walls of a museum-garden of antiquities belonging to the Archbishop of Cyprus, with mythological scenes of fauns and Bacchantes. The style could also be used to modernise the appearance of medieval towers, as was done for Tor Mellini.

The fashion for painted houses was influential in spreading the idioms of the style which is now known as Mannerism. Palazzo Branconio dell'Aquila, which is thought to have been designed by Raphael, was decorated in this way. The most notable example of the painted house which still gives some idea of the original appearance of this style is Palazzo Ricci, which is at the moment being restored. The amount of space apparently assigned by the builders for painted wall decoration makes the proportions of window to wall vary from the usual norm, though it may be that the paintings merely enliven a poorly designed façade.

(189)

XI

The most seductive manifestation of aristocratic classicizing taste was the Roman garden, which often amounted to an open-air museum. From the beginning of the century the same people who were building houses and palaces in Parione and Borgo were buying vineyards on the Quirinal, Esquiline, Pincio and Viminale, and making them into cultivated and well-kept walks and gardens, which served to show collections of classical monuments and statuary, often arranged with exquisite taste. One of the prototypes of these gardens was the Vatican Belvedere, which contained one of the finest collections of classical sculpture in Europe. The two great terraces of Bramante's Belvedere, surmounted by a great hemispherical niche and perhaps recalling the Temple of the Sun at Praeneste, formed a setting of immense splendour. The Laocoön, the Apollo and the Venus, were shown in specially built aedicules; round them were formal gardens planted with fruit and bay trees, watered by the fountains of ancient statuary; the "Nile", "Tiber" and "Cleopatra" fountains were set in grottoes as wall-fountains. When these gardens had been freshly established by Julius II, the devout humanist Giovanni Pico della Mirandola was so shocked by their pagan beauty that he wrote a poem describing the Belvedere as a grove of Venus! But the splendours of the Belvedere remained, and the collection was only added to as the century advanced. The ravages of the Sack on the gardens were repaired by the plantings of Paul III.

The main aim of the Roman gardens was to set off the collections of antiquities. This did not exclude a concern for horticulture. Julius III was particularly interested in rare trees and shrubs, and over 30,000 were planted in a short time in the gardens and walks of his villa. The villa of Cardinal Ippolito d'Este on the Quirinal possessed plantations so copious as to be described as a "sort of wood", and also included a labyrinth. Most gardens included the "private garden" (*giardino segreto*) in a medieval tradition. But the walks and beds acted, above all, as a setting for the antiques. These might be centralised in an *antiquarium*, which could be a sort of building, or a collection of walls specially built to form a courtyard or centre. In the great Cesi gardens in Borgo the *antiquarium* was a small, centrally-planned area with four short arms projecting from it; each wall contained niches to house ancient statues. Some of the walls in these gardens were decorated with *sgraffiti*, like those in the Del Bufalo gardens on the Pincio which were executed by Polidoro da Caravaggio.

Villa Madama possessed terraced walks, with statues mounted in the wall niches as in the Cesi gardens, and with elaborately decorated fountains in the grotesque taste, of which the "Elephant head" (a natural theme for the pontificate of Leo X, whose elephant made such a stir) is the best known, and still survives in a mutilated form. Fountains tended to occupy central positions in all the great gardens. Aldovrandi wrote of the Pio da Carpi gardens on the Quirinal that they were

> not only the most delightful spot in the Roman area and in all Italy, but indeed a terrestrial paradise. Nothing lacks in them; there are convenient and beautiful rooms, a garden, a most delicious and serviceable vineyard; an immense number of rare ancient statues and objects of interest, and as many loggias and places of recreation as a man could possibly wish. But the most extraordinary thing of all is the delightful and ingenious fountain, which has been placed in its grotto with such skill and taste that a civilised person could ask for no greater amenity or pleasure, of a sort entirely distinct from vulgar amusements. Such a man may enjoy there something which seems, as it were, a shadow of heavenly leisure.

Equally fine fountains were placed, after Aldovrandi wrote, in the Este gardens which adjoined those of Da Carpi on the Quirinal hill. Cardinal d'Este had fountains with statues placed in and round them in the lower garden on the slope of Monte Cavallo, in the garden "in the wood", and in the "secret" garden. The wood in the Este gardens was possibly a "sacred" wood, with a mythological meaning, on the lines of the sacred wood in Villa d'Este at Tivoli, or the later garden of grotesques at Bomarzo.

The movement to open new areas for gardens and villas went on continuously, halted for only a short time by the Sack. Some of the largest projects belong to the fifth and sixth decades of the century: the Este gardens which have just been described; Cardinal Jean du Bellay's gardens in the grounds of the Baths of Diocletian; Villa Giulia; Villa Pia in the grounds of the Vatican; the Soderini conversion of the Mausoleum of Augustus. Monsignor Francesco

Soderini made this neglected heap of ruins, which in the Middle Ages had been made into a fortress, into a smiling and elaborately trellised garden of antiquities. It is a gloomy thought that today the Mausoleum of Augustus is once more just as sad and as visually uninteresting as it was in 1549 when he began the excavation and transformation of the monument.

There is no logical division between Renaissance museum-gardens and the villas and palaces to which they were attached, since the antiquities often spread outwards from the house in a series of open-air rooms. Villa Giulia still offers an especially beautiful example of a series of garden rooms. A great entrance court backs onto an extraordinary sunken nymphaeum, which in its turn is quitted by a double helicoid staircase, above which is a casino. Wall paintings on the pattern of the ancient *topia* flanked the hemisphere above the casino stairs. Antique statuary was disposed throughout this large complex of buildings and gardens, but especially in the nymphaeum, which was the favourite archaeological device of later Renaissance gardens.

Some museums were housed in courtyards opening off the main palace, with climbing plants between the niches of the walls, and potted plants in urns in the court. The most important and well known of these was the courtyard in Palazzo Valle-Capranica. Two sides of the courtyard contained statues and busts in niches, in two rows of unequal height, with ancient reliefs also partaking in the decorative scheme; a third wall was more symmetrically arranged, and there were four free-standing ancient pillars. An inscription on the third wall made it clear that the museum was arranged not only for the benefit of the cardinal and his family, but for Roman citizens and foreign tourists. In this Cardinal Della Valle was following the example of another prominent Roman family which had pioneered the idea of a garden-museum, the Cesarini. The Della Valle collection was a very large collection of antiquities indeed, and it set the style for the absorption of the many small collections of antiquities in a few very great ones.

XII

The face of Rome was in general grave. In a city dominated by priests and bankers, this is hardly surprising. Roman gentlemen wore dark clothes and carried themselves soberly; Roman wives went out in the streets little, and when they did they too were soberly dressed and attended. "Marcher d'un grave pas" was du Bellay's ironic but literally meant opening to his sonnet on behaviour in Rome.

On the other hand, Roman feasts and festivals were, except during the drab six years which followed the Sack, extravagant and splendid, and the architectural scale of the decorations for some of these feasts was so great as to transform, for a time, the whole appearance of the city. The greatest of all these festivals, almost certainly, was the *possesso* of Leo X. The *possesso* was the taking possession by the pope of the physical control and the temporalities of the Roman bishopric. It involved a solemn procession from St Peter's to St John Lateran, by way of the Via Papale. The "triumphal arches" were decorated with hangings and with figures symbolic of the cultural and political policies which were expected from the new pope. Scores of these arches were erected over the streets through which the procession passed, beginning with Castel Sant'Angelo and ending with other *apparati* at the Lateran itself. The theme of the arches was Leo's role as peacemaker, as the continuator of the Lateran Council, and as the patron of letters and the arts. Many of the decorations were pagan, like those of the arch of Agostino Chigi, which had figures of Apollo, Mercury and Pallas; Apollo was the most frequently represented classical god. Like most of the festivals of this kind in the Renaissance, that of the *possesso* was not a frivolous extravagance, but a seriously intended political programme whose function was not only to show the power and splendour of the new papal regime but to emphasise its political direction. The second notable *possesso* procession during the period was that of the austere Paul IV in 1555, whose magnificence was intended to impress and overawe the Romans. The *possesso* and coronation festivities of the pleasure-loving Julius III, however, were not without *éclat*.

The ceremonies of the *possesso* were based on ancient religious rites. There were many other great public feasts whose origins were distinctly secular, some of them celebrated with a freedom unfitted to the city of the holy martyrs. The Roman Carnival, celebrated before the beginning of Lent, was a period of officially licensed delinquency. It was in origin more than this. The "games" celebrated on Monte Testaccio during the Middle Ages were a symbolic display of the po-

(193)

litical domination of the Roman Commune over the subject towns and villages of the Roman District, each of which was made to send a contribution of men, money or material. It was no accident that in the early sixteenth century this aspect of the Carnival, which emphasised Roman communal independence, decayed and atrophied. The games on Monte Testaccio were renewed, after the Sack, in 1536, but these barbarous displays of civic independence were not really acceptable to the cultivated despotism of Paul III. As a former member of the Borgia court, he enjoyed the bullfights. But the spectacle of live pigs packed into carts, which were released from the top of Monte Testaccio so that they splintered to bits on the bottom, and the populace could fight for their contents, was too disorderly and too rustic for the polished Farnese circle. In 1545 the last games took place on the Testaccio; the Carnival continued, but domesticated and urbanised. Masked dances and showers of perfumed oranges were more acceptable to the prelates of the Roman court than the old bucolic hooliganism.

A far more civilised and political manifestation of the Roman Carnival was the *Festa d'Agone*, the spectacles organised in Piazza Navona. A contemporary account of this feast in 1536, just before the coming of the Emperor Charles V to Rome, expresses the feeling of convalescence after a devastating illness which is typical of Rome in the early years of Paul III, still trembling from the Sack:

> Rome, which has suffered so much in the past, is coming to life under Your Holiness just as the fields throw off the frost in the rebirth of spring . . . as Carnival approaches, the few surviving Romans (as they might call themselves) have decided to organise the customary *Festa d'Agone*, both to please Your Holiness and to amuse the common people.

The floats and processions at this feast tended, from Leo's time onwards, to be in the same popularised idiom of classical antiquity which inspired the ceremonies and decorations of the *possesso* and the "painted houses" of the period. "Roman" chariots covered with "antique" reliefs were used in the Carnivals of 1536 and 1538, the first of which honoured Pope Paul by a representation of the triumph of the Consul Aemilius Paulus. The learned organiser of these "triumphs" was the inevitable Latino Giovenale Manetti, who held the civic offices of "conservator" and "maestro di strada", besides his curial positions.

To some extent these great pageants were the amusements of the court, and might be expected to exhibit the iconography of classical humanism which permeated the courtly ambience. But they were also popular entertainments, and it seems clear that a large number of Romans of the middle sort, members of guilds or sodalities, participated through these pageants in the learned pedantry of the aristocrats and their tutors. The floats of the Roman regions in the Carnival of 1545, which must have been financed by the contributions of relatively humble people, were almost exclusively humanist in concept. Paul III as Androcles with the lion (from whom he extracted the thorn of heresy), Constantinople besieged, the Hesperides guarded, the Arimaspians conquering the griffin, Heraclius and Trajan conquering the enemies of the Empire, are some of the topics chosen, most of which referred to papal struggles with heretics and with the Turks. The region of Pigna chose to show Cybele, mother of the Gods, holding the Pinecone known to all Romans from the great bronze pinecone in the atrium of the basilica of St Peter, a part of the old church which was still untouched by the builders. The choice of the Phrygian Cybele, "crowned with towers", referred to a celebrated passage in Virgil (*Aeneid*, VI, 784–787), in which the "mother of cities" Cybele is identified with Rome herself. One of the statues in the Roman collections was a Cybele "crowned with towers", and du Bellay invoked the same Cybele of Mount Berecyntus, borne in her chariot among the Phrygian towns:

> Telle que dans son char la Bérécynthienne,
> Couronnée de tours, et joyeuse d'avoir
> Enfanté tant de Dieux, telle se faisait voir,
> En ses jours plus heureux, cette ville ancienne,

comparing Rome, "in her happier days", with the Berecyntian goddess, joyful mother of so many gods.

Other feasts, fitted into the same kind of cultural dress, were the vehicles of more overt political propaganda. The conferment of Roman citizenship on Giuliano and Lorenzo de' Medici, nephews of

Leo X, in September 1513, was marked by an elaborate ceremony in a wooden "theatre" specially designed and built for the purpose on the Campidoglio. This theatre was a rectangular auditorium for about 3,000 people, with a large proscenium backed by frescoes *all'antica*, and by five large paintings which stood over the stage entrances. The political theme of the decoration was Roman-Florentine ("Roman-Etrurian") friendship. Although the citizenship conferred seems to have been that bestowed by the Roman Commune on any other friendly nobles, and not the "patriciate" whose origins were joined with those of the medieval Empire, the allegorical pageants which followed evoked ancient Roman majesty. "Rome" appeared first, with "Justice" and "Fortitude". Then, after the music of the "cory-banths" of Cardinal d'Este, an "ancient" chariot was drawn by two lions (referring to Leo X) onto the stage, bearing Cybele and a great ball (the Medici device) in the shape of the world. Cybele, as mother of the Gods and patroness of Rome, informed the audience that just as she had liberated the ancient Romans from misfortune and peril, so she (a pagan goddess!) had now placed Leo X at the head of religion, which would now be as well conducted by him as the chariot had been by the two lions. The orb then split open to the sound of thunderous cannon without, and "Rome", a beautiful young woman crowned and clad in gold, stepped out of the separated halves accompanied by a flight of birds. Camillo Porzio, the Roman notable who had written the entertainment, then had the "corybanths" scatter among the audience medals which portrayed Giuliano de' Medici on one side, and on the other "Rome" as a young woman clad in a light cloak and seated on shield-trophies, holding "victory" in her hand.

These expensive pageants were not given in a spirit of innocent classicizing fun; political aims were omnipresent. In the receptions of foreign ambassadors and potentates this was especially so. And yet there *was* a certain lightheartedness in the pageant of the elephant brought to Pope Leo X by the embassy of the king of Portugal in 1514. The political background of this embassy was the enlistment of papal support for the Portuguese war in Morocco and Mauritania. The Portuguese object was therefore to emphasise the riches of Africa, and also, incidentally, those of the Indies. Oriental beasts —horses, panthers, leopards—accompanied the elephant, which halted and knelt to salute the pope when it approached Ponte Elio, and Leo awaited the embassy in Castel Sant'Angelo. The elephant created a great literary and iconographical vogue, and its surviving memorials include the intarsia panel in the Vatican, the fountain in the grounds of Villa Madama, and the vault relief of Baldassare Peruzzi in Palazzo Massimo.

The most serious of the great political feasts was the visit of the Emperor Charles V to Rome in April 1536. This took place at a time of considerable papal-imperial tension, when the emperor had only just decided to relax the hostile attitude he had adopted towards Paul III, who had refused to abandon his neutral position in spite of the imminent Franco-imperial war. On the pope's side, the arrangements to entertain the emperor were designed to emphasise the pope's recognition of Charles's role as the protector of Christendom against the infidel, and hence of his supposed military success at the siege of Tunis. It was also expedient to remind the emperor that Rome, after the Sack of 1527 for which he was responsible, was emerging from "the frozen fields of winter" into a new papal spring.

All these factors pointed towards some novel entertainment which would substitute archaeological tourism for the traditional imperial routes and pageants, especially as these were linked with the ceremony of imperial coronation, which had already taken place six years earlier in Bologna at the hands of Pope Clement VII. In April 1536 Charles V approached the city from the south, from Naples, which was the opposite direction to that normally taken by the medieval emperors. The usual imperial route to St Peter's was from the north, skirting Monte Mario and entering the Leonine city by the Via Triumphalis, which brought the imperial cortège almost immediately to the "porticus" and so to St Peter's. Medieval popes and emperors did not want the imperial troops in Rome proper if this could be avoided, since riots and bloodshed were the usual result.

A completely new approach route was used for the imperial visit of 1536. Behind a huge procession of troops and dignitaries the emperor entered the city by the Via Appia (a route disused in the Middle Ages, and only reopened in the Renaissance), through Porta San Sebastiano, and thence past the Septizonium at the foot of the Palatine to the Arch of Constantine. His route lay through real and false triumphal arches. Decorations all'antica had been imposed over the medieval fortifications of Porta San Sebastiano. From the Arch of Constantine

(197)

Charles followed a route through the Forum marked by the Arches of Titus and Septimius Severus, and approximating to the Via Triumphalis of the ancients (instead of the medieval Via Triumphalis on the other side of the river). His path through the Forum had been prepared by extensive demolition of houses and churches, and of other buildings such as the medieval tower of the Frangipani. The planning of the clearances had been effected by the ubiquitous Latino Giovenale Manetti. The archaeological sights were explained to the emperor by Manetti himself, and by the Roman civic officials, who were for the occasion wearing ancient "Roman" costume.

As he emerged from the area of the Fora and of the former market of Macel de' Corvi, the emperor passed into the Piazza di San Marco through a great double "triumphal arch" constructed on the designs of Antonio da Sangallo the Younger. The Campidoglio was thought to be in too ruinous a state for him to be entertained there, and he therefore proceeded from San Marco down the Via Papale, through Campo de' Fiori (where there was another "triumphal arch") and Via dei Banchi, and finally across Ponte Elio. At the beginning of the Leonine Borgo he passed through the third and last "triumphal arch", and he was received finally in the square of St Peter's by Pope Paul.

As the imperial army passed down the long processional route, the waiting Romans identified among the troops the faces of some of the captors, extortioners and torturers of the terrible events of nine years earlier. But this was only a part of the significance of the imperial visit. It did indeed, as the Carafa pope was sadly to verify in 1558, spell out the dominance of Spanish military power in Italy. But it also pointed to a new Rome, in which the pope was no longer the venerated custodian of the shrines of the martyrs, to be approached by the German emperors-elect for the performance of coronation rites which would set them apart from all other kings, and would also bind them to the Roman bishop in an indissoluble relationship of protector and protected. In the imperial visit of 1536 this ancient liturgical symbolism was not prominent. The primary meaning of Rome in 1536 was not that of the city of the martyrs, the basilicas, the holy relics—relics many of which had been desecrated or dispersed by the imperial troops only a few years earlier. The primary meaning of Rome now seemed to be that of the temple of humanist culture: here the learned experts could reconstruct for Charles V the Rome of the Caesars, and the artists and architects could produce a lavish décor *all'antica*, whose programmes integrated the image of ancient Rome with that of modern Hapsburg power. The imperial route had taken Charles V first along a new tourist route specially conducted through the Fora, and then through the fine new squares, streets and markets which were the urban achievement of new, Renaissance Rome. The emperor had been shown the heritage of the Caesars, but in new Rome he was asked to admire not the Rome of the basilicas and of the medieval popes but the Rome built by the popes from Alexander VI to Paul III.

Chapter Seven

THE SPIRIT OF A CITY AND THE SPIRIT OF AN AGE

I

Religious feeling exists in the moral climate of which it is a part. In early sixteenth-century Italy that climate was one of disillusion. The prevailing mood of the lettered classes was one of cultivated scepticism, though not of specifically irreligious scepticism. The literary tool of some of the greatest masters was irony: in the case of Ariosto this irony was applied to the chivalrous literary conventions of courtly society: in that of Machiavelli and Guicciardini the irony was applied to political life.

The cool and critical mind of Guicciardini was characteristic of a ruling politician of an aristocratic class; that of Ariosto of a pensioned writer enjoying the patronage of the great clerical and princely courts. Not all Italian writers were either as privileged in social position or as detached in spirit. At the other end of the scale lay the literary tradition of the lampoon and the pasquinade, which became the particular province of a few freelance satirical writers who managed to live (though not always to flourish) in the short period between the expansion of a free press in Venice in the 1520s, and its control by the Inquisition and the government after the mid-century. The greatest and richest of the lampoonists, though he was far more than that, was Pietro Aretino, whose formative period was the time he spent in the camp of Giovanni de' Medici "of the black bands", and that spent in Medicean Rome.

Rome had its own place in the sixteenth-century literature of disillusion and satire. As in some other things, the antiquity of Roman tradition made Renaissance Italy seem callow. Satire on the abuses said to surround the Roman bishop goes back at least to the ninth Christian century, to which the "Invectiva in Romam" belongs. Satire on the Roman court is to be found in almost all the more important Italian writers of the early Cinquecento, and not only in the savage Aretino but also in the mild Ariosto. But there was also an internal tradition of Roman satire, which was influential on Aretino and on many other writers. Adjoining the palace of Cardinal Oliviero Carafa in Parione was a battered ancient statue known to the Romans as "Pasquino". Under Julius II this statue was annually decorated with hangings to which humanist poets attached verses in Latin or Italian; the feast was initially under the patronage of Cardinal Carafa, and then under that of the English Cardinal Christopher Bainbridge, and an anthology of the verses was each year published by the learned printer, Mazzocchi. But the decorous and academic period of Master Pasquino did not last long. Before the end of Julius's pontificate Pasquino became also the recipient of the mordant political lampoons which the Romans had at least since Sixtus IV's time delighted to compose against unpopular members of the papal government, or even against the pope himself. The humanist tradition of the neo-Latin epigram combined, in the pasquinade, with the vernacular late medieval tradition of the political lampoon. A typical victim of the pasquinade at this time was the notorious Cardinal Armellini, whose responsibility for increased local taxes in Rome, especially the tax on consumption or *stadera*, made him particularly disliked.

The aim of the pasquinade was biting abuse; libellous obscenity was Pasquino's stock-in-trade. The model of the neo-Latin pasquinade was Martial. But the vernacular writers could allow their fantasy to roam. The death of Paul III gave rise to a pasquinade which claimed that Pope Paul III (at the age of eighty-one) had died in child-birth, having aborted two stillborn cardinals! The conclave of Pius IV was marked by an ingenious pasquinade which assigned to each car-dinal a card of the Tarot pack. Accusations of sodomy against popes and cardinals were common form. Both Pasquino and du Bellay asked why Julius III did not make his monkey into a cardinal, since he had made one of his young monkey-keeper. Julius III's homosexuality made him particularly vulnerable to Pasquino. But Pasquino burst the dykes of abuse when Paul IV died; the violence and obscenity of the pasquinades against the Carafa outdid all others. It was for the com-position of one of these pasquinades that the elderly Nicolò Franco was hanged by a judgement of the Inquisition in 1570, though his ex-ecution was the result of Pius V's determination to avenge the Carafa rather than of Pius's recent decision to control pasquinades in general. Paul IV was after his death termed a demon, a tyrant, a drunken sot, a criminal, a hypocrite; he was made to write a letter to his cardinal-nephew from the depths of Hell. In some of the writings against him there is no trace of irony or humour; only of hate which has been long pent-up and is now released. Two poems celebrate the destruction of the statue which had been placed on the Campidoglio and destroyed by the mob after his death. The rest of the Carafa family was treated by Pasquino with equal brutality.

Pasquino was so topical that it is hard to find an illustration which does not need learned commentary. The following free translation deals with an unusually general theme.* It was probably written in 1512, when Pasquino was dressed up as a soldier, perhaps to celebrate the wars of the Holy League. Pasquino conducts a dialogue with "Marforio", another ancient statue at that time in the Forum; Mar-forio acted as Pasquino's foil. Pasquino in this poem complains to Marforio that he has been insulted by the vilest epithet which could be proffered to anyone: "Me ha detto d'ogni mal el magior male". When Marforio enquires what this horrible insult can be, it emerges that poor Pasquino has been slandered by being called a cardinal!

*Italian text in G.A. Cesareo, *Pasquino e Pasquinate nella Roma di Leone X* (Rome, 1938), pp. 168–69.

MARFORIO AND PASQUINO

M.   Why, Pasquino, you're armed right to the teeth!
P.   Because I've got the devil on my back
      With an insult that has placed me on the rack,
      And got my deadly knife out from its sheath.
M.   But who insulted you, Pasquino, what runt?
P.   He's a c—t!
M.   Then what was it?
P.   You stupid heel:
      I'd rather have been broken on the wheel
      Than ever have been called by such a name.
M.   He called you liar: what a shame!
P.   Worse than that!
M.   Thief?
P.   Worse!
M.   Cuckold?
P.   Men of the world shrug off such sobriquets,
      You simpleton! and just go on their way.
M.   Well, what then? Coiner? Simonist 'gainst God?
      Or did you get a little girl in pod?
P.   Marforio, you're a babe who needs a nurse:
      Of all things evil there is nothing worse
      To call a man than—"Cardinal!" But he
      Who abused me so won't 'scape death, e'en if he flee.

II

Whatever period of the history of Christian Rome one studies, it seems to emerge as a more typical bishopric than its apparently exceptional place would suggest. The Roman clergy were in few ways different from those of other sixteenth-century Italian bishoprics. The Roman churches were involved in the usual labyrinth of overlapping and competing jurisdictions. Basilicas, *tituli* of cardinals, collegiate churches, monasteries: all had their own privileged status, which affected not only these churches but others in Rome dependent on them. Nor were the hundred-odd parish churches in Rome all served by the clergy who were the legal owners of the benefices; a large number of the benefice-holders appointed vicars, whose literacy and competence were not high, and others omitted either to do their pastoral duty or to appoint anyone else to do it for them. Many of the beneficed clergy were unable to do their own parish duties because they were not in priests' orders.

In theory the pope's deputy for the control of the Roman clergy was the "Vicar" of Rome, usually a curial cardinal or bishop. In practice the Vicar's attempts to do his duties were frustrated by the number of privileged jurisdictions, and also by the number of beneficed clergy who could claim the status of courtier, and could therefore appeal to the jurisdiction of the Apostolic Chamber against his. The further competing jurisdictions of the papal Governor of Rome, and even of the city magistrates on the Campidoglio, made the legal complexities yet worse.

Under Paul III and his successors various attempts were made to reform the Roman clergy, and a comprehensive reform order was issued in 1536. But there is not much sign in the surveys of the Roman churches made in 1562 and 1564 that things were very different from their state in 1536, nor indeed from their state under Julius II, which was judged deplorable by two Augustinian friars. One of these was Giles of Viterbo, the head of the Order, and the other the young Martin Luther, who visited Rome in 1510 and formed a poor opinion of what he saw. But the Augustinians themselves were not blameless: under Julius II there was a scandal when the Augustinian friars in S. Maria del Popolo rioted in a struggle to secure the candles from a funeral procession in their church.

The failings and shortcomings of the Roman clergy were no different in kind from those for which church councils and reformers had been reproaching recalcitrant clerks for centuries. They visited taverns and gambling dens and went to the play. They neglected to wear the tonsure, they wore illicit forms of dress, including pinked buskins and gold-embroidered shirts (they were allowed to wear violet or tawny brown, or red in the case of papal familiars, so their authorised dress scarcely lacked colour). The main complaints against beneficed clergy were their failure to take priest's orders if the benefice required, and failure to appoint adequate vicars. The churches were often bare of the necessary ornaments and plate for the ordinary services, frequently in bad repair, sometimes open to the sky. The vicars were often neglectful and illiterate, lacking even the Latin with which to say a mass. Special rules had to be passed to insist that clergy in priest's orders said mass at least once a month, and on the obligatory feasts. There was also disquiet about the lax doctrinal and moral examination of men who were to be admitted to priest's orders in Rome. The rigorous Gian Pietro Carafa was empowered by Clement VII to examine such candidates, but after 1527 Carafa was absent from Rome; when he returned he was a cardinal, and had other duties to perform.

Nor was all well in the great Roman monasteries and basilicas. By taxing and forcing the great Roman churches to give them subventions, the Medicean popes made them sell or grant out their lands, and reduced their revenues below the level at which they could perform their proper monastic and liturgical functions. By granting Roman monasteries *in commendam* to great curialists, the popes used their incomes as pensions for papal courtiers. The number of monks in some of the Roman monasteries dropped below the minimum; Santa Saba, for example, disappeared from monastic life in this period. The canons of the great churches were often mere drones, neglecting entirely the collegiate liturgical life of their churches. In St Peter's itself the holy offices were often said in a negligent way, or by squalid, ignorant, dirty priests, wearing vestments "which they would not wear in a hovel".

In Rome, as in many other places, the churches could not escape from ancient folklore combined with modern hooliganism. On the Feast of SS. Philip and James (1 May) a popular jollification took place in the Basilica of the Holy Apostles (Santi Apostoli) which would make most modern Labour Days look like vicarage tea parties. The Colonna family, whose adjoining palace gave them direct communication with the church through doors and internal windows, sponsored the feast. Flocks of birds and animals were released into the church, and a pig was suspended from the roof, just above the heads of the crowd. As they struggled to get hold of it, jars of water were emptied over them from above.

Against this gloomy picture of an ignorant and worldly Roman clergy, some things could be placed on the credit side. The inspectors of churches in the early 1560s were impressed by the vitality of the Roman religious guilds and sodalities; churches controlled by these bodies tended to be properly run and cared for. On the other hand, the guilds sometimes used for meetings and business purposes churches where they had no legal right to be. Nor were all Roman priests negligent and hard of heart. In the mid-century S. Filippo Neri found himself part of a group of priests and laymen who were willing to devote themselves to spiritual reform and to the cause of the pilgrims and the Roman poor. It is true that only one of these priests, Persiano Rosa of Genazzano, was from the Roman area; though a layman of the Massimi family later joined the association. But the charity to which they attached themselves, San Girolamo della Carità, had from the beginning been Tuscan in inspiration.

Rome of the pilgrims was a Rome of genuine, if usually ignorant, devotion. Men and women who had trudged to Rome from all over the Latin Christian world were not feigning their emotion when they crawled up the Holy Steps, or flocked to the great basilicas for the Paschal ceremonies, where they could see a liturgical tradition which, if in some ways slackly observed, was unique in Christendom. Romans were not indifferent to religious emotion; the followers of Ignatius Loyola found no difficulty in reviving the practice of the visit to the Seven Churches, a visit which Michelangelo had made on horseback with Vasari in 1550. But in a city where religion had been, so to speak, industrialised, it was easy to treat religious ceremony in a "carnal" way, and to turn a coarse witticism in the midst of a pious observance. Castiglione in his *Cortegiano* tells without hint of moral blame a story about a gentleman who had attended the religious processions of the Lenten "stations" in Rome, and who in reply to a Latin epigram composed on the spot to celebrate the pretty girls who were present, replied with another about an equally pretty group of male homosexuals.

III

In some ways Rome and the Roman court were penetrated by ruthlessly thorough materialism, by jobbery, and by entire indifference to Rome's position as a great market for the sale of holy things. But at no point in the Renaissance was this the whole story. Idealism was always suspect in Rome: it is no accident that among those who received attention from the clerical police in the 1530s were Ignatius Loyola and the future Jesuits. Yet idealism and religious enthusiasm always existed in the Roman court, and not merely on the fringe but at the centre.

Even amid the sophistication and the money-grubbing of the courts of Julius II and Leo X there was an ascetic and unworldly strain. Its nature was typical of the court culture of the era, in that it was learned, obsessed by the antique, and rather cavalier in its approach to traditional theology. Giles of Viterbo was from 1507 to 1518 the Prior General of the Order of Augustinian Hermits, and so the head of the order to which Martin Luther belonged until his defection. Under Leo Giles became a cardinal. He was a scholar and a speculative thinker, a favourite preacher both of Julius II and of Leo X. That he was a religious man is clear: whether he was a profoundly religious man is less clear. The malicious Paolo Giovio attributed his pallid complexion not to fasting but to his wiping it with straw. Giles preached the opening sermon of the Fifth Lateran Council, in which he pronounced the phrase about men being changed by religion, and not religion by men, which is still quoted by historians. Yet whether Giles really believed in religious activism is open to doubt.

Like several other Renaissance humanists, Giles of Viterbo had a mystical vision of Christianity which was inspired not only traditional western Neo-Platonism, but by the version of Platonism which was mediated through the Jewish Kabbala. Giles was an enthusiastic student of Hebrew, in the pursuit of which he took the Jewish scholar Elijah the Levite into his household, and "kissed him with the kisses of his mouth, saying: Now, abide with me and be my teacher, and I shall be to thee a father, and shall support thee and thy house, and give thee thy corn and thy wine and thy olives, and fill thy purse and bear all thy wants". Giles was a milleniarist mystic, who took a good deal of his apocalyptic view of history from the twelfth-century mystical writer, Joachim of Flora. Nor does this exhaust the list of Giles's intellectual eccentricities. Like his countryman Annius of Viterbo, the forger of Roman antiquities, Giles was an enthusiast for ancient Etruscan history. He attached great importance to the presence of St Peter's on the right or the "Etruscan" bank of the Tiber, and he related the Christian saint, Peter, to the other keybearer, the Etruscan god Janus. In fact in spite of his official place in the papal court, Giles held mystical, milleniarist views which were no less apocalyptic than those held by the condemned Dominican Savonarola. Giles hesitated about the stage of cosmic history in which he thought he lived. He sometimes inclined to the optimistic view that the Church was on the edge of the tenth or golden age which had been prophesied by Joachim of Flora. At the time of the Sack of Rome he changed his mind about this, and pointed to Charles V as "the new Cyrus" who must punish the church before the golden age could be approached. Giles was not a pacifist, however: he tried (in vain) to raise troops to rescue Clement VII from Castel Sant'Angelo in 1527.

Hesitation between an optimistic and a pessimistic view of prophecy, with a decisive tilt towards optimism, was the essence of Giles's curial position. There was more than a little in him of the traditional Renaissance court panegyrist. He hailed Julius II as the new Solomon, Leo X as the precursor of the golden age. The central position assigned to Rome in his archaeological-religious view of things was only too appropriate for a courtier. Giles referred to the hill of the Vatican as the new Mount Zion, to Rome as the Holy Latin Jerusalem. The popes were the representatives of Elisha who bore the mantle of Elijah. In an almost hysterical oration Giles hailed seven-hilled Rome as the holy bride. Where the verdict of twelve birds had led Romulus to the site of the ancient city, twelve doves (the Apostles) were called by the "new Romulus" so that Rome might be Christian. They brought an olive branch to the holy Rostrum, so that the city could be anointed with peaceful oil, and the gate of Janus eternally closed in peace. "Hail, seat of Janus, now the true Janiculum!" Christian Rome fulfilled the destiny once preached by the Etruscan priesthood.

Giles called the stars, the moon, the sun, the heavenly spheres as witnesses to his prophecy of the eternal destiny of Rome. But the moral authority of that prophecy is very much weakened by Giles's omission to criticise the obvious failings of Julius II and his court. There is, in particular, no criticism in Giles's writings of the wars of Julius II. Far from being closed in eternal peace, the gates of the shrine of Janus were conspicuously open under Julius II: in fact the very oration which refers to the closing of the gates of Janus ends with what looks suspiciously like a reference to Julius's victorious return from a military campaign. The bitter attacks of Erasmus on the bloodshed for which Julius was, as a Christian bishop, responsible, find no echo in Giles, who managed in his sermon to the Lateran Council to include congratulations to Julius on his pacification of the papal state.

Like so many clever humanists, Giles of Viterbo lacked cutting edge. His culture was profound, but his political role in the service of the mendicant orders was essentially conservative. He showed, certainly, that clerks could adopt theories of apocalyptic prophecy and still remain orthodox church administrators. But his thinking betrayed the rhetorical diffuseness shown by other humanists of the Della Rovere and Medicean courts. He tended to play with apocalyptic or Utopian ideas, which he abandoned as soon as they approached points where they might have real political or moral application. Giles was an interesting and learned man, but his career was ineffective, and it is hard to forget that he failed to give his Order the leadership which might have dissuaded Martin Luther from leaving it.

IV

Other and more orthodox Catholic currents were stirring in Rome by the third decade of the century. In December 1523 the pious Venetian patrician, Paolo Giustiniani, described to his friend Gaetano da Thiene what spiritual life he had been able to find in the Roman Babylon. The most important elements were those which were shortly to form themselves into the "Congregation of Divine Providence". Giustiniani mentions Gian Pietro Carafa as a man present in Rome whose modesty, holiness of life and ability are such as to make it possible to hope that he will one day confound all the lovers of this world, and give joy to all those who thirst for the glory of God. Not a bad prophecy for the future Paul IV! Giustiniani also mentions a Spaniard and a Neapolitan nobleman who lead good lives, and a Franciscan friar who had prophesied that the emperor would soon come to Rome and seize the pope's temporal possessions: heretics would seize the remainder, and the Turks would finally come to destroy what was left. When one reads such prophecies, made less than four years before the Sack of Rome, it becomes easy to understand how the Sack was interpreted, when it came, as a divine judgement.

A few months after Giustiniani had described these reforming elements in Rome, they came together in a small religious group known as the Congregation of Divine Providence (they were later known as "Theatines", from the name of Carafa's bishopric of Chieti), which was approved by Clement VII in 1524. Three of the four founding members were curialists: Gian Pietro Carafa; Gaetano da Thiene of Vicenza, who was a papal scriptor; and the papal familiar Bonifacio de' Colli. The way in which the Congregation was originally financed was also typical of the curial world: Gaetano da Thiene and Bonifacio de' Colli sold their curial offices and placed the capital into a common pool, which was then aggregated with the proceeds of the sale of Carafa's movable goods. Though he was not a member of the Congregation, the help of the papal datary, Gian Matteo Giberti, was essential to facilitate the legal processes necessary for its approval, which would otherwise have been blocked by conservative officials.

The Congregation of Divine Providence was an association of clerks regular, who at the outset were financed neither by begging nor by appropriated benefices, but by their own private resources. Whether they would have remained in Rome in their modest house on the Pincio if the Sack had not driven them from it in 1527 is something which cannot be known. But once driven from Rome, the Congregation did not for many years return. Its next home was in Venice; at the same time the ally of the new Order, Gian Matteo Giberti, left curial office to take up permanent residence in his diocese of Verona. One suspects that both Giberti and the Congregation felt that Rome was the one place where the reform of morals could not be pursued, at this stage at least. Pietro Aretino wrote of Carafa's residence in Venice as expressing the disgust of "good religious men" for the "filthy life" of Rome—a hypocritical remark, perhaps, as Aretino detested Carafa. In 1536 Carafa returned to Rome to accept the dignity of the cardinalate, and from that time until his election as pope in 1555 he lived in Rome. But Giberti never returned to Rome, save for brief and essential business visits.

One of the most important needs of both personal and social reform in the Church was that men should set aside their particular

(211)

private interests (*la sua commodità propria*) in favour of the spiritual interests of the whole Christian family. The group who were to become known as "spirituals" (*spirituali*) aimed to renounce the "carnal" side of their church interests, which in the coarse, materialistic world of the Roman Court was bound to dictate the course of their lives if they accepted its benefits. The ablest and most striking example of the reformed curialist was Gian Matteo Giberti, the former datary, who in his "Apology" referred to the immense powers he had enjoyed in this position. When writing the "Apology" fifteen years after leaving the papal court, after long years of reform work in his diocese, Giberti perhaps rather glossed over the extent to which he had once served his own interests in the Vatican. It is doubtful if he had, as datary, behaved in a way very different from other "carnal" curialists. Though the knowledge that this was so may have become rather clouded over in Giberti's conscious mind, its subconscious force absolutely forbade him to return to Rome. The watershed in Giberti's life had been his imprisonment by the German soldiery during the Sack of Rome. After that terrible experience he was determined to do his religious duty by serving as resident bishop in his diocese. It was a decision from which he never went back: the renunciation of service in the Roman court was the foundation of his moral and religious life. In this he is to be distinguished from Gian Pietro Carafa, whose residence in Rome never compromised his moral position. The distinction between the two men was partly a social one. Carafa was not only a Neapolitan aristocrat of some distinction, but a man who first saw the Roman court in the household of his uncle, a rich and important cardinal. Giberti was the illegitimate son of a Genovese merchant, and he owed his brilliant career in the Roman court to his own personality and abilities. As a self-made man, Giberti could not look at the Roman court with the detached and contemptuous eyes of Carafa.

V

The "spirituals" raise the difficult question of heresy in Rome. That there was heresy in Rome is certain: how it is to be defined and whom it affected are questions by no means easy to determine. In much of Europe the first half of the sixteenth century was a period of religious revolution. There is no reason to believe that any inherent Catholicism of the Italian soul was responsible for the failure of organised Protestantism to develop in Italy. The intellectual and religious ferment affected the Italian clerical and learned classes as much as those of other countries. The reasons for the failure of Italian Protestantism were social and political. Only in one or two small centres like Lucca and Ferrara was there any real tolerance for heretical opinions. Italy is a striking instance of the iron law of sixteenth-century Protestantism, that whatever the degree of discontent with orthodoxy, an organised heretical church could not come into existence without the consent of the secular authorities. That consent could only be given on political terms: in Italy such terms did not exist. The guardian of Italian religious orthodoxy was the same as the guardian of Italian political conformity: the military tyranny of the Hapsburgs. Before the Council of Trent the desire of the popes to preserve orthodoxy of belief exceeded the effectiveness of the means at their disposal; heretical clergy often flourished under the papal nose. The real guarantee of orthodoxy in Italy was Hapsburg power. Small aristocratic enclaves of heretical thought could survive, like the circle of Juan Valdès and Giulia Gonzaga at Naples, or that of the Duchess of Ferrara. So could small pockets of millenialists and Anabaptists. But openly organised Protestant churches hardly existed in the Italian peninsula.

Yet heresy was in some ways more conceivable in the Roman court than among clergy in less privileged positions. Sixteenth-century Italian society was articulated from the top. Political theory was mostly either oligarchic or autocratic. In the Roman court the principle of social leadership by privileged groups whose rule was sanctioned by God was accepted without question. This was the theory behind the bishops who still believed in a conciliar solution to the problem of Catholic reform. In a more practical way some curialists working in the papal offices felt that they were in a position to ordain reform within the Catholic establishment, provided they could persuade the pope and the College of Cardinals to listen to them. Reform memoranda had been circulating in the papal bureaux ever since the time of Alexander VI. The "Advice" given to Paul III by the Reform Commission of Cardinals in 1537 was a particularly well-known, and in some ways influential, example of such memoranda: it was well known partly because it was against the wishes of the pope leaked to the printing press. From the time of the "Advice" of 1537 to the Diet of Regensburg in 1541, in which an attempt was unsuccessfully made by the Catholic theologians to come to terms with Protestant doctrine, it seemed that there was an opportunity for eirenic curialists whose theology was perhaps not very far removed from that of moderate Lutherans, to influence papal policy in the direction of compromise with Protestantism. It was a period of what would now be called détente, in which high officials who secretly sympathised with the opposing ideology, and who would in the 1950s have been termed "fellow-travellers", could try to guide papal policy in the opposite direction to that desired by Gian Pietro Carafa.

Both at the Conference of Regensburg and at the Council of Trent, the disappointment of these eirenic hopes was complete. But among these "doves" of the papal court there were men whose theological position as between Catholicism and Lutheranism was almost entirely indeterminate. These were the "delicate protonotaries" whom the reformer Jean Calvin attacked in his treatises against those who, although they had understood the Gospel, preferred, like Nicodemus who came to the Lord by night for fear of the Jews, to hide their true convictions under an exterior cloak of orthodox Catholicism. Such men walked in Italian society (one might add, particularly in the Roman court itself) on a razor's edge. Systematic ambiguity was a part of their way of life; their conversation and correspondence were strewn with vague and discreet references, and, particularly after the Roman Inquisition was founded in 1542, they lived under the threat of ruthless interrogation and terrible vengeance—a vengeance hideously travestied, as it was by all sides in the sixteenth century, as a parody of Christian justice and mercy. It was all very well for Calvin to chide the prevarication of the "Nicodemists", but Pietro Carnesecchi, the Apostolic Protonotary whom Calvin certainly had in mind when he wrote, went eventually to his death in 1567 following his condemnation by the Roman Inquisition. A "delicate protonotary", Carnesecchi walked to his execution in spotless white gloves.

According to Gian Pietro Carafa, there was indeed a problem of heresy in Rome. To Giberti in 1536 he wrote, "Monsignore . . . haven't you placed your hand in the wound? Haven't you seen this

evil thing, both in Venice and in Rome?" It was Carafa's conviction
that the Franciscan Friars were a large part of the trouble, and he
proved to be not entirely mistaken. The reformed friars who called
themselves Capuchins were able to call on the support of distinguished laymen and laywomen in Rome, especially on Vittoria Colonna and her brother Ascanio. The Capuchins had broken away from
the main Franciscan body only in the 1520s and they needed powerful help in Rome in order to maintain their independent existence. But
they produced some powerful preachers, of whom the most famous
and important was the Sienese, Bernardino Ochino. Ochino first
preached in Rome during Lent in 1534. He immediately became the
most fashionable and widely followed preacher of his time. During
Lent the next year he again preached in San Lorenzo in Damaso (the
church in the Cancelleria), this time on the Gospels. The church was
full to the extent that people sat in the roof; cardinals and nobles
(including his patron Vittoria Colonna) thronged the church, besides
the common people. Ochino had the traditional appearance of a
medieval friar, with a long, fair beard; he had a most musical and
commanding voice. He preached for two hours, and ended in tears,
together with most of his audience. He preached not only affecting
moral sermons on the Gospels, but denunciations of corruption in the
high places of the Church. This did not prevent his being the most
sought-after preacher in Italy. In 1539 (when Ochino was General of
his Order) Vittoria Colonna explained to Cardinal Ercole Gonzaga
Ochino's difficulties: if he accepted to preach in Rome he would be
accused of seeking advancement, if he refused he would be accused of
spurning or avoiding Rome.

VI

Most of the leaders of the "spiritual" party in the church in Italy
were among those called to Rome by Paul III in 1536 to prepare
a report on the reform of the Church. The "spirituals" included
the Venetian patrician Cardinal Gasparo Contarini, the Englishman
Reginald Pole, who was made a cardinal in the same year, and Gian
Matteo Giberti, who reluctantly left his diocese of Verona for the task,

but refused to accept nomination as a cardinal. Carafa and Sadoleto also sat on the commission. In summoning Contarini, Pole and Giberti, the pope had convened the three most distinguished members of the *spirituali*. In the Reform Commission they had to work with Carafa, and the Reform "Advice" which they produced—whose "leaking" to the printing press was one of the major political indiscretions of the period—was a synthesis of the varying tendencies in the Commission.

Reginald Pole was an eminent English political refugee, the grandson of the Duke of Clarence. His opposition to Henry VIII's policy over the divorce and the schism was politically important because of his birth and his ability. But he was also an extremely devout man, and a learned one. He had studied in Italy, and was more at home in Italian society than anywhere else. His close relationship with the imperial court made him even more important: in the Conclave of 1549 he was to be very close to the papal tiara. Such a man was not only able to conduct his own theological speculations without much fear of interference, but was also able to give support and protection to others of like mind. From the mid-thirties onwards, the Pole circle was a pious group whose central activity was the reading and commentary of the New Testament. They were "spiritual" rather than "carnal", "evangelical" rather than "scholastic". They had access to Lutheran literature, and they were influenced by the doctrines which Juan Valdès was enunciating in Naples. A member of this circle, the humanist Marcantonio Flaminio, the former secretary of Giberti, revised for publication the influential little book, *Il Beneficio di Cristo*, which carried the evangelical message of Calvin to the Italian devout. Pole and Flaminio were not Protestants—Protestant is hardly a fit name for Pole, who gained the repute of "tormentor and executioner of the Anglican Church". But recent research has rightly emphasised the view that Pole held: "Heretics be not in all things heretics. Wherefore I will not so abhor their heresy that for the hate thereof I will fly from the truth."

It is most unlikely that Pole had wished to settle in Rome. But his having been called there and given the red hat in 1536 led to his presence there, save for absence on diplomatic missions, or for the momentous absence at the Council of Trent (1545–1546), until his return to England in 1554. From 1541 until his departure for Trent in

1545, Pole was not actually resident in Rome, but serving as the governor of the papal Patrimony of St Peter in Tuscany, and so living in Viterbo, about forty miles from the city. This undistinguished post was a strange one to give to an eminent cardinal of the Roman court. Its conferment on Pole may have been in order to give him an official residence within easy reach of Rome, and also to give him a small income, since he was a "poor" cardinal. But it is also possible that the principal intention was to place a cardinal whose doctrinal ideas were suspect in a post where he could do little harm in matters of faith, and in which he could be surveyed easily from Rome. Viterbo was a day's journey from Rome. Marcantonio Flaminio, who was a member of Pole's *famiglia*, wrote a piece of light Latin verse in which in the guise of a lapdog he begged for a ride in Pole's coach to the city. Vittoria Colonna, the aristocratic patron of Ochino, left Rome to take up residence in a convent in Viterbo. For three or four years Viterbo was the centre of the Italian *spirituali*. Small wonder that, both then and later, the Roman Inquisitors took a keen interest in Cardinal Pole's *famiglia* at Viterbo.

The attitude of Paul III to the curial cardinals and great officials who were suspected of crypto-Lutheranism is a problem which historians have not yet solved. No doubt the supple diplomacy of the pope envisaged the possibility of a theological compromise with the Lutherans: this was indeed the purpose for which Cardinal Contarini was sent on his abortive mission to Regensburg in 1541. Pole's special position in relation to both the English Crown and the emperor gave him additional immunity. It has been suggested that the *spirituali* were in possession of information about the scandal of Pier Luigi Farnese's murderous attack on Cosmo Gheri, the bishop of Fano, and that Pope Paul was therefore afraid of them. But Paul III was by no means blind or insensitive to the message of the Catholic evangelicals, and did not need to be blackmailed to be made to understand it. His choice of the great devotional paintings of Michelangelo for his private chapel means that he had some idea of what the message of St Paul meant to the "spirituals".

VII

The most distinguished of the Roman laity among the *spirituali* was Vittoria Colonna. The widow of Francesco d'Avalos, the marquis of Pescara (whose rather murky political career she chose to ignore), she was a high-born aristocrat and a woman whose character and intellectual gifts seemed remarkable to her contemporaries. Unlike her friend Giulia Gonzaga, protectress of the Neapolitan *spirituali*, Vittoria was no great beauty. Her patronage was thought valuable by men like Paolo Giovio; but other writers and artists sought her company for its own sake. She certainly assented to the *spirituale* doctrine of justification by faith: evidence of this is her satisfaction that Cardinal Pole left the Council of Trent in such a way that he did not have to assent to the Trent definition of justification. Her opinion of the official clergy was that although men might keep silent about their deeds, the very stones would one day speak.

A large part of Vittoria Colonna's poetry was religious; much of it suffers from conventional rhetoric. Only occasionally, as in the sonnet "Quand'io riguardo il mio si grave errore" ("When I consider my serious failing"), which may refer to the crisis of Vittoria and the other *spirituali* in 1542, does her piety speak simply and effectively in her verse. Too often she reminds the reader that by the late 1530s the "spiritual" sonnet of religious repentance had become a convention, widely practised by writers as far from Vittoria's kind of piety as the libertine Francesco Maria Molza and the courtesan Gaspara Stampa.

Michelangelo stood on the edge of the *spirituali* circle; he was a part of it in that he met Vittoria Colonna in 1536 (or perhaps as late as 1538), and remained her very close friend until her death. If they met in 1536, she was then forty-six years old and he sixty-three; there is no sign that there was a sexual element in their friendship, which was a communion of distinguished and passionate minds. Using the masculine gender, Michelangelo wrote of her at her death that "Death took from me a great friend" ("un grande amico"). They shared an intense piety, whose manifestation was even more baroque in Michelangelo than in Vittoria. But Michelangelo's religious feeling was not dependent on the tradition of the Roman *spirituali*; he was in Florentine terms a *piagnone*, drawing his religious experience from the life and doctrines of Savonarola.

Michelangelo's religious experience was not an aspect of his art but central to it, and its manifestations can be found in the frescoes of the Sistine ceiling, in the youthful period of his work, just as much as in the frescoes of the Last Judgement and the Capella Paolina, or in the

Rondanini Pietà, the works of maturity and old age. The more specifically "spiritual" experience of conviction of sin and of turning to Christ for forgiving grace is clearly expressed in poems written by Michelangelo in the mid-1520s, such as the "Vivo al peccato, a me morendo vivo". "Dying spiritually, I live in my lower and sinful self; my life goes on not on my behalf, but on that of sin. My health is given from heaven; my sickness is caused by my own unbridled will, of whose control I am deprived". The much later poem "Ben sarien dolce le preghiere mie" shows (in Wordsworth's translation) how close he came, towards the end of his life, to *spirituali* views on saving grace:

> The prayers I make will then be sweet indeed,
> If Thou the spirit give by which I pray:
> My unassisted heart is barren clay,
> Which of its native self can nothing feed:
> Of good and pious works Thou art the seed,
> Which quickens only where Thou say'st it may;
> Unless Thou show to us Thine own true way,
> No man can find it.

Michelangelo and Vittoria Colonna would meet at the Church of S. Silvestro on the Quirinale, where the anti-Lutheran preacher, Fra Ambrogio Caterino, expounded the letters of St Paul to them in the presence of the Portugese artist, Francesco d'Ollanda. Even if we allow for literary convention in its expression, there is no doubt that Michelangelo's feeling for Vittoria was profound. "A man, indeed a god, speaks in her woman's mouth, and on hearing her I am no longer my own man, but hers." The religious feelings which preoccupied them were a great deal more than conventional. He made for Vittoria a drawing of a Deposition from the Cross; on the stem of the cross was inscribed the Dante quotation: "You take no thought of how much blood was shed [for the Gospel]" ("Non vi si pensa quanto sangue costa"). Vittoria wrote that Michelangelo was conceded "supernatural grace" to execute this drawing. On Vittoria Colonna's death in 1547 Michelangelo committed himself to extravagant grief, if his poetry is to be believed. But the conventional element in such memorial poems is always high: his simple reference to her as "a great friend" is more touching.

The most enduring physical monuments of the *spirituali* are the two Michelangelo frescoes in the Capella Paolina in the Vatican, executed between 1542 and 1550. No greater testimony can be imagined to faith in a saving grace given by God to man whose works are utterly inadequate to protect his personality from self-destruction. In the "Conversion of St Paul", a startling vertical descends from Christ's hand to the apostle's face and makes an awkward but dramatic right angle with the leg. In the later "Crucifixion of St Peter" human impotence and the divine initiative are even more starkly stated by making the crossing of the two shafts of the cross into the only dynamic element in the composition. In both frescoes the inability of the spectators to participate more than passively in the divine drama, their heavy, leaden treatment, their lack of physical grace, are utterly unlike Michelangelo's earlier art. The contrast between the sensuous beauty and grace of the frescoes of the Sistine ceiling, Michelangelo's first great work in Rome, and those of the Pauline Chapel, is far more profound than the contrast between the work of a young artist and an old. We may see in it, if we wish, the gulf between the exuberant and confident culture of the Rome of Julius II and Leo X, and the introspection and doubt which had invaded that environment by mid-century. But one must also admit the force exerted by the *spirituali* on Michelangelo, which made him cast their doctrines in this unforgettable mould. Michelangelo painted the Capella Paolina frescoes in this way not because his powers were failing—he was still to be the sculptor of the Rondanini Pietà—but because his convictions imposed on him this way of viewing his faith.

The year 1542, the year in which the Capella Paolina frescoes were begun, saw the final collapse of the hopes of the *spirituali* to influence the Roman Church. That summer the Capuchin General, Bernardino Ochino, and other "spiritual" leaders in Italy, fled to safety in Protestant territory. Their flight marked the end of a recognisable orthodox group of "spirituals". On 15 July 1542 Ochino had been summoned to Rome. He visited Cardinal Contarini, as he lay at that time on his death-bed at Bologna, and according to Ochino Contarini had hinted that the Capuchin should fly the country. The political climate in Rome was changing disastrously for the *spirituali:* cardinals were named as members of the future Roman Inquisition on 4 July, and the bull setting up the new organisation of the Inquisition was published on 21 July. Cardinal Carafa, impatient of delay, purchased the locks and chains for the new prison of the Inquisition at his own expense. Contarini died on 24 August. Vittoria Colonna, panic-stricken by the flight of her protégé Ochino, wrote of him that "the more he tries to make excuses, the more he shows his guilt; and the more he tries to save others from shipwreck, the more he exposes them to the Flood." The less emotional Giberti wrote to Cardinal Gonzaga that "as our spirituals have been such a disappointment, partly because of death among them, partly because of their becoming fugitives, I think it best to quit their company." With this harsh little sentence he wrote the epitaph of the *spirituali* as an effective force in church politics.

Yet in political terms the deluge which the surviving *spirituali* feared might engulf them in 1542 was not released. Cardinal Pole was still a very powerful man, and the canny Paul III may have felt that the political tide might still turn in Pole's direction rather than in that of Carafa. Pole's group at Viterbo was closely surveyed by Inquisition agents, but it was not disturbed, and no arrests were made. The members of Pole's *famiglia* at Viterbo who were papal curialists were employed again by the Roman court subsequently, and some were given important posts. Flaminio was offered the secretaryship of the Council of Trent, though he refused it. Far from being frightened to live in Rome, Flaminio returned there in 1546, and remained there until his death in 1550. Once more Flaminio frequented the learned circles in their delectable gardens on the Janiculum and the Quirinal. He had, however, to put up with the inexorable interest of Cardinal Carafa, whose interest in Flaminio's orthodoxy was so insatiable that he made a dramatic and unwelcome appearance at the poet's death-bed. As Flaminio lay dying in the house of Cardinal Pole on 17 February 1550, Gian Pietro Carafa followed the priest carrying the last sacraments into the house. First concealing himself in the room, Cardinal Carafa listened while Flaminio (at the ministering priest's request) recited the Creed and expressed acceptance of the doctrine of transubstantiation. Then Carafa came to the dying man's bedside and comforted him until his spirit left him. This was the macabre and melodramatic scenario which he supplied for the last hours of a luminous and sensitive mind. With not untypical subtlety Carafa chose to have Flaminio interrogated about transubstantiation (on which he knew Flaminio's views to be orthodox), rather than about justification by faith (about which he rightly suspected his views to be heretical). As many priests have done at Christian death-beds, Carafa mixed Christian charity with a taste for ecclesiastical scalp-hunting. Flaminio was claimed for orthodoxy as well as for heaven.

VIII

The uncertainty of religious allegiances in Rome under Pope Paul III can be illustrated from the so-called persecution of Ignatius Loyola and his companions in 1538, the year in which they arrived in Rome. The Lent sermons at S. Agostino were preached by one Agostino Mainardi of Saluzzo, who at the time was considered one of the main ornaments of his Order. This did not prevent Ignatius and his companions from denouncing Mainardi for heresy: they confided their doubts about him to some Spaniards living in Rome. Unfortunately for Loyola the sympathies of his confidants turned out to be on the other side. They launched a counter-attack on Ignatius and friends, and denounced them to the Governor of Rome for suspected heresy, claiming that charges of heresy had already been brought against them in Spain and in Paris. The charges were untrue, but their refutation was by no means easy. Eventually, having got help from Cardinal Gasparo Contarini, and having also obtained access to the pope, the leader of the future Jesuit Order managed to bring a lawsuit which cleared his name. In the course of the lawsuit it became clear that the agents of Cardinal Gian Pietro Carafa were spying not only on the Augustinian preachers but on Ignatius and his companions.

Agostino Mainardi revealed himself in 1541 as the "Lutheran" that Ignatius Loyola had suspected him to be. But the interest of his case lies not in the accuracy of Loyola's suspicions but in the complicated and ambiguous ambience in which they were formed. The picture of hostile Augustinians and Jesuits in Rome, with Gian Pietro Carafa spying on both, and the *spirituale* Cardinal Contarini lending his support to Loyola, is one of religious cross-currents and blurred alle-

(222)

giances. In 1538 Agostino Mainardi could find protectors in Rome as powerful as those of Loyola. Things would not have been the same five years later.

None of the first members of the Society of Jesus was a Roman. Yet the Jesuits are the only important religious order whose formative experience actually took place in Rome. When Ignatius and his companions arrived in Rome in 1538 they regarded their stay there as a stage on the pilgrimage which they intended to make to Jerusalem, and they were not yet clear about their intention to form a new religious order. In the event the organisation of the Society of Jesus took place rapidly: the bull authorising the Society was issued on 27 September 1540. Ignatius lived in Rome until his death in 1556: the Rome he knew was what we call "Renaissance" Rome, and not the Rome of the "Counter-Reformation". It was a city where he and his friends had taken root immediately and profoundly, from the early days of their reception in modest lodgings by the Roman gentlemen, Garzoni and Frangipani, to the foundation of the Church of the Gesù and of the Collegio Romano in the early 1550s. The Roman charities founded by Ignatius, particularly those for converted prostitutes and for prostitutes' daughters, were rescue operations which demanded an intimate knowledge of Roman social conditions. The close connection between the new Society and the Hospital of S. Spirito in Sassia linked the new religious order with one of the most ancient Roman charitable foundations.

The papalist political purpose of Ignatius brought him into the highest councils of the popes within a short time of the Society being approved. But Rome fitted the saint's aristocratic viewpoint no less than his authoritarian policies. It was a place where the intense and flame-like charm of this lame little man, and his immense administrative ability, were swiftly understood and exploited. The Jesuit concept of the formation of an educated religious elite was also one to which Rome lent itself: the idea of the Collegio Romano, when it had taken shape, exerted great influence on Rome as a city as well as on the Catholic world as a whole. As a city Rome suited the Jesuits: it was a place where their vocation could easily and fittingly be expressed. There is a striking contrast between the confidence with which the Jesuits settled in Rome in the 1540s, and the inability of the

(223)

Theatine reformers to do so a generation earlier. It is not surprising that Jesuit building had made such an indelible impression on the face of Rome by the end of the sixteenth century.

Other new boundaries in the spiritual map of Rome were marked by the setting up of the Roman Inquisition in 1542. But change was gradual: for a long time the practice of the Inquisition was moderate and cautious. Popular preaching in Rome was controlled more strictly by the Inquisition after Paul III's death in 1549. Not until Paul IV became pope in 1555 did severity and the general practice of denouncing suspects for heresy begin to turn Rome into a different city. The long delay before the Inquisition became deadly to deviant belief in the Roman court can be illustrated from the career of the Florentine Pietro Carnesecchi, one of the "spirituals" who formed part of Cardinal Pole's Viterbo group in 1541–1545. Carnesecchi had been for many years a rich and powerful curialist: he had been the favoured adviser of the last years of Clement VII, whom he had been said to dominate in all things. Carnesecchi was later in direct contact at Naples with the group of Juan Valdès and Giulia Gonzaga, and by the time he was with Pole in Viterbo Carnesecchi had reached "heretical" conclusions about justification and grace. The Inquisition brought charges against Carnesecchi in 1546; they were graver than had been expected, but his friends, who included Cardinal Pole and Cosimo de' Medici, the ruler of Florence, managed to see that they were dropped, though he was not formally cleared of them. Carnesecchi went abroad for a time, but after the death of Paul IV he returned to Rome to take up his lucrative curial employments once more. Not until 1566, twenty years after the first accusations, where the charges brought by the Inquisition which led to his condemnation and beheading in the following year.

IX

It is hard to decide, as we reach the point where what we call "Renaissance Rome" becomes "Counter-Reformation Rome", what real changes took place below the surface. When life in Rome in the first half of the sixteenth century is contrasted with life there in the second half, the differences tend to be of style and atmosphere rather than of social organisation. Some things simply cannot be determined: we cannot know how many good and holy men there were in the court of Pope Leo X, any more than we can know how many religious hypocrites there were in the courts of Popes Pius V (1566–1572) or Sixtus V, when piety was more fashionable. But we do know that the social structure of the Roman court was immensely durable; moreover, the essentially conservative purpose of the Counter-Reformation meant that little was done to change it in the course of the sixteenth century. The setting up of the Congregations as organs of government by Pope Sixtus V had some effect on it, as did the enforcement of the obligation of residence on Catholic bishops; and so did the economic and social decline of the Roman nobility. By the beginning of the seventeenth century clerical wealth tended to be concentrated in the hands of a few very favoured office-holders, rather than spread as widely over the clerical class as it had been in Rome during the earlier Renaissance. But the clerical oligarchy remained rich and powerful nevertheless: it was encouraged by the papal government to build fine houses; it collected beautiful objects; and it passed on its property to its heirs.

The atmosphere of Rome at mid-century can be best sensed in the writings of Giovanni della Casa. Monsignor della Casa was a talented Tuscan who had passed in the 1540s from a life of literary bohemianism to the single-minded pursuit of advancement in papal service. By an irony typical of his times, this ex-libertine was responsible for the promulgation, while he was papal *nunzio* at Venice, of the first Counter-Reformation Index of Prohibited Books. Della Casa obtained an archbishopric, and was for a time an important figure in the administration of Paul IV, but the highest prizes of papal service, in particular the cardinalate, eluded him. The author of some of the finest lyric poems in the Italian language, he died an embittered man in the same year as Ignatius Loyola, 1556. Della Casa's best prose work deals almost exclusively, under one disguise or another, with the arts of pleasing the rich and powerful. In the Roman court which had educated Della Casa, first place went, as he saw it, "not to learning, not to age, not to noble birth, not to talent, but to wealth, office and power." In his manual of gentlemanly conduct which became known all over Europe, the *Galateo*, this harsh doctrine was toned down, but it lies behind his main principle that a gentleman should "moderate and order his behaviour not according to his own pleasure, but to that of the persons whom he frequents." How far is this sombre advice from the confident assumption of equality of relations among the well-born in Castiglione's *Cortegiano!*

Nonetheless there was still a *douceur de vivre* in papal Rome: an easy, civilised, worldly discourse which belonged not so much to the great palaces as to the vineyards and gardens where the secretaries and men of letters drank their wine at their ease. This was a Rome which survived from Medicean Rome before the Sack into the Rome of Paul III which Monsignor della Casa had known as a young man. It was a way of life which persisted not only into the Counter-Reformation but beyond it: it endured in one form or another as long as papal Rome. Certainly it was still to be found in the dark days of the rule of Paul IV, when it was expressed by Joachim du Bellay in a sonnet addressed to Maraud, the poet's companion in the service of Cardinal du Bellay in the office of *valet de chambre*. Du Bellay speaks for one side of the spirit of Rome just as surely as the passionate austerity of Ignatius Loyola speaks for the other. The sestet of his sonnet is a piece of hedonistic philosophy which turns on an image from the urbane life of a cardinal's household. The poet proposes to his companion that though their lord the cardinal is still sitting on some dreary commission, it is time for them to go to the cardinal's garden—which we know to have been in the grounds of the Baths of Diocletian—and to lay out their supper:

> Come then, my dear Maraud, and while our lord,
> Born for the public weal, sits on some board,
> With cares of others frets his life away:
> Go to the vineyard: get our supper spread:
> Tomorrow you'll perhaps be sick, or dead;
> The only life is life we live today.

Select Bibliography

What follows is very far indeed from being a list of all the books and articles consulted in preparing the text. It is a selective list of the books (and a few of the more important articles in learned publications) which have either been of particular importance in writing the present book, or which seem to me to be useful for someone who wants to read more extensively about the subject, or about some aspect of it. It has been impossible to confine this list to books written in English, but I have tried to indicate relevant works written in English where they exist.

I have borne in mind that there are full bibliographies of the material on social history in Delumeau's book, on urban history and architecture in that of Portoghesi, and on cultural history in that of Dickinson. With a few exceptions (like that of W. von Hofmann's book, which although very technical and hard to read has been terribly neglected and under-estimated) I have emphasised the more recent work.

I have not included many biographies. A number of the more important biographies of cardinals are referred to in the article of D.S. Chambers quoted in the list of books for Chapter V.

Editions of Italian sixteenth-century authors quoted in the text are listed in the manual of Borsellino and Aurigemma which is quoted below.

GENERAL TOPICS

The number of books about Rome is proverbially countless. So is the number of books about the Roman Church.

For those with a good digestion, L. von Pastor, *The History of the Popes, from the close of the Middle Ages*, Vols. i–xvi, is a wonderful book to read. both as an introduction and as a source book for the whole period. The great modern master of Church history of this period is H. Jedin, whose *History of the Council of Trent* (Eng. trans., 1957-in progress) is fundamental not only for the Council itself but for the period leading up to it.

For the social history, J. Delumeau, *Vie économique et sociale de Rome dans la seconde moitiè du XVIe siècle* (Paris, 1957–1959), is indispensable. For urban and architectural history there is a new book (a collective work in spite of its publication under the name of a single author): P. Portoghesi, *Roma del Rinascimento* (1970). There is an English translation, *Rome of the*

Renaissance (London and New York, 1972), which lacks the text of the second volume of the Italian edition. Portoghesi's book is invaluable, but is not always accurate in detail. The only relatively modern treatment of both the social and political history is that of P. Pecchiai, *Roma nel Cinquecento* (Bologna, 1948), which is old-fashioned by some ideas of what social history ought to be, but based on a good knowledge of the sources. G. Dickinson, *Du Bellay in Rome* (Leiden, 1960), is a most useful book for the social and cultural background. The best guide to Rome published in English is that of G. Masson, *The Companion Guide to Rome* (1965).

There is a useful collection of essays, two of which (by Cantimori and Delumeau) touch directly on sixteenth-century Rome, in *The Late Italian Renaissance 1525–1630* (ed. E. Cochrane, 1970). The literary history is well treated by N. Borsellino and M. Aurigemma, *Il Cinquecento dal Rinascimento alla Controriforma (La Letteratura Italiana: Storia e Testi,* iv, Rome and Bari, 1973). S.J. Freedberg, *Painting in Italy 1500 to 1600* (1970), is a helpful guide, though written in a style which I do not always find lucid. J. Shearman, *Mannerism* (1967), is a stimulating essay. The sections by Lotz in L.H. Heydenreich and W. Lotz, *Architecture in Italy 1400 to 1600* (1974), are also helpful.

BOOKS AND ARTICLES ON SPECIAL TOPICS

Introduction and Chapter I

J. Hook, *The Sack of Rome 1527* (1972).

H. Lutz, *Christianitas afflicta. Europa, das Reich und die päpstliche Politik im Niedergang der Hegemonie Karls V. (1552–1556)* (Göttingen, 1964).

M. Mallet, *The Borgias. The Rise and Fall of a Renaissance Dynasty* (1969).

B. Mitchell, *Rome in the High Renaissance: the Age of Leo X* (Norman, 1973).

C. Roth, *The Last Florentine Republic* (1925).

Chapter II

A.V. Antonovics, "A late 15th-Century Division Register of the College of Cardinals", *Papers of the British School at Rome,* xxxv (1967).

W. von Hofmann, *Forschungen zur Geschichte der kurialen Behörden vom Schisma bis zur Reformation* (Rome, 1914).

F. Litva, "L'attività finanziara della Dataria durante il periodo tridentino", *Archivum Historiae Pontificiae,* v (1967), pp. 79–174.

M. Monaco, *La situazione della reverenda Camera Apostolica nell'anno 1525* (Rome, 1960).

P. Partner, "The 'Budget' of the Roman Church in the Renaissance Period," in *Italian Renaissance Studies* (ed. E.F. Jacob, 1960).

——, *The Lands of St Peter* (1972), Chapter 13 ("The Papal State at the End of the Middle Ages").

Chapter III

M. Armellini, "Un censimento della città di Roma sotto Leon X", *Gli Studi in Italia*, iv, v (1881–1882).

D. Gnoli, "'Descriptio Urbis' o censimento della popolazione di Roma avanti il sacco borbonico", *Archivio della R. Società romana di Storia Patria*, xvii (1894).

G. Masson, *Courtesans of the Italian Renaissance* (1975).

M. Maroni Lumbroso and A. Martini, *Le confraternità romane nelle loro chiese* (Rome, 1963).

A. Martini, *Arti mestieri e fede nella Roma dei papi* (Bologna, 1965).

A. Milano, *Storia degli ebrei in Italia* (Turin, 1963).

M. Romani, *Pellegrini e viaggiatori nell'economia di Roma dal XIV al XVII secolo* (Milan, 1948).

"The English Hospice in Rome", *The Venerabile*, xxi (Exeter, 1962).

Chapter IV

J.S. Ackermann, *The Cortile del Belvedere* (Vatican City, 1954).

C. Dionisotti, *Geografia e storia della letteratura italiana* (Turin, 1967).

L. Dorez, *La Cour du Pape Paul III* (Paris, 1932).

R.M. Douglas, *Jacopo Sadoleto (1477–1547): Humanist and Reformer* (Cambridge, Mass., 1959).

H.W. Frey, "Regesten zur päpstlichen Kapelle unter Leo X", *Die Musikforschung, viii–ix (1955–1956).*

F. Hartt, *Giulio Romano* (New Haven, 1958).

J. Shearman, "The Vatican Stanze: Functions and Decoration", *Proceedings of the British Academy, 1971 (1973).*

Th. von Sickel, "Ein 'ruolo di famiglia' des Papstes Pius IV", *Mittheilungen des Instituts für oesterreichische Geschichtsforschung*, xiv (1893), pp. 537–588.

E. Wind, "Michelangelo's Prophets and Sibyls", *Proceedings of the British Academy*, 1965 (1967).

Chapter V

U. Aldroandi, "Di tutte le statue antiche, che per tutta Roma . . . si veggono", in L. Mauro, *Le antichità della città di Roma* (Venice, 1558).

A.V. Antonovics, "Counter-Reformation Cardinals 1534–90", *European Studies Review*, ii (1972).

D.S. Chambers, *Cardinal Bainbridge in the Court of Rome: 1509 to 1514* (Oxford, 1965).

——, "The economic predicament of Renaissance Cardinals", *Studies in Medieval and Renaissance History*, iii (1966).

F. Ubaldini, *Vita di Mons. Angelo Colocci*, ed. V. Fanelli (Vatican City, 1969).

Chapter VI

J.S. Ackermann, *The Architecture of Michelangelo* (1970).

T. Ashby, *Topographical Study in Rome in 1581. A series of views with a fragmentary text by Étienne du Pérac* (1916).

F. Cruciani, *Il teatro del Campidoglio e le feste romane del 1513* (Milan, 1969).

H. von Einem, *Michelangelo* (Engl. trs., London 1973).

C.L. Frommel, *Der Römische Palastbau der Hochrenaissance* (Tübingen, 1973).

J. Lees-Milne, *Saint Peter's* (1967).

A. Marabottini, *Polidoro da Caravaggio* (Rome, 1969).

G. Masson, *Italian Villas and Palaces* (1959).

——, *Italian Gardens* (1961).

F.C. Wolff-Metternich, *Die Erbauung des Peterskirche zu Rom im 16. Jahrhundert* (Vienna-Munich, 1972).

Chapter VII

G. Alberigo, *I vescovi italiani al concilio di Trento* (Florence, 1959).

R. De Maio, *Riforme e Miti nella Chiesa del Cinquecento* (Naples, 1973).

D. Fenlon, *Heresy and Obedience in Tridentine Italy: Cardinal Pole and the Counter Reformation* (Cambridge, 1972).

P.F. Grendler, *Critics of the Italian World (1530–1560)* (Madison, Milwaukee, London, 1969).

H. Jedin, *Kirche des Glaubens Kirche der Geschichte* (Freiburg-im-Breisgau, 1966).

C. Madison, *Marcantonio Flaminio: Poet, Humanist and Reformer* (1965).

P. McNair, *Peter Martyr in Italy* (Oxford, 1967).

J.W. O'Malley, *Giles of Viterbo* (Leiden, 1968).

——, "Man's Dignity, God's love and the Destiny of Rome. A text of Giles of Viterbo", *Viator*, iii (1972).

O. Ortolani, *Pietro Carnesecchi* (Florence, 1963).

A. Prosperi, *Tra Evangelismo e Controriforma: G.M. Giberti (1495–1543)* (Rome, 1969).

Index